A. W. Jervis
1919

ON SOCIETY

MACMILLAN AND CO., LIMITED
LONDON · BOMBAY · CALCUTTA · MADRAS
MELBOURNE

THE MACMILLAN COMPANY
NEW YORK · BOSTON · CHICAGO
DALLAS · SAN FRANCISCO

THE MACMILLAN CO. OF CANADA, LTD.
TORONTO

ON SOCIETY

BY

FREDERIC HARRISON

MACMILLAN AND CO., LIMITED
ST. MARTIN'S STREET, LONDON
1918

TO

MY WIFE

PREFACE

At the close of a very long and busy life I now collect my last thoughts as a real *testamentum in procinctu.* Bidding farewell to history, biography, and letters, I wish to gather up some of the attempts to teach the people—which now for more than fifty years have been the serious purpose of my life. I am the only survivor of those at home or abroad that had personal interviews with Auguste Comte, whom I went to see in Paris in 1855. In books, such as my *Autobiographic Memoirs,* 1911, *Creed of a Layman,* 1908, and elsewhere, I have stated the very gradual steps by which the Positive Philosophy —and ultimately the Religion of Humanity— absorbed me; and when a body of men and women who shared this belief began to form in England about 1870, I took part in the task of making these known to the public. From 1880 to 1905 I was chosen to lead the society which had its centre at Newton Hall. From that time my main business was engaged, by lectures there and by essays in the *Positivist Review* (1893–1918), to develop the moral, social, and religious meaning of the Positive system. This book is a summary of what we sought to popularise and to teach.

It will appear from these addresses that we had no idea of forming either a *sect* or a political *party*, nor even a Church in any narrow sense. From the first all those with whom I was associated, and myself as leader and guide, treated the scheme of Comte as an Ideal which the future might work out, but of which we could only form a School to influence opinion. Everything we did was open to the public, gratuitous, and informal. We made no terms for adhesion in any degree, no rules or pledges, no attempt at legislative action. We were simply a group of men who aimed at guiding public *opinion*—attacking none, never disturbing any genuine faith, not seeking any personal power or privilege. The Lectures I now issue were part of the Courses which I gave frequently at Newton Hall and elsewhere to several Positivist Societies in various cities. As there was nothing in them of exclusive dogma or formal sect, they were delivered or repeated to sundry Ethical or Free Thought Societies in England and in America, at which I had been invited to speak.

The second Part contains as specimens some of the Annual and Occasional discourses which I gave regularly at Newton Hall; and these will show the scheme of education and the kind of propaganda which we sought to make known. Almost without exception, those who took part in the movement had been bred in homes and in schools devoted to Gospel and Church. And the majority of those who lectured had been trained in Science as their profession. Our School has been maintained now for more than forty years on the same lines; and when our younger men return from War service, it will no doubt be developed with fresh energy and experience.

This book, therefore, is the plain record of the practical work of a School for the People. It is not a systematic scheme of philosophy, much less does it pretend to literary art. The chapters are spoken lectures printed in the exact words in which they were uttered—always designed so as to be easily understood by the general public, at times using popular and unconventional form. As the audience was somewhat fluctuating, and those who came might not have heard preceding lectures and might not hear others, the course was purposely infused with not a little repetition. Reiteration of thought is a familiar instrument of the teacher of Ethics; and it was not necessary to delete this altogether. It will be observed that the terms Humanism and Positivism are used as practically equivalent; and Scientific or Demonstrative are taken as meaning Positivist.

I have thought it right to include my replies to the elaborate criticisms of Mr. Mill on Comte. For the earlier career of Auguste Comte, Mill was a whole-hearted supporter; and to the last remained practically a Positivist with some very deeply opposed convictions of his own. These were specially marked in his famous book *On Liberty*—to which this book *On Society* is in some sense a rejoinder. I am well aware that the reputation and the influence of Mr. Mill are much less in 1918 than what they were in their high-water mark of 1868. But, as he had long known and studied Comte, had carried on constant discussions with him, and, above all, as he had supplied the literary and scientific critics of Comte with all the best of their materials; and since Mr. Mill's objections to the religion and polity of Positivism still retain their hold on many minds, I have met his arguments as those which Positivism has to meet if it can win the attention of Liberal Thought and Religious Reform.

I follow too the beautiful example of Mr. Mill, who associated the work of which he was most proud with her to whom he owed so much inspiration and guidance. I dedicate this, my last public utterance, to my Wife, who heard these words spoken and who lived and died in perfect sympathy with all that they maintain. They are hardly more my own thoughts and hopes than they are the thoughts and hopes of Her, who is to me ever while I yet live:—

—viva adhuc et desiderio carior.

BATH, *August* 1918.

CONTENTS

PART I

LECTURE I

LECTURE II

LECTURE III

LECTURE IV

LECTURE V

LECTURE VI

LECTURE VII

LECTURE VIII

LECTURE IX

LECTURE X

LECTURE XI

LECTURE XII

NOTE

PART II

PART I

LECTURE I

(*Newton Hall*, 1893. *Philadelphia*, 1901)

THE ETHIC OF HUMANISM

AN ethical and human religion (like every real religion whatever) must go at once to the root of the matter, which is—how to purify the human heart—how to elevate the human nature—how to make good lives.

And this it must do in the way that every system which ever influenced mankind has done, by having its own view of human character, and by having its own mode of appealing to the dominant motives in human hearts.

It was a great step in morality when the old moralists said—*Do unto others as you would be done by*. It regulated conduct, it made justice—equity—the rule of life. But this is an appeal to *external act*—not to the heart. It makes *self* the standard of duty. And there was great danger of its being interpreted to mean—give what you get—treat men as they treat you—*Do ut des*.

It was a great advance when Christ said—*Love thy neighbour as thyself*. The same words had been used by Confucius very much earlier, and by others. But the Gospel made this rule a central principle, and forced it deep into the conscience of men. The new principle became not *Justice*, equality, or reciprocity—but *Love*. *Love thy neighbour* involved social sympathy—*Humanity*. This is the key of all the beauty of Christian sentiment, of that exquisite idea of Paul's—Charity, *i.e.* Love—Goodness of heart.

Let us examine this as a dominant maxim. Is this the last word of morality and religion? Is it complete: is it final? The *principle* to which it appeals is Love: but the standard of measurement still is *Self*. It calls upon self to be the test of unselfishness, as if it were true that Devils could only be cast out in the name of Beelzebub. There is another quality in the maxim: it is an appeal simply to sentiment, to feeling: the purest feeling, but feeling only. Action and Thought are not included, they receive from this maxim no guidance or control. Now Action and Thought are very powerful forces with strong instincts of their own, which very readily tend towards self. We see how very willing are Action and Thought to take their own lines and to gratify their own imperious demands, fully accepting the view that religion does not address itself directly to them and therefore does not concern them. They are quite content to welcome a religion which comes crying out—My kingdom is not of this world. The instincts of energy and of intelligence concern this world very much: those of energy exclusively so; those of intelligence for all but occasional and mystical meditations. And thus the instincts of energy and intelligence are quite unconcerned with a religion which expressly disclaims any relation to their sphere of activity.

Consider next the motive, or inspiring force. Why love my neighbour? Why forgo so much that is desirable for his sake? The answer of the Gospel is simple. For fear of God's wrath; by the express command of God; in order to win the reward He promises, in order to escape the penalties He threatens. The morality of the Gospel is summed up in this: He that loveth his neighbour as himself shall save his own soul, and have eternal life.

No reasonable mind can deny that this Gospel—this message of gladness to the contrite heart weary of evil-doing and fearful of retribution—has, in its history, done great and glorious things. But, viewed as a final and complete Gospel for mankind, it has these three undeniable defects.

1. *Its sphere is strictly limited to sentiment.* The Evangelical and Catholic ideal is attained when the *heart* is perfect. That is certainly an immense gain; and vast consequences for good

must follow. But it is very far from all. The whole range of the intellectual and active life stands outside of it. The religious type of the Gospel is complete without inspiring a single intellectual or active quality. Hence came monasticism, mysticism, quietism, quakerism, and all the various forms of meditative seclusion and withdrawal from the work and thought of the world which take such a hold on Catholic and evangelical communions everywhere. Ever since the rise of Christianity, this ideal has held sway over the tender-hearted, the emotional, the pure—and also over the indolent, the dreamy, and even the hypocritical. It has assumed a wide range of forms, from the hermit of the Thebaid and Simon Stylites down to the Calvinistic fanatic who would spend his life in prayer and psalm-singing. This unworldliness, or rather "other worldliness" is of the essence of the Gospel whether in the Catholic or Protestant types. Indeed, to speak plainly, it is the real Imitation of Christ, the supreme law of the Gospel, if the Gospel be taken literally—which happily is not done by the majority of Christians. But this type—this ideal of other worldliness, which it is impossible for the sincere Christian evangelist to repudiate, explains and justifies the profound inner revolt of the strong natures and the intellectual temperaments against this religion of sentiment, with its feeble and morbid renunciation of all that is noble in man's character and brain.

2. *It centres the religious life round self.* For the end of the religious life is personal salvation. Personal reward, personal fear dominates its moral and religious life. Hence the individualist, egoistic side of all deep and vital Christianity, so far as its dogma extends. No doubt the soundness of human nature is constantly correcting this very questionable creed. But in an absolute creed, the paramount duty of saving one's own immortal soul is necessarily of infinite moment compared with any consideration of this transitory life on earth. The material welfare of oneself or of one's fellow-creatures, in this fleeting and miserable state of trial, is dross when weighed in the balance with a crown of eternal glory, or a hell of eternal torment. A true Christian, who was able to avert a plague from his generation by freely accepting damnation for himself would be bound by his own religion to save his own soul, and to count the death of thousands as of no moment beside the joy of the Angels over a sinner rescued from the Evil One. Such an one might be superior to his creed, or might practically disbelieve his own creed and listen to the innate moral instincts within his own heart. That is to say, the Creed would break down on any real trial against sound human nature. And this dilemma arises. Heroism and Genius seem

often to force men to be bad Christians, *i.e.* by neglecting their own souls and ceasing to dwell on the hope of Heaven. The letter of the Gospel seems to force Christians to be bad and worthless men, when torpid hermits and idle recluses dream away their lives in religious "exercises."

3. A third difficulty is this. The love of God, the fear of God, the will of God, are not homogeneous with the love of one's neighbour. It is a matter of pure conjecture what God would have us do for our neighbour. What kind of love of our neighbour does the will of God inspire? Not necessarily of course his earthly good. Hence have arisen such strange, vague, and some abominable ways of showing one's love to one's neighbour in order to find favour with God. The burning, torturing, or outlawing of heretics has been for the whole Christian period a very orthodox mode of giving practical expression to one's love for one's neighbour. Even now, after eighteen centuries of Christian civilisation, it is maintained by the priesthood, that those who worship in a chapel may not lie in the same cemetery beside their neighbours who are Churchmen. As a matter of fact the apparently beautiful precept of the Gospel—Love thy neighbour as thyself, so that God may feel justified in taking your soul into Heaven—has led to spiritual pride, mysticism, idleness, the mere impotence of devotion, to cruelty, uncharitableness, and un-

neighbourly scorn, has been found compatible with practical self-absorption in action, in a life of engrossment in ambition for wealth, power, or fame, or in an unscrupulous use of intellectual superiority. It has led to a conversion of the whole nature to mere intellectual vanity or curiosity in men who all the while conscientiously believe themselves and are believed by others to be devoutly following the behest of the Gospel to love their neighbours as themselves, and to be constantly meditating on the world to come.

In the meantime the world that is stands delivered over to the natural man, to the instincts of ambition, greed, the thirst of power, or the insatiable curiosity of the intellect. For the old Gospel rule, beautiful at first sight, touching and pathetic as it is to the loving-hearted and the poor in spirit, proves to be too vague, too unreal, too narrow to command the strong and intellectual natures, and to those whom it does command it appeals in secret to the very self of their selves.

This principle of the Gospel rests of course upon a doctrine. Every religion has its doctrine about human nature, its cardinal rule of life.

The doctrine of the Gospel about human nature is this: The human heart from the very first generation has fallen from the purity in which it was designed, has become depraved by its second nature, is desperately wicked and evil continually, so that it seeks evil as the sparks fly upwards. And yet into this blackened nature a Divine Spirit, called Grace, mysteriously descends, illumines it, conquers nature; and so the nature is born again, is regenerated, and in some supernatural way becomes perfect, pure, and unable to fall from Grace.

We know what have been the consequences of this doctrine of fallen and blackened human nature working with this principle of saving our own souls by fixing our whole mind on a Heaven and a Hell that transcend this earth and which offer an eternity beside this fleeting moment. The Inquisition, the religious wars, Calvinism, Puritanism, the long and odious history of Church Orthodoxy, of sectarian bigotry inside and outside all the churches, the vast record of spiritual inhumanity and spiritual hypocrisy, give the answer, and all their works of evil in men and in societies of men.

This doctrine is utterly false. It is vague; it is fantastic; one-sided, inhuman, and degrading in its extravagance. It makes out human nature most untruly black, to make it the next moment, by some spiritual legerdemain, to be as untruly ecstatic. It libels our nature with as much falseness as it transfigures it. Human nature is too good and sound for this vilification: and yet not etherial enough for this sanctification. Both forms of exaggeration are hysterical, and wildly disturbing. They undermine morality, whilst they turn ethics into nonsense.

We know very well that men of the world professing the Gospel, and indeed all the more enlightened theologians of to-day use no such language as their creed, and they may be ready to deny that Christianity rests at all on any such central maxim. Well! they may throw over the Sermon on the Mount, and all the explicit words of Jesus of Nazareth. But what else is the Creed? What Gospel or sacred Scripture anywhere teaches the ethical theories of modern philosophy? Sermons we know are preached daily on the ethical basis of Comte, or Herbert Spencer, or Mill. But that is because rational Christians have completely abandoned the plain words of the Gospel and their own creeds, whilst using the poetry and mysticism of Christianity as a mere colouring for modern and rational philosophy.

Let us not be carried away by the pathetic vision of the divine reformer of the shores of Galilee, by the tremendous drama of the Passion —a drama which I do not hesitate to call the most sublime creation of all human poetry—let us not be misled even by the burning enthusiasm of Humanity as we know it in the life and letters of Paul, and ever forget how wrong, how cruel, how crazy is this vaunted scheme of the dead human heart and its miraculous regeneration into a transcendent and immaterial Heaven—which is the true message of the Gospel—and its only message to man.

Humanity is strong and noble indeed that it can have drained this potion to the dregs, and still have lived on good and healthy!

Let us turn to the Ethical form of the central maxim of Religion. It is this. *Life belongs to Humanity*. At first sight it may not appear that this differs very widely from the Gospel rule—*Love your neighbour as yourself*. But a little examination will show that it differs subtly, widely, and fundamentally. Comte's French *Vivre pour autrui* is usually translated *Live for others*. But I am hardly satisfied with this. The literal equivalent for *Live for others* in French would be *Vivez pour les autres* which would be a stiff and narrow version. When I remember how deeply Comte has suffered from crude anglicising of his phrases such as *culte*, *vénération*, *unité*, and so forth, I am careful to note how these maxims of his should be translated. We have no exact equivalents of the impersonal *vivre* and for the collective term *autrui*.

The nearest equivalent that I know is *Life belongs to Humanity*. Live for Society. Individual life is bound up in the life of the social organism. One sees at once how much this differs from *Love thy neighbour as thyself*.

Life applies to the whole nature, and is not

limited to the heart. It includes Action and Thought as much as Feeling. The life of intelligence, of activity, of enjoyment, of effort—industry, art, meditation, study, family life, public life, politics, science, religion—all alike belong not to our neighbour, but to the Humanity of which we and our neighbours, our forefathers and our descendants form infinitesimal units.

It means not simply *love* your fellow-men; but think, work, plan, observe, dream, if you will—but develop life in all its many sides—Live in a word for the *Man* that is, that has been, that is to be.

How real, how practical, how comprehensive, and yet how definite is this rule of Life. *Life belongs to Humanity.* Nothing can be wider than life. Nothing on earth can be broader than Humanity. The one includes the aggregate forces of the individual: the other the whole human race outside self, and indeed including self. Nothing, be it said, earthly; nothing within the sphere of our planet. Anything transcendental is doubtless beyond the sphere. But that which is transcendental is infinite, without limit, and hence to me at least unreal, and incomprehensible. Let me guard myself here from the assumption that I am putting Humanity in any sense in antagonism with God. About the Creation and Moral Government of the Universe I say nothing—for I know nothing, and to those who know that they do know—also I say nothing. They maintain of course that to live for Humanity is to live for God—nor shall I dispute what they say. I am concerned now with the immediate and visible sphere of Ethical life—which is obviously our human kind and our earthly abode. That Ethical life may pass onwards through Humanity to an Almighty creator, and beyond our planet to an Infinite Heaven, I neither affirm nor dispute. I can speak to you only of what I know, and the immediate object—if you please you may call it the intermediate object—is Man, and his life here.

In this maxim there is nothing one-sided. There is no setting the heart against the brain and the energies. There is no special appeal to emotion. Life implies the due development of the nature all-round. Again in the object or motive: there is no transcendental or disparate object proposed. It does not say—"Live a material life as a man on earth, in order that you may hereafter enter on an immaterial life in Heaven as an Angel without organs and without functions." There is no motive of an ultimate life entirely disparate from the actual life of which we have experience. When the fear of God is proposed as the motive to a right life, it is a matter of interpretation to know what this means. Every Church, every teacher, every man may understand it in different ways. Live according to the will of God may imply fifty ways in which that will may be understood. But when we say *Live for Humanity*, it is possible to understand this differently in details, but it is a practical matter of moral and social science. It is very difficult to assume that burning people alive and baptizing savages by force and fraud, or extending the Gospel by war, or enlarging the boundaries of Christendom by maxim guns, or doing any downright evil in order to save souls and spread the glad tidings of peace and goodwill amongst men—can be *Living for Humanity*.

It is an obvious and very fair question—What is then to be the motive ? Why should we—Live for Humanity rather than for ourselves ? The charge often made against Humanist morality is that to give up Heaven and Hell is to open the door to arrant self-enjoyment. " Eat and drink, for to-morrow we die," and so forth. Why should we live for Humanity ? That is, no doubt, the key of the problem.

The ethical reason why we should live for Humanity is this, that it is the natural way of living; that human nature is so organised that this is the only way of living a life at once free, complete, harmonious, happy.

The ethical rule rests on positive proof—it lies at the base of social and moral science. If it is not at first sight obvious, it is a clear result of observation. There is nothing at all extravagant or hysterical about this maxim, if we understand it fairly. It has been said—even by Mr. Mill amongst the rest—that "Live for others" means that life is to have self expurgated out of it. It is not so at all. Live for Humanity simply means that social, sympathetic, collective life which is natural to Humanity. "Life belongs to Humanity" implies that self is part of Humanity. This life of self is part of the groundwork of all life. In order to begin to live for Humanity we must begin by living for self—but in a due measure, in a right degree. We cannot live for Humanity, without so living for self that we make ourself part of Humanity.

The sympathetic, social life is the life of self, in a true sense. We do not cease to be ourselves by loving, thinking, working for Humanity. We *become* ourselves. We develop, realise, manifest ourselves. We do not live other people's lives. We live *our own* lives. Why ought we to live for Humanity? Because *we must*. We are so constituted by nature. Because we only live by Humanity, in Humanity, through Humanity, just as Humanity lives by, in, and through us. We can live no other life, unless we choose a broken, partial, unnatural kind of half-life—alien to, an outcast from, Humanity.

Humanity bred, bore, tended, nursed, and clothed us—for our parents and guardians were only the instruments of Humanity, using for our benefit the resources of Humanity. Humanity taught us to speak our mother tongue—for our mothers assuredly did not invent language—we sucked in Humanity with our mother's milk. For years our existence depended, minute by minute, on the care of Humanity—for there again our parents were only in part the organs of society, the agents and ministers of others. So does our existence depend on Humanity in sickness, and, indeed, if you only think it out, in every hour of life, and so will it depend at the end till the last breath, nay, until our return again to our mother earth.

So also to others we become the instruments of Humanity. When we think or study we use the thoughts of Humanity. When we work we are only applying, directing, giving some new form to some previous result of the labour of others. Crusoe on his island, cut off from men, was still living on the products of civilisation, reading his Bible, using human knowledge, arts, and experience. He was only living a human life, because he had saved from the wreck fragments of man's accumulated knowledge, and because with his cats, dogs, and parrot he was imitating a human family. The most lonely philosopher would be a savage but for his possessing the stores of human thought, and his most splendid ideas only add something fresh to that store. The most powerful ruler is only one who induces many men to do what he urges them to do, for Caesar and Napoleon (if they could have induced no one to follow and obey them) were less able to win a victory than one naked African brave.

The wealthiest capitalist is merely one whom Humanity suffers to say what shall be done with the products accumulated by countless men and women and children: and (apart from this co-operation which Society ratifies) Rothschild and a beggar are equally rich. The most cynical voluptuary cannot drink a glass of wine or a cup of coffee without putting in motion thousands at the other end of the planet. The most sordid miser is only one who keeps together for a few years and accumulates some of the produce of Humanity, and often saves it for a useful destination. The worst misanthropist can only curse Humanity in the language taught him by Humanity. The worst tyrant can only work his inhumanity by the help of Humanity and by the sufferance and consent of Humanity. The very rogue and murderer works out his crimes by the agency of Humanity, and plunders others or takes life by the skilled appliances of Humanity, and often by the highest ingenuity of science, economics, and applied mechanics. The Anarchists and Terrorists, whose aim is to blow up civil society with dynamite, profess that they do so in the cause of Humanity and under a sense of devotion to Humanity.

We necessarily live by means of Humanity. The simplest act of life is impossible without it. And in one sense we can only live for the sake of Humanity. Every act of life, except, perhaps, mere eating and drinking, and we may add solitary smoking and idle reading, and such other silent and sensual indulgences, concerns and affects others, obtains the co-operation of others, and, if it does this, it must be to the interest or pleasure of some others. Every human being must in some sense "live for Humanity," otherwise he would not live at all. The very baby at the breast lives for others as well as by others. In one sense the most luxurious live for others; for their personal aims and desires can only be satisfied by indirectly conferring benefits, rewards, or mere subsistence on those they employ or need. A man can only, in the strictest sense, cease to live for others when he is at once dead and infamous. And this is undoubtedly the Ethical equivalent of Hell.

Thus, since it is impossible for a living man (however bad) not to live for Humanity in some degree, it may be in a degree infinitesimally small or extremely low, so to live for Humanity in an enlarged and honourable sense can only mean—Live for Humanity in the natural and scientific conception of human nature. The low, petty good that is done, without intending or perceiving it, by the debauchee or the ambitious or the tyrant, is only conferred on a few, and those the least worthy, and that in a part, and the least worthy part, of their lives. The work of the good man is done to a far larger number, to their higher interests, and it belongs to the highest interests of Humanity, and helps to carry on the permanent growth of Humanity. Thus Live for Humanity really means—Live for the best interests of Humanity in the widest sense. Live for others means only Live a complete, a free, a useful life—and life is only complete, free, and useful according as it is in true relation with the sum of human life in the vast organism of which we form units.

This of course rests on a theory. Every religious scheme must have a doctrine of human nature, as well as a code of duty. What is the scientific doctrine of the moral problem ? It is this :

Man, as all ethical analysis combines to prove, is a composite organism made up of very various propensities which stir him to everything he does. Some of these are self-regarding ; some of them regard others. Of the desires we may say : Those which regard self are (1) the more numerous, (2) the more energetic, (3) the more constant.

On the other hand, the desires which regard

others, though fewer, weaker, and less imperious are :

1. More able to give permanent satisfaction.
2. Can alone keep a permanent ascendancy.
3. Can alone be indulged freely without bringing us into collision with our fellows.

That is to say, mere appetite, the simplest of all appetites, that of self-preservation, affects us all, men, women, and children, every day, and with most of us in a civilised state several times in each day. If not satisfied, it affects us to madness or extreme violence, and till it is satisfied more or less, the other human attributes are distorted or paralysed. There are many such personal appetites :

1. That for food, air, nourishment of the body.
2. That towards mating with our kind.
3. That impelling us to breed and rear children.
4. The desire to destroy, overcome, or contend.
5. The desire to construct, put together, devise, and make the beautiful or the useful.
6. The desire to have power over others.
7. The desire to win the approval of others.

In other words, the instinct of nutrition, of sex, of parenthood, of destruction, of construction, of ambition, of vanity. These seven are here placed in the order of their decreasing vehemence and increasing social dignity. The most common, the most imperious, and the most purely personal, the craving for food, stands at the bottom of the scale, sexual love leads on to higher moral uses, and the care of offspring to higher; construction, which is industry, is nobler but less violent than the passion for removing what is evil or troublesome, and not so liable to frightful abuse; and the desire to win the approval of others is usually nobler than the desire of controlling others. Both are liable to odious depravations, but both may be converted to great social ends.

The instincts which impel us to seek satisfaction out of self in the good of others are not seven but three. They are far less imperious and occupy a smaller part of our lives. They are:

1. Attachment for our equals and colleagues.
2. Respect for our superiors, teachers, guides.
3. Benevolence, sympathy, charity in the Apostle's sense—the desire to feel for, help, please each and all.

These instincts towards promoting the good of others, or of impelling us towards others are steadily active, apart from the moment of fruition. They give us a far higher and more enduring satisfaction. They may become a ruling motive without disturbing the harmony of our nature. And they may be indulged to any limit without bringing us into conflict with our fellows.

A life of selfish appetite cannot be lived without constant disturbance within, and risk of perpetual conflict with others. It is only a wild beast, and a wild beast of superior strength and ferocity, which can live a life of consistent indulgence of appetite. A tiger in the jungle or a gorilla kills its prey, and gorges itself, seeks its mate, feeds its cubs till they can kill for themselves, and wars on all things living till it meets its match, or dies of starvation and isolation.

A man who tries such a life of wild beast is shortly brought up and put in restraint. If he is to live like a man, in human society, he must be faithful, respectful, helpful, affectionate in some degree, to some persons, under some conditions, or the gallows and the prison ends his career of violence. If he simply desires to indulge his lower sensual appetites, he must get the means of self-indulgence, by industry, co-operation with others and some social qualities, or he will be an outcast and an object of suspicion, dislike, and hostility to his fellow-men. If his life is to be really adequate, happy, and free, he must live in the social spirit conforming to the true life of men about him, helping, loving, and in sympathy with the great sum of human life around him.

Such is the analysis of the human instincts given by Comte as a fundamental part of his philosophy. It is constantly repeated in his works, and may be taken as the scientific analysis of human nature. It is included in a variety of our publications, and is bound up with the *Calendar* and the *Library* and the other *Tables* and *Laws of Thought.* I have myself been familiar with it for some fifty years, and have pondered over it, used it, searched it, and compared it with all the leading forms of psychical analysis from Aristotle to Herbert Spencer. The more I consider it, the more entirely luminous, scientific, and fertile does this analysis seem to me. It is, I have no doubt, one of those permanent contributions to philosophy, which may be so classed, with the Law of the Three Stages, and the Classification of the Sciences.

I will not venture to say that the progress of philosophy may not bring some modifications in minor respects, but I know of none, and I have seen no criticism which appears to me to touch it or to modify it. It has completely entered into my own mental structure, so that I cannot think or reason about human nature without resorting to it. Nor, indeed, can I find any analysis of human nature which can fairly be said even to compete with it, or in any way to suggest an alternative theory.

Now the moral problem, as stated by Science, is this—Of our ten primordial instincts *seven* are self-regarding, and are far the more vehement, though far the least noble; *three* are directed to others, and if less energetic are higher in quality.

A sound and natural life is the just balance between our self-regarding and our social instincts. But this balance or rather harmony (for it is the combination of all working together) is very far from easy. The self-regarding instincts, as we see, are the more numerous, more vigorous, and most persistent. Sympathy may be dormant for long periods, but if appetite were not gratified we should die in the course of a few days, and neither Simon Stylites nor an Indian fakir could wholly subdue the craving for food. Hence the harmony between the two sets of instincts can only be maintained by continual effort, by education, by social influences, by daily cultivation of the nobler instincts, by daily discipline of the lower to accept their minor functions.

There is in this no extirpation of the self-regarding propensities, no crushing or mortification of them, no exaggerated estimate of the higher instincts. All the instincts are necessary to life, and thus are necessary to Humanity. All are in some degree good and useful, because human nature would not be itself without them. But the full development of human life, the freedom of life, the higher pleasures of life, are only possible by the systematic reining-in of the self-regarding instincts to be confined to their due, indispensable, but lower functions, and the systematic rousing of the social instincts to their due place of superiority and rule.

In a purely individual life one selfish passion might be supreme. But there is no such thing as an individual life; it is as impossible as life without oxygen or without sensation. Life being always in constant and necessary relations with others, if waged with utter regard to self, involves a life of constant struggle and ultimate destruction. Even a man-eating tiger does not last long; and now and then a man of tiger-like nature and bestial cunning attempts a purely egoistic synthesis, or life of criminal indulgence—but he speedily ends in prison or the scaffold. Happily, all the instincts of selfish enjoyment imply some co-operation with others, unless it may be the lowest of all, the craving for food and the means of life—which, as we all know, usually takes a sociable form. Any one of the selfish passions indulged without restraint would lead to a short life and a stormy one—not at all a happy one. Again, the selfish passions, if freely indulged together, must conflict with each other. Indulge appetite too freely, and love of power and of praise would be sacrificed. Indulge the love of power and of praise, and you must sternly control appetite. Pride kills vanity: vanity kills pride. It is not easy to be a popular tyrant, or an ambitious self-admirer. The constructive and the destructive instincts can hardly be indulged together, and if either is indulged inordinately, it can only be done at the expense of the strictly family affections and the atrophy of the two essentially public instincts. Hence harmony is impossible on the basis of giving the control to any one of the selfish instincts. An egoistic synthesis involves a life of storm, suffering, struggle.

Hence, for various reasons, harmony of the nature is only possible on the basis of giving the unselfish instincts supreme control. These usually combine—and do not neutralise each other. So much so, that some philosophers have doubted if there is any analysis of them possible, if the instinct to help others be not one and indivisible. The unselfish instincts steadily and necessarily lead us outside self. They force us into society and into being welcomed by others. Our love, regard, and desire to aid others never brought us into collision with others—quite the contrary. It is only the sense of this outside overwhelming pressure which keeps the violent selfish instincts in hand. Starving men refrain from seizing the food before their eyes, because along with the generous sense of duty to others goes hand in hand the irresistible social repression of crime. So in marriage, the affection of the married pair is fortified for the most part under all the strain of disagreement by the social pressure of submitting to a public and irrevocable bond. "The being, whether man or brute, who loves nothing outside himself, and really lives for himself alone, is by that very fact condemned to pass his life in a miserable alternation of ignoble torpor and uncontrolled excitement" (*Pol.* i. 566).

This harmony between our instincts—the only mode in which regular life is possible to a social being—conspires with the life of Humanity about us, enables us to join in that life, and secures that our work shall be incorporated with it. In a word, in living for Humanity we live for our whole selves and our true selves. We fulfil our natures only in living for others. Our life becomes a success, a joy, a poem only when we raise it to the life of the whole. We obtain harmony in our souls within and harmony with our kind around. In other words, the law of Happiness is the law of Duty.

Thus personal morality demands a twofold effort:

1. Constant discipline to restrain the self-regarding instincts in their due place.

2. Constant cultivation of the unselfish instincts to maintain their ascendancy.

In other words—First, discipline; and next, religion. That is:

(1) Practical habits to check the violence of appetite.

(2) Continual stimulus to the affections to fix them on some worthy object without.

We may apply to each side of life in turn the rule—*Life belongs to Humanity.*

Take the simplest, lowest, most imperious of our instincts, that which prompts us to satisfy our bodily wants—appetite for food is the type and the most obvious, but all bodily and material wants may be included. Give this instinct a social turn by applying to it the maxim *Life belongs to Humanity*, and then we feel that food, warmth, shelter, and clothing, external activity, and the enjoyment of physical life of a certain kind are absolutely essential to life, at any rate to any efficient and normal activity. And so far the satisfaction of the instinct is just and indispensable. But it does not limit us to considerations of health, decency, and good sense. Place the personal and primitive duty of maintaining the body in full activity on a social ground, and we must say—If *Life belongs to Humanity*, then, not merely bestial excess in food and drink, but preposterous extravagance in luxury are odious and sinful.

Nay, we must go on to say—It is not only the quantity of that which we consume which we must consider, and its wholesomeness to our bodies, but the quality and proportion of what we consume to our own gratification which is to be considered. All flagrant misappropriation of the common stock is an abuse, even though such abuse have in it no infringement on our own health, or on the conventions of society. The man for whose bodily wants hundreds have to suffer and toil, even though he never eat or drink so as to affect his health, is living in breach of the moral law as much as the drunkard or the glutton; and he may possibly, in a more refined way, be doing a wider social wrong. Nor is his case mended by the shallow sophism that his personal extravagance may be good for trade. Nothing is good for trade which wastes human industry upon one pampered and surfeited egoist. The drunkard mars his own power to serve Humanity. The spendthrift engrosses an inordinate share of the services of Humanity. If we place our personal temperance on a purely selfish ground, we may oscillate between an irrational and ecstatic asceticism and a cynical indifference to anything but the claims of our bodily health. Duty to society is a measure which covers ground far wider than any personal standard whatever; it goes deeper; it acts more constantly.

If *Life belongs to Humanity*, then temperance means not only the care of our own health, and the dignity of our own bodies, and the fulness of our own powers. It is this—all this—and much more. It is the temperate acceptance of a fair share of the common human produce. And he violates the rule who pampers the appetite with waste, who insults and degrades his neighbours by display of luxury, who humiliates them by hiring them to give him unworthy service, who perverts the industry and the ingenuity of Humanity to be the mere instrument of his insolent extravagance.

And so, if time allowed, we might go through all the personal instincts and show what new meanings they acquire by the light of the maxim *Life belongs to Humanity.* Continence would be seen to consist not only in a formal chastity or personal indulgence within the strictly legal restrictions, but in constant and scrupulous regard for all those consequences by which the claims of family and society can be affected by our acts and our habits and lives. Our parental instincts would be controlled not only by continual regard for the interests of our descendants, but also for the interests of society.

And so we may pass through all the range of human desire and on every side find fresh illustration of the truth—that to guide, control, and spiritualise the tremendous instincts of self in the human heart, we must cease to appeal to any motive that is based on self either in this world or in the world to come, and we must base morality on the omnipresent and circumambient Humanity—which is the natural object of our unselfish efforts and activities, and which is the sole external Power by which our selfish instincts can effectually be disciplined and curbed.

LECTURE II

(*Newton Hall*, 1893. *Ethical Societies*, 1895–1900)

FAMILY LIFE

THE last lecture showed that the balance and organic working of the complex human system required a double effort :

The first, to restrain the selfish appetites.

The second, to educate, enlarge, and stimulate the unselfish emotions.

Both ends may be trained in the light of the central moral maxim : *Life belongs to Humanity.* The last discourse dealt with the first. Let us turn to the second—the cultivation of the nobler affections. One has to realise what this cultivation really is in our scientific scheme. The French word *culte* is often inadequately translated *worship.* Many people who turn to the human religion in a superficial way are inclined to revolt at the idea (as they fancy it) of being asked to " worship " their fellow-men. They say —" No more bowing down the knee for us—and certainly we will not bow it down to the many-headed million, whom we do not greatly love." All this is a parody, a mere misunderstanding. *Culte*—*cult*—means the rational, scientific, practical training of our generous feelings of attachment, reverence, love—for our family first, our country next, lastly for the human race and the future of civilisation. "*Worship*" is an utterly narrow and ambiguous equivalent for this concentration of our sympathies, gratitude, and affection towards the beings around us with whom our life is cast, and with whom we have to work and live.

Family is the first, the permanent, the elemental sphere of social life, of morality; and consequently, is the source of religion. It is an obvious truism that in the Family, as members of a Family, we first come to know and to exercise our sentiment (1) of *attachment*, comradeship, fellowship, (2) of *reverence* for those who can teach us, guide, and elevate us, of love which urges us to protect, help, and cherish those to whom we owe our lives and better natures. That is to say, the Family is the fundamental, primordial unit of society.

It is one of the most crucial of all our social doctrines that society is made up of *families*—and not of *individuals*. That is to say, anatomically, or arithmetically, any given social organism can be analysed into single persons. But socially, it can only be analysed into families: the real social life is composed of the aggregate of families and not of individuals. Most of our modern anarchical theories come from our looking upon society, as made up of individual men and women, instead of looking on it as made up of family groups. Socially and morally considered, family groups are the smallest units into which social life can be resolved.

Of course in the abstract we can think of men as individuals, just as we can think of their bony skeleton apart from the rest of their bodies. And, no doubt, to the eye we see the individuals distinct. Individuals eat, drink, sleep and move in a separate physiological life—but not as a separate social life. We can think of individuals, just as we can think of the mind, or the body, or the nervous system. But strictly speaking, mind, nervous system, digestive system, are mental abstractions and not substantive and independent organisms. There is no such self-supporting, living, entity as a nervous system, or brain. You can dissect out the brain, or this or that set of nerves—but they are then dead, functionless, inert—not at all living and acting. Anatomically, we can find the corpses, or dead physical forms, of brain, digestive apparatus and so forth. By a process of mental abstraction, we can imagine the action of brain, or digestion, as living organs of a complex organism. But we can never get at *living* brain as a separate unit or being.

Just so, an individual is an abstraction—

a mental image, not a living entity. There is no such thing as an independent, self-supporting, living individual, and there cannot be. Of course, we mean not living as an effective and worthy member of a civilised community. There might be living and breathing animals in human form, devoid of every human and social quality, living as the hippopotamus lives in his tank. But when we consider human beings as living a human life however primitive, they are necessarily members, in any normal state, of some larger social organism. The smallest real, substantive, self-contained social organism is the Family. When a great social philosopher imagined Crusoe on his island beginning to live a human life again, he had to give him a quasi-family—first a dog, a cat, a household, and soon a son or young friend to be educated.

You might as well analyse society into stomachs, brains, or spinal chords as into individuals. It would only be carrying the mental abstraction one step farther. There would of course be no society, if there were no individuals; and so, there would be no society, if there were no stomachs. You cannot look on society as made up of individuals, any more than you can look on it as made up of stomachs, brains, and the rest of the physical organs of man. Brains and stomachs cannot live *per se*. Nor can individuals live *per se*—At least, not the individuals we call men, the organisms we conceive as forming human societies.

Abstract in thought one single solitary individual, mentally conceived as having neither parent, nor mate, nor offspring, nor any human kindred either natural, or artificial—no human quality or faculty, no endowment or enjoyment which we derive from family, acquire in the family, or exercise by the help of the family. Such an one would be without speech—for speech is only learned in the family and could not be acquired alone—not the faculty of articulate utterance. Such an one would have no descendants, no future, nothing human. He is a pithecoid biped—a two-legged, pair-armed, monkey-like brute, without the characteristic endowments of man. Now society is not made up of brutes, but of men. Society implies (1) a succession — an inheritance of knowledge: accumulations, gifts, and faculties from generation to generation—the transmission of useful knowledge and useful things. (2) It implies a combination of efforts on the part of numbers working in unison to a common end, (3) a distribution of different functions, adapted to the respective faculties of differently qualified members.

Some of the more intelligent animals show these in some partial degree, some of the monkeys, beavers, bees, and ants. But man only exhibits them all in a very high degree, especially the first, which is the peculiar distinction of man, the transmission of products and experience from generation to generation. This is the one essential gift which marks off man from the brutes, and really constitutes his pre-eminence. Some brutes show the family instinct; some the accumulative instinct; some, especially bees and ants, the tribal or swarming instinct. Man alone combines the family, the tribal, and the racial instinct and has found out how to combine the family, the tribe, the species without effacing either: man is the only animal which can transmit his experience to his race. But this unique human faculty is acquired, learned, and maintained in and by, the family. That is to say, human society is the creation, not of individuals, but of families.

Plant a million individual men in any suitable land—bound to live strictly as individuals—not associated in life in any way, not co-operating with, or doing anything for, one another—each solitarily living his own life—like a man-eating tiger, eating, drinking, devouring, dying alone. You get nothing that can be called human society out of that. But take one family—a pair and their offspring and descendants—with different functions, nurturing, helping, training one another with the human faculties and feelings, however low, even suppose them to be the sole denizens of this planet—you would have a small but a real human society, living human lives, a continuous group of beings, having transmission of faculties and possessions, succession, combination of efforts, distribution of function, permanence of organic union, in other words a human society.

Modern anarchists talk of society as made up of individuals, men and women, equal and independent. There is a gross error in this calculation. About half the human beings on the earth are children :—the infants (say up to three or four years) depending on others for their existence, hour by hour ; the children (up to fourteen or fifteen at least) depending for their moral and intellectual life wholly on others. No one, not even an orator on the rights of women, can venture to say that the infant at the breast is an equal independent unit. Nor is the child of three, or of five, or even of twelve. And of these there are millions, some in almost every house. The children have to be placed somewhere. They are half of the human race ; they are potential men and women ; it would be absurd to count them as independent units of society. Where are they to be classed, since they cannot stand alone ? It is easy to say off-hand, the babies in arms go with their mothers, though it is a very poor kind of an independent unit that can be made by a mother with a baby in arms. But there are millions of children which are not able to stand alone, and yet are too old to be thrown wholly on the mothers. Their daily existence depends on the men, and yet they cannot be classed exclusively with the men.

About half the whole race, then, are necessarily shared jointly between the men and the women—the men providing for their material existence in the main, the women in the main providing for their moral and intellectual training. Plato and other socialists who propose to take children away from their parents and bring them up in public phalansteries, may consistently speak of men and women as independent units. But without this Platonic and Spartan Utopia, the human race could not be continued on the unit system. The unit hypothesis is an absurdity, if regarded as anything but a mental abstraction. And if we take into view all the millions of those who form artificial or voluntary family groups, all the sick and feeble and those who are in the moral and intellectual condition of the children, we come to this—that the ultimate units of human society cannot be *individuals*, but must be *families*; for more than a majority of the human race need both men and women jointly, and also all but a small minority of any society are jointly required to give their lives for others, and to live a common life with them.

The instances of either men or women who are really free "to live their own lives" quite independently, are peculiar exceptions. Here and there a few single men and women with intellectual aspirations, and here and there a few childless and unencumbered adults, may nurse the idea that they are living for themselves alone: but their condition is so abnormal, so unnatural, and their mental and moral constitution is so morbid, that their opinion is not worth considering, and their demands should excite nothing but pity. There are people who object to the institution of marriage and some who believe in polygamy; we have known persons who think it wicked to kill sheep or to cook food with fire. But we cannot stop to confute all such wild theories.

It is the foundation of the scientific view of life to regard society as composed of families and not as resolvable into individuals. And the value of this is—that it accustoms us to start in our social theories with the interest of the *family*, and not of the *person*. The Family becomes the root and key of man's social, moral, and religious existence.

We are too prone to think of *family* as meaning three or four, or more children, living in one dwelling, or else as a number of persons related by blood, but possibly living at a distance apart and in utterly disparate lives. Neither of these views is adequate. The first is too narrow: the second is too wide. It will not do to narrow the family down to a few children. Very many modern theorists on this question (indeed the large majority of them) have no children: and they come to consider the Family to be no affair of theirs.

Family has a much wider sense. A man or a woman may have neither spouse, nor child, nor brother, nor sister. Yet all have family relations. The most solitary theorist has or has had parents. And it is a *lusus naturae* almost if they have not some close to them in blood relationship or in artificial relationship of a kindred sort. A man or woman whose parents are dead, and who has no living relative, may fancy that he or she has no family life possible to him or her. But the case is rare. And it is part of the scientific scheme to diminish the separation which is caused by death; and to make Death itself a means of spiritualising and intensifying the moral bond between parents and children, brother and sister. And it is also part of the scheme to revive the system of the artificial family by means of adoption, so largely practised, and to such good result, in ancient times.

In a normal state, the cases would be rare, and as hard as they are rare, where men or women would have neither any natural family relation at all and no one to whom they stand in any relation of family, whom they feel morally bound to regard as something more than an outside friend. At any rate, a large number of such stand in the domestic relation as it is called of being servant or mistress in one way. And if persons carefully live a solitary life, it is more perhaps their fault than their misfortune. No philosophy can provide for quite exceptional cases. Normally speaking, the bulk of mankind have, and will have, definite if incomplete family relations. In their complete form these are five. (1) Parental, (2) conjugal, (3) filial, (4) fraternal, and (5) domestic, understanding these in their widest sense, as embracing all those who, living together, stand in this relation to each other, by blood, by adoption, by office voluntarily assumed, legally or morally,—by any voluntary association which practically creates this family bond; and the last, the "domestic," embracing the relation of service where it is a more or less permanent bond in the same household, forming as it should a quasi-family tie.

The Home is the primeval and eternal school where we learn to practise the balance of our instincts, to restrain appetite, to cultivate affection, to pass out of our lower selves—to *Live for Humanity.* The Home it is where men are made, where characters are formed, where the first great problem of life is solved—how to reconcile self with unself.

What is the inspiring force—the genius of the Home? The instinct of mankind, the hearts of us all, poetry, art, the commonplaces of ordinary speech with one voice answer the question with the name of Woman !—the mother, the wife, the sister, the daughter, the serving-maid (*bonne* is the expressive French word)—Woman who is the nurse of our infancy, the nurse of our sickness, the cheerer of our labour, the allayer of wrath, the teacher of childhood, the counsellor of youth, the companion of manhood and of old age, the inspirer of the highest sentiments and truest thoughts.

By virtue of what do women hold this place ? By the positive fact of biological and psychological science that the moral and emotional nature of women—that which we call *goodness*, the readiness to bear, work, live for others, the habit of restraining appetite, the capacity of living in a sustained atmosphere of the purest emotion—all this is stronger and deeper in average women than in average men.

One cannot argue so subtle and general a truth. People must feel it : we must appeal to common language, the ideals of mankind, to eternal poetry. We know that some women (possibly here and there a man) deny it. Some women think it due to robustness of mind to deny it : some men think it shows robustness of heart to deny it. One never can tell what grotesque paradox will not be dictated to its adepts by "strength of mind." Let us appeal then from the strong-minded to the heart and the sense of mankind. No sober-minded man will deny (it is often wiser to be sober-minded than strong-minded)—that women are as a rule—(1) Less the victims of selfish appetite than men—(2) More the creatures of unselfish affection than men. No poet ever places the moral influence of the father on quite so high a level as the moral influence of the *mother*. Is the brother ever all that the *sister* may be ? Is the son all that the *daughter* may be ? Is there any relation between man and man not related by blood which reaches the noble and beautiful devotion of the nurse to the children of the household, seen at its best and truest ? Alas ! these natural bonds are not seldom discredited, forgotten, distorted, and degraded, as are all things moral in human nature ! But we can consider them—and justly should consider them—in their highest ideal.

Could Sophocles have given the heart of *Antigone* to a brother, or would his tragedy of *Œdipus at Colonus* gain, if the blind exile were attended by two sons instead of two daughters ? Would Shakespeare have been more " strong-minded," if he had given the devotion of Cordelia to a *son* of Lear, or the love of Ophelia for Hamlet to Laertes and not to a woman, if he had attributed Desdemona's majestic resignation to the husband and not to the wife ? Could Dante have dared to present the moral influence of the poet on his lady as the equal in spiritual beauty to the moral influence of the lady on the poet? Where would be the poetry of the *Heart of Mid-Lothian*, if Jeanie Deans had been the brother—not the sister of Effie? The great poets at any rate knew the human heart—and their judgement is unerring on the subtler problems of Psychology.

Take all that poetry and tradition records from the time of Ruth, and Rizpah the daughter of Ayah—down to Mary Magdalen, and Mary of Nazareth—all the aureole that piety has painted round the image of the Virgin-Mother and of the Virgin Martyrs that bear her company, all that Chivalry has woven round the ideal of the Lady-love, all the halo that modern romance, from Ariosto to Walter Scott and Tennyson, has thrown round the heart of woman—ask any of us whether in the supreme moments of life, in the first agony felt by the child, in the last agony of the man, ask which of us would rather share these hours of passion and of horror with a man or with a woman, with a father or with a mother, with a brother rather than a sister, ask which of us would rather have our dying eyes closed by a man and not by a woman—think upon all this and say if "strength of mind" requires us to deny the first great truth of human nature—the moral superiority of women! And all this world of truth, poetry, and spirituality is to be replaced by gruesome cant about equal rights and adult suffrage.

If we ask what is the highest level of this truth, what is the centre and root of the family, the deepest expression of *Life for others*; it is plainly, Marriage, the relation of Husband and Wife. And the end of Marriage is as plainly—the mutual perfecting of man and woman; the moral refinement and elevation of man by the sympathy of woman, the moral strengthening and broadening of woman by the practical energy of man, the purification and consolidation of the nature of both.

In old days, the continuance of the species was regarded as the end of Marriage, at other times the convenience of men, or the support of women. And even still, Theology with its notion of the individual soul and its wild hallucination about the human heart, retains the vulgar, brutal, blind view of marriage, and to its shame consecrates it in the very marriage service.

We are very far from meaning that every man or woman can only find a complete life in marriage, or that to be unmarried is to be debarred from the highest life of Humanity. No, no, indeed that would be a cruel pedantry. With very many under our actual conditions it is often not only a necessity but not seldom a duty of the first order to live unmarried. And some of the noblest lives are attained by those who live single, and would even (it may be) in given circumstances be marred by Marriage. Philosophy must deal with general and not particular cases. Marriage of course is the source of Family and the typical centre of Family. And what is meant is this, that Society must be looked on as a combination of Families. And that a true moral standard takes the Family as the root of Morality.

Now a Family is a society in itself. And a society implies distribution of function, organisation, government. All of these are typically present in the Family. Distribution of function and harmony of organisation imply subtle differentiation of parts. And it is the differences of nature in those who compose the family which brings about its natural and easy organisation. There cannot be two governments of the same sphere in one society. Hence man or woman, parent or child, one or other, must govern for the same things. There can neither be two independent material forces, nor two independent moral forces in the same society. And when we have got so far as to understand this, there is little difficulty in assigning the material force as the function of the man and the moral force as that of the woman.

This is the key of the vexed problem of our day, the respective work of men and women in society. If the question be looked at thus, that our individual life is our true life, that Humanity exists for the individual, any incoherence is possible. The equality, or rather the assimilation of the sexes, the identity of duties, the identity of capacities, the absolute interchangeability of parts, as if the moral and intellectual functions of members of the family could be as easily interchanged as the chairs, plates, and napkins they use, is an idea that follows from the theory of individual units.

But it is far otherwise. Humanity exists for Families; it is composed of Families; it is represented and typified by Families. Family is the organism which reproduces Humanity in miniature; and it is with reference to Families that the moral and social life of men and women has everywhere and always to be considered.

It is only in the Home that Humanity is revealed to Man in all its majesty and charm—for there only can we get so close to each human soul, see it transfigured in such sympathetic light, and watch it in all the subtlety of its working—as to be able to know all that the human heart can be. In the Home only do we learn the habit of daily, hourly self-discipline, so that restraint of the self-regarding instincts becomes habitual, regular, and easy. This is true, of course, only of normal members of a healthy Home, for we know too well how the Home itself may be perverted into being the occasion and nursery of selfishness. And it is in the Home that the three forms of affection—attachment, reverence, sympathy—become known in all their intensity, purity, and continuous vitality.

This threefold affection is concentrated and perfected in the union of husband and wife—the only human relation which unites attachment, veneration, love in equal degrees and all in the highest degree. For no human beings can know each other as husband and wife learn to know each other's souls, no other human relation makes such incessant appeal to the whole character and every fibre of our capacities. There friendship is idealised and perfected by being the indissoluble lifelong union of two beings, like yet unlike, bound together in a partnership from which every germ of rivalry or of opposing interests is purged, and wherein every hour of existence is a new variation on the dominant theme—that to live means—to Live for others.

Well might Comte say that the whole of life is too short to enable two beings, of nature so subtle and so complex, of character so finely differenced, fully to know each other, perfectly to love each other. Well might he in his vision of the future look forward to a time when the part borne in this union by the instinct of passion—the indispensable, normal, and honourable part I am ready to add—should be raised to such a standard as that which we find in the purest ideals of poetry and romance.

Well might Comte look to a future which should recognise the marriage union as indissoluble even by death, for it is the material and not the spiritual attributes of marriage which are taken from us by death. The touch, the voice, the sight, the vital grace have gone: their magical power remains only in memory; but the fellowship of spirit remains, purified often and transfigured by death. And the revelation of the spiritual nature of another which marriage begins is not seldom enlarged and deepened by Death with all the bereavement and solitude it brings.

Here, again, we must be careful to be clear that such language, such expectations are possible only to the normal marriage, to the happy and successful union. Many there are which fail to reach such an ideal, and not a few which are a cruel mockery of such a type. There are men and women to whom marriage becomes but a fresh field for their self-absorption, a new descent from Man to Brute. The greater is their damnation.

No part of Comte's ideal has given more unreasonable offence than his canon that it is a moral and social duty for men to support women, so as to free women as a sex from the drudgery, the conflict, and strain of a public career, and professional labour outside the Home. They would be left free, he foresaw, to devote their lives within the Home to the moral education of society, the perfecting of the Family, the furtherance of religion, worship, education, art. It does not seem that this is a narrow field, if we give these things all the extension they demand. Home is the proper seat of real education, paradox as this sounds in an age when education has become almost equivalent to getting away from Home. But even in these days, Home is admitted to be the sphere of the moral education, where such a thing as moral education is recognised at all. But it is also the sphere of not a little of the intellectual education of the more simple kind, and of the practical education which forms the character. The scientific, professional, and technical parts of education which are the business of schools and academies are really special, and exceptional parts of education as a whole. The normal education is the moral standard, the ideal of life, the practical judgement about men and things, the qualities of action, compared with which that which we get from books is rather an acquirement or an accomplishment than the substance.

In the whole of our up-bringing (regarding man as a whole and not as a mere linguist; and taking men in the bulk, and not the few who fill the technical professions) no part of our education is so critical, so determinate of the whole life, as that which we receive from birth till the age of fourteen. Even in this age of infantine and puerile barracks, *Kindergarten*—I protest against their being likened to gardens—and the competitive system for the young, a very large part of the real moral, spiritual, and ethical training of boys and certainly of girls is admittedly given in the Home. Even anarchy itself admits that it is a fine ideal when possible, where a competent mother herself gives their first education in the Home to her girl and even to her boy. No education through life so deeply impresses the nature, abides so long, and rises, when adequate, to so pure a level.

"Competent mother"—"adequate education"—we were forced to say. How much lies in that qualification! How few, alas! of our actual mothers are competent! How rare would be that "adequate education" even amongst those adventurous spinsters who aspire to be Home Secretaries, Lord Chancellors, and Archbishops of Canterbury. Many of them, I suppose, are more fit to-day to adorn the woolsack or the Treasury Bench than they would be to do what they never think of trying—to give a truly adequate general education to a young person—meaning by that to form the moral judgement, implant the rudiments at least of a common-sense philosophy, and discipline the habits of action and firmness.

I say this. The mother who is not competent by herself alone to give such an education as this to her children—say till the age of fourteen or fifteen—is not fit to be a mother. And the grown woman who is not fit to fill the part of a mother is not fit to be a woman.

The first word—the last word—in the true belief about Family Life is *Education* in its full and due sense. Family life is an education in itself. The Family is the proper centre and root of all education. Home—Education—Women—these three great factors of existence, are inextricably woven one within the other. Each will suffer when any one is violently wrenched from the other. It was a grand word of Comte's that the true work of women is to create men—not meaning to bring forth babes and to suckle infants, but to make citizens, to form the boy and girl into the worthy man and woman, to stamp on the life of the age its moral and spiritual tone, to humanise and raise the son, to develop the strength of the husband, to cherish the parent, to help the brother, to shame the impure, to abash the cruel, reward the generous, and spread everywhere mercy and tenderness—in one word, to inspire young and old with the spirit of womanliness.

Is not this enough? Is this task so obvious, so easy, that it may be made the bye-play of women's life, so that their serious hours may be given to conveyancing, book-keeping, and attending ward committees and so forth ?

When I think of all that education means, all that it implies to bring up a family of young persons in firm habits of morality, common sense, and resolution, of all that is meant by the management of one pure, happy, and noble household—when I think of all that might be done to teach men their moral and social duties, of all the misery that women by tact and sympathy could soften, of all the brutality and selfishness that women could shame into self-effacement, all the uncared-for children whom they could cheer, all the loneliness and dullness of life that they could brighten, all that they *might* do for husband, child, brother, friend, neighbour, and servant, if they only knew more, and felt more, and rose to a sense of their true mission—I am aghast to think that there are good and thoughtful women to-day who complain that they are degraded, because they cannot grub in the parchments of a law office, and make speeches in Parliament—nay, because any kind of distinction is still retained between men's work and women's work or that the Family should be treated as anything but the common lodging for a time of men and women who happen to have the natural relationship of blood.

The absolute assimilation of men and women

means the extinction of the Family and Home—and the extinction of the Family and the Home means the annihilation first, of the womanliness of woman—and soon after that—of the humanity of man.

LECTURE III

(*Newton Hall*, 1893. *Ethical Societies*, 1895–1900)

THE FUNCTIONS OF THE STATE

If there is one thing which is more peculiarly characteristic of scientific Philosophy and Scientific Polity, it is this: that it looks on society as a living organism—an infinitely complex organic system of mutually correlated organs, indispensable to each other, and having really no independent life. Human nature is not a bundle of sticks or a sack of potatoes. It is a living body; and it can no more be truly separated into parts than a living man can be separated into a digestive apparatus and a nervous system.

Society is an Organism and it must be treated as a whole. The elements of society (*i.e.*, of Humanity) can be separated only in thought—not in fact. The State, the Church, Law, Public Opinion, Economics, Ethics, are subjects which we may reason about separately, and detach in the abstract. But for all purposes of concrete application we must consider them as depending one on each other.

Now the popular social and political schemes treat society piecemeal, in arbitrary sections. They study society in analytic groups, and then they begin to act as if these groups were separable factors. It is as though physicians and surgeons, after studying the physical organism first as skeleton, then as nervous and digestive apparatus, then as a circulating system—were to begin to treat any one of them by itself, as if bone, heart, or brain could be treated by drugs or instruments apart from the rest of the body, and without reference to any reaction such treatment might cause elsewhere. The Socialist, the Communist, the Co-operator, the Democratic reformer, the Land Reformer, the suffrage reformer, the Temperance or Sex agitation, confine themselves to one definite element or capacity in human nature, and go for their own particular remedy without any regard for the rest of the social organism.

Now our scheme, true to its uniformly synthetic character, treats society organically. Every one of the institutions, methods, doctrines it puts forward has to be viewed with reference to every other. It is an attempt to restore health to the body politic by a comprehensive treatment of the whole constitution, and not by applying local remedies to particular parts or organs. This proviso should prevent many objections which are made by hasty critics. They estimate the Humanist Synthesis, bit by bit, in the light of their own analytic notions, quite overlooking the truth that each institution and doctrine in any really synthetic scheme implies the rest. And underlying all is the institution of a strong and active public opinion, resting on an organised education, moral as well as intellectual, common to all, and modifying habits and all forces. Without this vigorous public opinion, all social and political schemes are little more than *nostrums*. Having this public opinion to moralise the whole social organism, the weaknesses of institutions may be corrected and supplemented All institutions and political devices need this.

Positivism is simply this proposal—Try the effect of a right moral education in the world, before you seek to pull things to pieces by legal and practical revolutions. Thus when Positivism rejects Communism as the solution of the industrial problem, it proposes as the basis of an industrial society a moral (not a material) socialism. That is to say, it proposes to obtain the end by transforming opinions and habits, and not by violently revolutionising social institutions. But how are we to transform opinions and habits, the Communist asks? By forming, we reply, a new public opinion, by a complete education, by an educating body, by a common religion of Duty.

But it also presupposes as an antecedent condition of such public opinion, a transformed State: one in which the workman is guaranteed all that the State can give to improve his material condition without injuring the rest of the community, and a real Republic: that is, a State wherein the ultimate power rests with the body of the people. By Republic we mean a commonwealth resting on the will and devoted to the interests of all citizens alike; having these three qualities—(1) with no hereditary functions or privileges, (2) with no class excluded, (3) no property in any public thing. A Republic is a commonwealth where the whole common force is directed to the welfare of all citizens equally, as its *raison d'être*. This is the normal and only permanent form of the body politic in advanced civilised communities of free citizens.

This Republican type is practically, but imperfectly and irregularly realised in England. In form, but in little more than form, we retain a Monarchy, which an acute and conservative observer described as the "theatric," or show part, of the British Constitution. The Monarchy preserves certain traditional features of England, exerts a steady and uniform pressure to keep society in an organic form, and at times no doubt serves certain useful purposes. But we know that in all the larger things, and directly the nation is roused and has a will of its own, the throne becomes a mere symbol, without the smallest power even of retarding a definite policy.

The other obstacle to the Republican type is the existence of a hereditary Chamber, which, under the growth of democracy in the Lower House, is becoming perhaps more powerful as a resisting force than it has been for the last sixty years [1893]. An hereditary Chamber is obviously irreconcilable with any Republican principle; and when this chamber is in the theory of the constitution the equal of the elected Chamber, and under given conditions is able for a time to make its equality felt, it becomes a very serious source of disturbance and embarrassment. Still, since it is admitted that the resistance of the Upper House is a purely temporary one, that its action is dilatory only, that it has no originating power to force on the country any policy of its own, since it becomes a merely formal registering body whenever a conservative majority exists in the elective Chamber, and since it can never under any circumstances interfere in anything touching finance and expenditure—it must be taken that the House of Lords has an indirect and retarding effect on the body politic, but not a decisive or dominant effect.

Both Monarchy and House of Lords, from

time to time, affect English political development for evil: especially the second; but neither of them separately, nor even both together, neutralise the principle, that England is a Republic, a democratic Republic, modified by powerful aristocratic and monarchic institutions. The Republican type is fully realised in the United States, in Switzerland, and practically in many of the smaller States of Europe, such as Greece, Norway, Holland, Denmark, even though all of these retain a ceremonial Monarchy, and it is essentially but not completely realised in France. A typical Republic implies the complete extinction of all hereditary institutions, of class manners, and of all privileged orders, or Churches, and France retains all of these things, though in very vanishing form. The United States and Switzerland are as yet the only complete types of the pure Republic; though many persons will think that the unscrupulous power of wealth in America, and the low inorganic condition of social life in Switzerland present evils as bad as the aristocratic institutions of England, if not worse than they.

The Positive Synthesis, to begin at the beginning, is hostile to every proposal for aggrandising the State, whether of the Imperial or the Communistic type. As it trusts the main influence in the moral and spiritual sphere to education, so it would commit the main work in the political sphere to public opinion. As in the moral world the problem is to organise education: so in the political sphere the main problem is to organise public opinion. If we could accomplish that, all the schemes for increasing the power of the State may be reduced to a *minimum*. Positivism has carefully considered the mode of organising public opinion, in the first place by providing for the people a common education of a high and complete sort; next by greatly increasing the leisure of the people by reduced hours of labour and constant holidays; thirdly, by the regular institution and immense increase of workmen's clubs and meetings for political discussion; fourthly, by the wholly new institution of requiring public appointments to be submitted to the test of public approval; and lastly, by guaranteeing, as a social and religious institution, complete freedom of speech. With this, the form of government would become a thing of minor importance.

We are all so saturated with ideas of Parliamentary government that we do not easily imagine any other as possible. Parliamentary government in England is quite a special national product, apparently innate in the British race, and indigenous in our peculiar social type. I am not prepared to deny that it may continue for many generations to work under a revised form in Britain; but it seems quite unfit for France and most other countries of Europe, and to be rather a scandalous parody even in the United States. From the point of view of sociology and of human society, we could not regard what is an anomaly in the British islands as a normal type. So that, what we say as to parliamentary institutions may require some modification when applied to this country.

Comte proposed to retain (for the present) a Parliament elected by manhood suffrage with complete control over the expenditure, but not directly charged with administrative functions. For the effective control over the Executive government he would rely far more upon public opinion than on Parliament. And that is what we are now coming to do. Parliamentary government still retains a vast power over the imagination and even over the affections of Englishmen, because it really represents to us the Republic: it represented the People and Progress in the great struggle with Monarchy and Feudalism. To us, Parliament is the only instrument whereby a despotic Executive has been curbed and shorn of its intolerance. Its glory is that it has been the moderating and humanising force of our Monarchy. But now that the Monarchy is a shadow, and Parliament has no function as a counterpoise, and when the two Houses of Parliament are now balanced in such a way as to produce a chronic dead-lock [as in 1893], men are seriously asking themselves if

Parliament deserve this regard and affection. What is there to show to-day that Parliament is the normal executive organ for an advanced Republic? Do we see it to be so in the United States, or in France? On the contrary, in the only great and complete Republics we have seen for the last two generations, the tendency of Parliament elected by universal suffrage is to make a stable and vigorous Executive impossible, and that whilst failing to pass any sound system of industrial and social legislation. Like every other system devised and perfected to act as a check and a counterpoise on tyranny, Parliaments are impotent in the ordinary course as efficient organs of progressive government.

Parliamentary government is not truly Republican except in great revolutionary crises, when it may become for a time a mighty engine of reform. The Long Parliament of 1640, the Convention of 1689, the first American Congress, the French States General and Convention, our Reformed Parliament of 1832 all did tremendous work of a revolutionary sort. But when Parliament settles into a mere institution, especially when it undertakes the administrative machinery of a vast aggregate of States, it soon ceases to be either truly Republican, or really practical. In the first place it passes largely into the hands of the rich, or of those who are seeking to become rich or who are the creatures of the rich—as we see in England, in France, in the United States. Secondly, it passes under the control of the professional debaters, whether lawyers, journalists, or office-seekers, whose eloquence and activity is as little inspired by the welfare of the Republic as that of an Old Bailey advocate is by the virtue of his client in the dock. Under the combined influence of the ambitious men of wealth, and of the professional men of the tongue, Parliament too often sways backwards and forwards, doing nothing but debate and rearrange Ministries, retarding, obscuring, and falsifying public opinion.

Parliament, in this country within the last two centuries and particularly within the last two generations, has completely changed its original character and function without any definite change in the constitution, or any formal authority for the change. We still call it the Legislature; but it is much more of a huge executive committee than a Legislature. It passes new laws very slowly and occasionally: its financial business is settled in a few nights, often without any serious examination. But it devotes violent and prolonged debates to very small executive details, and brings the conduct of the State at last to something rather like government by public meeting. A common legal proceeding in Connemara or Shetland, the act of an official in British Columbia or the banks of the Nyanza are equally the subject for vehement debates. Is Parliament a consultative body, a ratifying body, or a law-making body—an initiative or a Court of Appeal? Is it a Legislature, or is it an Executive? It claims to be, and acts as if it were, all of these at the same time and much more as if it were—King, Lords, Commons—public meeting, High Court of Justice, international arbitrator, the grand official Journal, and controller of all public officials, great and small, from a Lord Chancellor to a doorkeeper.

It is difficult to see how Parliament is to be at the same time a Legislature and also an Executive—for the body which controls, cross-examines, and modifies the Executive, day by day, *is* the Executive. The difficulty about a Parliament being the real Executive arises when Parliament is not homogeneous. At times the two Houses are in direct and systematic conflict. The plan is, for the large minority in the Lower House, leagued with the enormous majority in the Upper House, to make legislation impossible and Executive government as difficult as possible. Whilst the House of Lords remains untouched, that state of things is certain to continue; and it is difficult to see how popular legislation or a really democratic party can succeed, without some constitutional change. In the meantime, Parliament divided against itself is neither Legislature nor Executive in any active and free sense.

The legislative function of Parliament is not a reality so long as nine-tenths of the hereditary House decline to attend, to listen, to consider, or to understand the points under debate, and yet have an equal voice in all legislation with the elected representatives of six millions. The executive functions of Parliament can only be exercised for harm so long as every petty administrative act or order is liable to be debated by a miscellaneous crowd of 680 talkers, many of them ignorant, ill-informed, unscrupulous, and eager not to do what is right, but to win credit for themselves and bring discredit on their rivals. Such is the ignoble end of the Mother of free Parliaments.

There is a great deal of solemn cant still pervading our superstitious reverence for Parliamentary government. What does it mean? Parliamentary government means literally—government by a talking assembly. But the real deliberative and critical assembly of the nation is a much larger and freer thing. It is the nation itself, quite as well informed of the facts as the M.P.'s, and meeting in ten thousand unofficial parliaments by day and night. The deliberative functions of Parliament are now quite superseded by public opinion; and the House of Commons is a very belated, imperfect, and often perverse representative of public opinion. It is easily converted into a retrograde and retarding force, as we see when a Bill which all parties in Parliament profess themselves anxious to pass, the principle and general lines of which have been heartily accepted by an overwhelming weight of public opinion almost without any definite difference of purpose, is opposed by factious and frivolous amendments.

There is much more to be said for the doctrine of pure democracy—as now practised under the *referendum*—the direct vote on a definite measure of the entire body of citizens. But a pure democracy of the Athenian type cannot be worked except in such a small community as that which met on the Pnyx—where the bulk of the active citizens in the State could all be assembled within the hearing of one man's voice. And the *referendum* or direct vote is only possible where the vote taken is a bare Yes, or No; the mere acceptance of a particular law, measure, or minister. No modification, qualification, or other variation is possible under any system of *referendum* or other type of direct democratic vote. Government cannot be carried on by crowds, or in crowds. A House of 680 members, coming and going, intriguing and grouping anew day by day, has some of the worst faults of a crowd.

The arguments for pure democratic government, for reaching directly the whole body of citizens, are all negative. They aim at getting rid of some evil: they do not pretend to claim any direct advantage. They appeal to the sentiment of jealousy, self-interest, and self-assertion. Their sole claim is to neutralise the effect of aristocratic or monarchic pressure. The most daring publicist has not ventured to assert that pure democracy, or the direct intervention of all in government, is *per se* the best method of obtaining efficient government. He only prefers it as a mode of preventing the people being forced to submit to what they hate, and plundered by those whom they cannot resist. The pure democratic principle was designed to combat gross abuses, ancient institutions, and rank superstitions. It has often served this end with striking success.

But the whole problem is transposed by the Positive scheme which would take from government its power for evil, and strengthen the people by a new organisation of public opinion. Real Republican sentiment is accomplished by this far better than by any conceivable reform of the franchise or system of checks.

The first condition is a strict limitation of the sphere of government.

1. The chief and foremost limitation is to reduce the military function to pure defence [1893]. No one can pretend that this is possible at this hour [1918]. We are not here discussing what this Government, or another, are likely to do about the Army and the Navy. We are

looking forward to a time when industry, not empire, shall be the end of human ambition and the desire of true patriotism. Standing armies might then be replaced by such an adequate militia, of which we already have types in the Swiss and the American Republics. There, no doubt under very special geographical conditions, but conditions totally different, a free and proud people have organised a militia amply adequate to protect their independence, at a *minimum* drain on the freedom of the population, and a *minimum* of expenditure on the taxes of the country. Their scientific services, their staff, and in the case of Switzerland, their military organisation, and powers of mobilisation, are judged by experts to be ample for mere defence, and no other object can ever cross the mind of a Swiss. Wild as it sounds to-day, the day is at hand when Europe may abolish its huge armaments, renounce all military habits and prejudices; and having paid off the vast debts, the sinister inheritance from past wars, at one stroke reduce the national expenditure by one-third, or even one-half [1893, *eheu !*]

2. Next, of course, these vast aggregate Empires must disappear. They are all the creation of war, they all exist only by chronic war, or preparation for war; and they all mean oppression and race tyranny. The Russian, Austrian, German, even the British Empire are

all more or less oppressive aggregates, with their origin in conquest, and their standing character of race ascendancy [1893]. Nor are France, Italy, Spain, and Sweden without elements of the same kind in less marked degree. All of the vast tyrannous empires must dissolve before we can reach a normal state, which will be that of smaller, homogeneous, industrial, and peaceful republics, of which these islands might easily make four.

3. Without vast armies and fleets, without scattered empires, and with no subject races to coerce, the sphere of the central government would be simple enough. It would be confined to maintaining order, providing for health, promoting and assisting industry in all its forms, and supplying a simple, cheap, and scientific system of law.

4. Lastly, the temporal government would have nothing whatever to do with any moral, intellectual, or spiritual concern whatever—neither with any Church, sect, or creed; with no matter of education, with no academy or learned society. All these things would belong to independent, moral, intellectual, and religious movements.

Relieve government of its absorbing military duties; take it out of any class interest; remove from its sphere all religious questions, and suppose extinct all those vexed international questions, and incessant frontier wars in all parts of the globe—and the sphere of government becomes simple enough and hardly a matter for desperate contention between rival parties.

The sphere of government would be reduced to this—Protect the nation from foreign enemies; organise an efficient police; administer equal, cheap, speedy law; protect, assist, stimulate, and moderate industry; prevent groups encroaching on others; stop bands of marauders who seek to make aggression on other peoples, civilised or barbarous; provide for the health of great cities and of rural districts by establishing local bodies charged with providing air, open spaces, recreation grounds for the people, pure, unlimited, gratuitous water, which stands on the same footing as air, primary education, healthy comfortable homes for the people, museums, galleries, libraries, and other means of culture. These are the natural business of the local bodies: the task of the central government is to stimulate, control them and arbitrate upon their mutual conflicts and rivalries. When government is reduced to these six great departments, when it is relieved from the care of vast armies and vast fleets, from the load of debt, from irritating questions of religion and education, from ecclesiastical patronage, from all direct care of education, from all hereditary pensions, from the absurd paraphernalia of courts, embassies,

Messrs. Macmillan & Co. will be glad to receive a copy of the issue containing a notice of this work.

The price of the book is [illegible] net.

MESSRS. MACMILLAN & CO., LTD., will be glad to receive a copy of the issue containing a notice of this work.

The price of the book is 12/- net.

and sinecures, little would be left to struggle for. The national expenditure, even if doubled and trebled for public works, central museums, galleries, libraries, and so forth, might be reduced to one-third of our actual budget expenditure—which should easily be raised by a real land tax, a graduated income tax, increased succession duty, and customs and excise on luxuries only [1893, *eheu !*].

The furious struggles of our modern states, ranging from revolutionary anarchy to imperialist tyranny, come from the claim to determine a set of questions all of which take their rise either in military or feudal habits. The ambition of Tsars and Emperors to dominate Europe, the ambition of our own imperialist parties to extend an Empire scattered over the planet, create a tyranny, against which a desperate reaction sets in. Note the questions about which in this country our rival parties have been struggling for the last ten years, indeed for twenty years—they may all be ultimately traced back to war, to thirst for domination, aggrandising the Empire, securing the ascendancy of some conquering race or order, or maintaining the privileges and ascendancy of some Church or creed. Jingoism, the foreign wars in Asia, and in Africa, Zulu, Ashantee, Matabele wars, Egyptian, Soudan wars, Burmese, Afghan wars, the Irish struggle, the education struggle—all have their origin in the effort of one race, or party, or sect, or order to domineer over others. When we rightly understand what is within and what is not within the sphere of normal government, and have forsworn war, class, and sect, the rage to wield political power will be found to be extinct.

We should then be no more consumed with the desire to direct the government of the nation than we now desire to determine in what part of the city shall be the beats of the A Division or the X Division of Police. The ordering of such matters of internal administrative will naturally pass into the hands of those who have special interest and experience of such details. The difficulty will be to induce capable citizens to concern themselves enough in such burdensome problems. With a sound system of public responsibility, entire freedom, organised clubs, the habit of complete publicity, the body of the people will exercise an ample general control. But, in the main, under the influence of a healthy education, they will be content with seeing that the work is well done, rather than insist on doing it themselves. If government were in a healthy state, and the people thoroughly educated intellectually and morally, if the sphere of government were strictly limited, and incapable of abuse by having no coercive power, we should as little hear of persons insisting on governing themselves as of making their own boots and shoes.

There is an enormous fallacy involved in the formula about people governing themselves. Strictly speaking, such a thing is impossible. It usually means that some govern the rest, usually one or very few govern certain groups, and then one out of several groups gains the ascendancy for a time. Government means taking some one definite course out of a hundred. That one definite course in any complex case must originate in one directing mind, which impresses other leading minds, and these obtain the assent of more or less powerful groups, and ultimately one of these groups becomes strong enough to compel the more or less reluctant acquiescence of the rest. All government and all legislation, whether the government be that of a Parliament, or of a Tsar, or of a President elected by universal suffrage, means ultimately the will of some one, acquiesced in by overwhelming numbers. The despotism of the Tsar or the Sultan means that the decision of a ruler invested with divine right is supported by the superstitious reverence of a body of people strong enough and organised well enough to sweep down any opposition, the millions paying imperial taxes, and submitting to enter the imperial army without a murmur. The government of a Parliamentary party means that what a popular statesman thinks it wise and feasible to do, he induces his Ministry to accept, and after a great deal of talk, and compromise, the Parliament assents to the measures, or the Minister retires and another Minister carries his Bills. That is much the same with a President in the United States or in the French Republic. There is no essential difference between all five cases. The people govern themselves strictly neither in America, France, nor England, any more than in Russia or Turkey. Ancient superstition in Russia and Turkey produce a more absolute and imposing authority for the time. With us, a Prime Minister is liable to be checked and put out of office by Parliament or a general election. Tsars and Sultans are liable to be blown up by Nihilists or strangled by conspirators, and they have just as much trouble with students, ministers, and ulema as any Prime Minister with Parliament.

The future we may be sure will reduce Parliament to its natural functions of inquiry, financial control, and legislation pure and simple. The elected Parliament would meet for moderate sessions at regular intervals, and would have withdrawn from it administrative work, the supervision of ministerial routine, and any power to overthrow a Ministry by a single vote. The Presidential form of government, as recognised in the United States and partly in France, is a more natural type of government—the President being directly responsible to the body of the people, and appointing his own Ministers, without any limitation of his choice to members of Parliament, or Parliamentary approval. It is a vain bugbear to raise a cry of Dictatorship. We mean simply efficient government with direct responsibility to the nation: the indirect responsibility to Parliament only tends to neutralise and falsify public opinion.

The Positivist Utopia of good government then would be that—all hereditary and class institutions being eliminated, the sphere of government strictly limited, and a universal education being established—the people would be content to trust the temporal management of material interests to trained experts subject to those conditions:

1. That they have no great military force to compel obedience.

2. That their measures and appointments shall be submitted to ample public review before they are finally ratified.

3. That complete freedom of speech and criticism be a strict *sine qua non.*

4. That the budget be voted by a Chamber elected by manhood suffrage.

5. That the Government be directly responsible and removable by proper machinery: but not by a chance vote of a miscellaneous assembly.

The essential difference between the ideals propounded by Positivism and those of any despotic or any revolutionary school are these. The Positivist ideal would tend to reduce the authority of government whilst greatly enlarging the power of public opinion. The despotic and revolutionary schemes aim at getting into their own hands the whole existing force of governments in order to set up institutions even more violent, arbitrary, and pitiless than those which exist. Positivism equally repudiates the tyranny of Tsar, Emperor, demagogue, or Nihilist [1918]. It is wholly averse to the Black Terror and to the Red Terror. It protests equally against both in the name of Humanity—past, present, and to come. It rejects the claim of Romanoffs, Bonapartes, Hohenzollerns, Bourbons, or Habsburghs to crush society in the mill of divine right and supernatural revelation. Nor can it recognise any kindred right in revolutionists to enforce their own crudities and dogmas on Humanity at large. It refuses to place the interests of Humanity, past, present, and to come, at the mercy of a majority of the adults of any nation for the moment. The male adult voters in any country are always a minority of a minority in any population; and it is a mere metaphysical figment that they have any moral claim to recast society by a vote.

The interests of human Society are those which Humanity has created after about 20,000 or 30,000 years of toil; the institutions which the genius, labours, and martyrdom of myriads of men and women have slowly built up; the interests of the living children and minors who are always a majority of the population and the interests of the vaster majority of unborn children in the infinite ages to come. Positivism refuses to acquiesce in the resort to bayonets, police, or force in any form (be the agents of State authority adorned with eagles or with caps of liberty) to impose on human life any kind of institutions by State authority. And it is so completely sincere in this refusal, that it would refuse with horror to have even its own programme or institutions imposed by State intervention.

The social evils of Society do need a complete reorganisation; but by moral, religious, and intellectual agencies; and on these the physical force revolutionists have even less to offer us than the reactionists. We do most assuredly need a higher code of duty, more social and less selfish habits, a deeper and more moral education. But it is no more in the power of a Terrorist than of a Despot to decree virtue and good citizenship. The Positivist ideal of the Republic is one in which these—the main ends of social life—are attained by moral means, by religious training, by education, by an intensely active social opinion. The main work of Positivism, the main instrument of Humanity in the future is Education, in the highest and widest sense of the term. The State, or material system of external order, is merely the condition, the preliminary ground for this Education. The State has to defend, protect, sanitate, and beautify the conditions of civic life. It must keep order, promote health, comfort, enjoyment, good citizenship, by suppressing nuisances and all overgrown or anti-social forces, to prevent citizens or groups from encroaching on the free life of other citizens.

A truly industrial, peaceful, cultured, and free life cannot be imposed by any kind of armed force or arbitrary law. These institutions must grow, spontaneously and normally. The Republic, reduced to a manageable size and population, freed from all warlike ambition and from all fear of attack from its neighbours, will have little to do but to allow the moral and intellectual life of its citizens to develop in a healthy way, to prevent the encroachment of any on the lives and labours of others, and to furnish forth the material life of all with adequate means. The citizens will not want to burn down capitals, to blow up public buildings, to have a revolution once every ten years in order to secure these ends. They will be willing to entrust power to really capable hands, watching, supervising the way in which these functions are performed, discussing the way they are performed, making their own wants, complaints, and suggestions plainly heard, ready, if need be, to take the authorised modes of replacing these functionaries — if they prove finally untrustworthy—but not eternally correcting and embarrassing them, and not insisting on having every petty detail whether of administration or legislation voted on word by word in public and settled in furious party contests.

Such is the ideal of the Republic—an ideal not applicable, perhaps hardly likely to be considered either to-day or to-morrow. For it is an ideal which assumes as its antecedent condition the existence of a living Religion of Humanity.

LECTURE IV

(*Newton Hall*, 1883)

A STATE CHURCH

One of the most significant facts of modern politics is the degree to which politics tend to run in religious grooves.

Here Ministries have changed, and parties are dissolved and reconstructed by questions which have more of theology in them than politics. The Education Bill, the School Board Elections, Irish Education, the Disendowment of the Irish Church and Home Rule, Disestablishment questions in Scotland and England, the Oaths Bill in the House of Commons, cemeteries, and other questions, etc. etc.

Abroad it is so still more. France is rent about questions of ecclesiastical orders, education, secular burial, etc. etc., the government of *Moral order* under the Duc de Broglie.

So Italy—her history for years has been in a main degree a struggle between Church and State. In a sense it has been only this from the

Middle Ages. In fact, in many countries the issue is really one about Religion, and shall secular or Catholic principles control the forces of the State ?

In a matter of this kind Principle is of the most vital importance. It is a thing that can hardly be touched without a firm and profound hold on fundamental truth.

I am reluctant ever to boast about the wonderful creations of A. Comte's genius ; but I make bold to say that, in this question, our doctrine is the only sure and firm ground, and that every other school and party are involved in endless contradictions.

The outline of Positivism is that high civilisation is impossible without a systematic teaching of moral principles, nor without the regular enforcement of rules of law. The Spiritual and the Temporal can never be mixed up without evil.

Those who teach should not govern. Those who govern should not teach. All schools and common sense admit this in the main—in a loose rough way. All agree :

1. That philosophers, priests, or schoolmasters ought never to be trusted with political power.

2. That magistrates, statesmen, the State, are not to teach people what to believe nor what is right and wrong, true and false—but simply what is practical and lawful, in things political.

All classes of politicians agree to this. But this is a very rough rule, not adequate, and allowing compromise and inconsistency. Those who protest loudest against priests having secular government often suffer Governments to do a good deal of priest's work. We must go much further.

The contrast between the *Moral forces* which tend to affect men's conscience and thoughts, and the *Practical* forces which tend to govern men's acts and conduct, is the same as the contrast between Church and State, or between Preacher and Ruler, Religion and Law.

But it is also the same as the contrast between Theory and Practice, between Persuasion and Force, Conscience and Legality, Spiritual things and Temporal things, Moral and Material forces.

This great dualism runs through the whole of life, and it is only by strictly following it in all the inevitable conclusions that we can get any firm ground for action.

Government implies a hard-and-fast line. All must obey the law without exception.

But this implies *averages*, in practice: not the highest, but the best available; that standard, to fall below which a magistrate can treat as justly deserving of punishment.

All ideals are justly suspected by rulers. Rulers never can, or ought to say, *fiat justitia ruat caelum*—they must (and ought) to look at consequences all round.

Per contra—in all intellectual and moral things, ideals, individual peculiarities, abstract standards are all very important.

In intellectual and moral things, freedom—indefinite freedom of opinion, is of the essence. No progress is possible without it.

In Politics—freedom from law is really impossible. There must be one law for all—no exceptions are admissible.

Theory is and must be general, comprehensive.

Practice must be special, elastic in details.

Conscience, if it be limited to strict law, becomes hypocrisy, and conventional dullness results.

If the standard of legality is raised to cover conscience, tyranny is the result.

In spiritual things we must require the utmost personal purity and unselfishness in the guide.

In temporal things, skill is compatible with grave defects of a moral kind.

Material force in government is most necessary, but only in material things. The external welfare of the community presupposes uniformity.

It is impossible to exclude minorities: *e.g.* in the case of a tax, peace or war, the only true respect for minorities is limiting the sphere. On the other hand, moral force loses the whole of its moral weight, if it is charged with power to compel; it arouses resistance, fills the atmosphere with insurrection and strife, and stimulates mischievous opinion by encouraging the spirit of legitimate opposition to tyranny.

See the amount of irritation and political confusion produced by trifling attempts of the civil power to enforce opinion, *e.g.* a clause of an Education Act; the oaths question in England and France, the Church question in Ireland, the Papal question in Italy, the May laws against the clergy in Prussia (1883). Hence the great and wise rulers of the type of Cromwell, Frederick II., Walpole, Cavour, Lincoln, all showed an instinctive dread of touching questions of opinion —by law. No moral, intellectual result can be obtained by force.

"A man convinced against his will," etc., is not convinced. A man who pays taxes against his will pays his taxes all the same.

All parties roughly admit this. But all make exceptions in favour of themselves. There is no real consistency. Elements of persecution still lurk in these party programmes.

The common sense of Europe repudiates the idea of allowing coercive State powers to any sort of priest, schoolmaster, philosopher, but there is in every country of Europe remnants of priestly, scholastic, or philosophical functions, reserved to the State: and the result is everywhere tyranny and false teaching. [The fatal results are seen conspicuously in Prussia, 1917.]

Besides, many Liberal schools, and even the Revolutionary schools, rejecting Theology, are eager to use the State forces to propagate their secular or atheistical opinion; wish for compulsory education and that of a particular kind; seek to protect Atheism by penal laws, even to establish Atheism by State privileges. Paul Bert in France would do this (1883). In England we do not yet go so far. But here Liberals desire a sort of bureaucratic State Church, as a cynical Lord said, "to protect us against Christianity." Others would seize Educational Endowments and use Journalism as a mere party weapon to carry their party to power and to keep it there.

Now the Positivist view of all this is directly contrary. Our view is that:

It is absolutely essential to all healthy society to pass very clear, precise, and uncompromising principles in all this and to recognise the need of two real, independent, co-equal, very different spheres of social work, different men, and different instruments. These are:

1. The practical, hard-and-fast, legal force of the ruler and magistrate.

2. The moral, free, theoretical, and purely persuasive force of the teachers.

And also it is necessary to keep these absolutely

distinct—so that never, under any circumstances, shall—

(*a*) The magistrate force any *opinions*, or give any prerogative, or preference to opinions, be they religious, philosophical, scientific, or moral.

(*b*) The teaching of opinions shall never have legal force, no prerogative, no endowment from the common taxes.

The whole tendency of English history for 200 years, of European history for 30 years, has been tending to this. But the lesson is not yet learnt.

Positivism insists on all these things as essential:

No State Churches, no State religions, no religious tests. No State control of Education. No State endowments of Education. No State restriction on uttering of any opinion, other than utterances directly tending to disturb public order, or distinctly to injure individual citizens, in such a way as can be estimated in damages.

Generally State action must be rigidly confined to the material interests of citizens.

Positivism resting on Demonstration implies unlimited freedom of challenge.

Contra, it urges (but not as a matter of law) true guarantees of any real teaching; (*a*) publicity (no anonymous teaching); (*b*) personal character in the teaching body; (*c*) entire renunciation of political aim, or power for self, or for a party; (*d*) renunciation of State control, or endowment, or establishment, or privilege; (*e*) renunciation of pecuniary gain or personal glory, or unworthy object, to win credit or excite amusement for selfish ends in a reckless disregard of the social results.

The unwillingness of modern Liberals of all schools, Whig, Radical, or Revolutionary, to admit the very existence of such free teaching perpetually disposes them all to vicious theories of State action.

They seek to ignore all systematic moral education, all organised and independent teaching, and hence they find it impossible to avoid investing the State with some minimum of teaching authority.

Their opponents are more consistent—they do not assail the idea of Churches or priests, or public teachers—they stick to the old mediaeval theory, utterly hopeless and unworkable as it is.

But all schools of Liberals and Revolutionists, here and abroad, repudiating the very existence of Church and organised teaching forces, or desirous to reduce them to a minimum, find it in practice impossible to get rid of all appeals to opinion, and so they are constantly tempted to throw this minimum on the State.

The answer of Positivism is the only true one.

Recognise, as of old, the great sacred social function of teaching; realise what is it to have a religion, a systematic education in Science, moral and social philosophy; conceive the power of a Church, if you like so to call the moral association of men; cultivate to the utmost the respect for pure, true, and unselfish teaching of all kinds—and then you will find this is only possible when the State is strictly debarred from touching the sphere of opinion and education, morality, conscience, learning; and when the teaching and the teachers are raised to a high moral level and invested with a true social spirit.

Then we shall see the handling of public questions in a spirit of social responsibility and moral earnestness, utterly beyond the reach of the hireling and partisan journals of the day.

Then we may have a true public opinion when those who form it are neither office-seekers nor the *posse comitatus*, the paid agents, and creatures of office-seekers.

Then perhaps there may be journals, not owned by men avowedly scheming for party prizes.

Then we may have teaching not merely scientific or academic in purpose, but based on a religious and social philosophy, and animated at every step of its career by religious, moral, and social enthusiasm.

Such is the ideal of Positivism, and I make bold to assert that it is the only solution of the everlasting conflict between the Physical force of Government and the Moral force of Conscience; and that any attempt to balance the claims of the Government and Conscience on foundations less deep and wide must fail.

The only possible way to avoid tyranny and confusion in Society is frankly to recognise, nay, to welcome, the rise of a really free, independent, moral, spiritual force in Society.

It is the nemesis of mere negation, mere atheism, to find itself perpetually entangled with some of the worst traditions of spiritual tyranny; for it is ever seeking to seize and to use for its own purposes the discredited weapons of spiritual despotism, of the old Churches and empires.

It is curious in this matter to notice how dangerous and mischievous is the smallest compromise or paltering with the question. Once admit that there are *any* opinions which the State should uphold by penalties, and you are logically in the position of the Spanish Inquisition.

Once admit that there are any material and State prerogatives which you seek for your own opinions, and you are accepting the principle of State Church, State Religion, and State Academies.

What we find in practice is this. Every party and school really wants as much State power and money, protection, or monopoly, as they can get for their own opinions, and then they draw the line somewhere far or near below themselves and their friends. The old Popes burned all heretics, and would like to burn Luther and Calvin. Calvin burnt Servetus; no doubt Servetus would burn the Anabaptists; and the Anabaptists, the modern Atheists, and certainly some French Atheists would use the temporal arm against Jesuits. So we go round and round. Many will remember Mr. Gladstone's early essay on State Churches which Macaulay criticised. Mr. Gladstone then (1838) thought Dissenters ought to be excluded from office.

Into this absurdity we must all fall, if we do not scrupulously apply the right rule which is:

No opinion on any matter, social, religious, or scientific, shall, on any condition whatever, be officially adopted by the State or be protected by the State, or be placed by the State under any sort of public disability, or be invested with any sort of State precedence.

But the only way in which these views can be consistently maintained under every stress is that they who earnestly labour for the assertion of a real moral force should teach, and form opinion and character, until social respect for this and all who undertake that function is recognised. Those who really feel all this will be the first to see how it is poisoned in its source by any kind of State interference with opinion, any attempt to control conscience by prison and fine.

I am not about to argue the general case of

no persecution for opinion. But I insist on consistent application of this rule.

Most persons agree to have no religious persecution, but all will not admit what they call irreligion in the State.

State Church, State disabilities, and persecution, all stand on the same footing.

If belief in certain opinions is a condition of serving the State, or enjoying any public faculty whatever, the State is using its force to give certain opinions the preference; and the fact that these are the opinions of a majority does not prove their truth, nor has truth anything to do with it. The moral strength of true opinions is poisoned in its source, when the State persecutes, or bribes, or offers material advantage, or withholds them from those who do not hold this or that opinion.

There is one common argument against disabilities which comes from the high social qualities and great public usefulness of men of different opinions. Dissenters, Catholics, Unitarians, Deists, Jews, prove to be excellent members of the public service. There was first a start made in relieving from disabilities Catholics; then Dissenters; then Jews. The State, men said, must have a purely Protestant character; then it must have a Church of England character; then a Christian character, and so on. The argument that admits capable Dissenters to serve the State, admits all forms of Dissent; and that argument admits Unitarians and Deists; and the same admits Jews.

No rational limit can be drawn at any religious belief.

No theism of any kind, no religious belief of any kind, can be consistently maintained as necessary for public service.

Arguments in favour of keeping the State Theist are just as shallow as those of keeping it Christian. Some may say, If Theist, then why not Christian, and if Christian, then why not Church of England?

Positivists are not Atheists. Our Creed is not —There is no God. It is this—There *is* Humanity.

We are so far utterly opposed, not only to the Atheist, but to the Secularist type of mind and system of ideas, both in theory and in practice, in that we hold religion to be the deepest and profoundest part of human nature—to lie at the foundation of the peace and prosperity of human nature; in that we think the most precious things of civilisation are religious principles, habits, and institutions; and in that we mean by religion and religious habits the devoting of our souls and our lives to a Supreme Providence that rules our efforts towards good: one whom we can love, serve, and adore.

And yet, saying all this, we insist, that it is a condition of all healthy public life that all men shall be equal in the eyes of the State, whatever their religion, or their irreligion—whether they believe or not in God or Devil.

The retention of an Oath is merely the last relic of the old theory of persecution which has come down to us from the Catholic Church, and which dies so hard. No State can be on a sound foundation which subjects to any disability the Atheist, any more than the Wesleyan or the Catholic. The distinctions attempted to be drawn are futile. There are M.P.'s and officials quite as distinctly Atheist as the late member for Nottingham.

All possible legal distinctions are inapplicable as between a believer in God or the followers of Moses, or the Pope, or of Auguste Comte, or Mahomet.

The old rule of law was that "Christianity is part of the Common Law." This is now very doubtful (1883). [It was denied by the Court of Appeal, May 1917.]

Why Christianity? What is Christianity apart from some sect? Does Christianity imply the Divinity of Christ? Are Unitarians Christian? What was the real fact in the Resurrection? All these are speculative questions; but until they are decided, it is impossible to give any meaning to the rule, that "Christianity is part of the Common Law."

The Judges who decide common law are or

may be Catholics, Jews, Unitarians, Deists, Secularists, or Atheists.

The most eminent Judge, the head of the Equity side of the Law, the Master of the Rolls, the *ex officio* head of the Court of Appeal, is a Jew (1883). Imagine the outrageous inconsistency of calling on a sincere and devout Jew to punish a man for infringing the rule that "Christianity is part of the Common Law."

To administer this law you ought to have ecclesiastics, bishops—persons who have adopted given opinions, are pledged to them, and are at least outwardly expected to believe them. But, of course, a devout and sincere Hebrew is not expected to believe in them. Any Judge feels himself free to disclaim all theological opinion. The law and its administration is derived from the Star Chamber, and that was derived from the Catholic Church.

I will now enter on the case of a recent trial[1] (*Reg*. v. *Foote*, 1883).

Needless to say that we do not share the ideas of the *Freethinker*. Nay, far more. No men, whatever their creed, can look with more real disgust and indignation on any moral

[1] I retain much of what I said in public and which I also wrote in the *Pall Mall Gazette* of March 1883, on the case of *Reg*. v. *Foote*. The judgement then given by a very eminent Judge has now been set aside, and so flagrant a case of intolerance is not likely again to recur. But the case should not be forgotten—and it affords even now a striking illustration of the argument in this chapter.

offence committed by wanton insult to the conviction of others, than do consistent Positivists. To us all ribald mockery of things held sacred by others, and especially of things which, right or wrong, do as a fact hold together masses of men and bind up their moral and social existence in any appreciable way, all this is to us utterly hateful and abominable, and should be earnestly suppressed by us by every means in our power, so long as these means are moral and religious, and appeal to the conscience and not to jails or penalties.

Not only we ourselves are never guilty of reviling or ridiculing Christianity, but we regard such ridicule as an attack upon hopes and beliefs that are amongst our most sacred possessions.

How could I, standing in this room to promote the teaching of a man who has spoken in such admiration of so many of the greatest names and works of Christianity, having before me, as I speak, the image of Paul, the revered founder of Christianity, and the revered founder of Mosaism, and amongst them the images of two others at least of the most illustrious types of Christian civilisation—how can I treat Christianity with contumely, or speak of those who have exposed its believers to ribald mockery with anything but heartfelt repudiation and antipathy.

But none the less, must I speak of the punishment inflicted on the *Freethinker* as a crying attack on the freedom of conscience, as a gross perversion of the power of law, and a striking example of the hold which mediaeval theories still have on us.

I make no complaint of the act of the Judge; but it is impossible not to see that he acted in a spirit of theological zeal, that he was using language which could only be fitly used by a spiritual person, whose function it was to propagate certain religious theories, and not as a secular magistrate whose business is with material not with speculative concerns.

In the first place, this rule of law is not under Statute; it has only twice been acted on during the present half of a century, the latest was twenty-five years ago. It has received the greatest criticism, and, as a very learned Judge (Sir J. Stephen) tells us, the "offences against religion can hardly be treated as an existing head of criminal law." The law, if enforced, is sufficient to crush every criticism of Christianity, even the circulation of such a book as Strauss's *Life of Jesus*.

Note the extreme danger of using obsolete law, restating it, as it were, dropping half of it, and applying it to some particular branch of the offence.

There was no sort of ground for saying that the law is specially concerned with gross mockery. Note the injustice of this attack on obscure and poor men for what is at most an offence against good manners.

A bishop has held up the Old Testament to elaborate criticism, practically amounting to ridicule.

Mr. Matthew Arnold laughed at "the third Lord Shaftesbury." This was a wanton insult to wound persons and religious sentiments. If this is not ribald mockery, what is?

But Matthew Arnold is perfectly safe; he is the friend of bishops and ministers and M.P.'s, actually a school inspector, a State official, charged to see that little boys and girls are properly taught their Bible.

Mr. Arnold systematically protests against the idea of a Personal Creator. He describes Him as a "Power not ourselves that makes for Righteousness."

I am told that the object of the prosecution, the Christmas *Freethinker* (which I have not seen), was a copy of a French book having a large circulation.

This French book was shown to me and to others by the librarian of one of our great institutions, who had received it from highly respectable publishers, and it can be bought of any foreign bookseller in London.

I know that eminent Justices have been heard to give circulation to certain remarks far exceeding anything in the *Freethinker*.

Well, these eminent Judges would say: We are not bishops, our brethren on the Bench are Jews, Unitarians, Infidels, and Secularists: We take no test, and are not, in our official capacity, required to believe in any particular creed or to profess any; our business is to punish crimes and decide questions of property and order. Yet these are the men who have to lay down that Christianity is part of the law of England and decide upon what is a blasphemous libel. This shows the inherent weakness of the case. Such a law ought to be administered if at all by spiritual persons, men who are officially pledged to believe certain doctrines.

Such was its origin, coming from the Ecclesiastical Courts to the Stuart Judges, and then lying dormant for a century.

What makes this case so serious is, that it has been defended by what are called organs of Liberal opinion on grounds which logically imply a State religion, and by specious and clap-trap arguments which are utterly sophistical and misleading.

It is said that we are not to have vile outrages bawled into our ears. Well, nothing has been bawled into our ears.

There was no obtrusion (that I know of), no forcing of this book on the unwilling. No one could see it who did not buy, beg, or borrow, or steal it. As to its being placarded, this is not so. The book had been put in a shop window as other books are.

I quite agree that there are certain things which police may fairly remove from offending the public sight. I only wish they were a little more consistent in so doing.

For example, a grotesque caricature figure of the Pope, or of General Booth, paraded like a guy down the Strand would be a public offence. This is a police question, and the limit of interference is where outrageous and offensive things are bawled out in public, or paraded in public so as (*a*) to risk peace, and order, (*b*) to be forced on the ears or eyes of unwilling persons.

Then, I agree, a police question arises, and possibly a fine point of possible police interference may be made out for displaying the pictures of the *Freethinker* in a shop window. But whatever is the legitimate limit of police interference? Removal under a magistrate's order, and, in case of refusal, a small fine. There used to be a gigantic Guy Fawkes of the Pope in the Strand, in every way more dangerous to peace, and more blatantly offensive.

At most the police could seize the figure, and possibly a magistrate would inflict 40s. fine. Would the contrivers be sent to prison for one year? No! the worse outrage would pass because the religious feelings of millions of

English Catholics and of the majority of this Christian nation are not protected by law.

In other words, there is a State religion.

Some people think that it is sufficient to say, the prevailing religion. Well, what is the prevailing religion? Who is to decide, say in Switzerland or the United States, or in Paris, or in London?

It can only be decided on principles of Mr. Gladstone's Essay on Church and State. If there is no adequate protection for Catholics, is there any for Mahomet; would there be any for us, or for Secularists?

Reverend and right reverend persons are free to heap any outrageous insult they please on the idea of Humanity, and to treat the reverence for it and the idea of service to it as a piece of buffoonery—and they are not within the scope of blasphemous libel. "Blasphemous libel" cannot be applied to many creeds, it can only protect one; and to say the creed of the majority, or the prevailing creed, and to protect that one specially by law, is exactly to fall into the doctrine of State religions, the antithesis of the Positivist principles that the State shall not and cannot know any religion.

But another argument is now used freely. An attempt is made to distinguish gross and ribald insult from serious argument.

And a leading Liberal paper puts it thus—

"It ought to be legal to argue for any position whatever, but not to wound or outrage the consciences of the majority." This is an idle distinction. It is said—"I have a right to be protected against scurrilous abuse of what I hold sacred!"

Here again this position is only tenable on the theory of the sacred feelings of the majority, *i.e.* on the theory of a State religion. It is curious that this argument is urged in a paper which has long been known for its liberal views, the editor of which has distinguished himself by incessant defiance of that which is sacred to a majority, and who had more loudly maintained the sacred right of the conscience of minorities. But a journal whose editor is a pledged member of the Parliamentary party in power is not the place to which we should look for independent judgement on the violations of their own principles by the Government of the day.

And the argument will not bear a moment's consideration.

Who is to say that ridicule is never to be used in argument; and who is to say that ridicule is used with a malicious or wanton spirit, or in the highest spirit of religious controversy. Luther and Latimer, Christ and Elijah, often used ridicule in its bitterest form.

Perhaps Mr. Matthew Arnold will say that his third Lord Shaftesbury is not wanton lampoon but serious argument. Ridicule, even lampoon, is resorted to daily by all parties in philosophical, social, political, moral questions, and religious; and is one type of religion to be protected on the theory of a State religion?

Every day the windows are full of odious and brutal outrages on the dearest feelings of Irishmen, of Catholics, of teetotallers, of Trade Unionists.

Punch used to be full of gross and scurrilous caricatures of the Pope and of Irish Catholics.

Literature has been deluged by outrageous lampoons on Mr. Gladstone, Lord Beaconsfield, Mr. Parnell, General Booth, and the like, and on the causes they represent, and no one thinks of protecting them.

There are probably no scurrilous lampoons more wanton than those of favourite orators, no insults and caricatures more dangerous to society than some Irish letters. Yet who is to say that this or that lampoon is wanton outrage and not political argument?

It is sometimes said a jury must decide it. Unfortunately we know that juries are now a class institution: there is no class in the three kingdoms more violently partisan on certain things than a London jury to-day, where the mass of the workmen are not represented at all. On such a matter you had better have a jury of London curates than a jury taken from the average class of chapel-goers.

But to say that lampoons on the Pope, or the Salvation Army, or Ireland, are a totally different thing from lampoons on the Trinity and the Bible, is not this to protect the Trinity and the Bible as no other belief is protected ?

This is the very thing we here protest against, *i.e.* the making one set of opinions, absolute, above discussion, sacred from ridicule, no longer in the region of proof, but *supernatural.* This is to accept a theological and absolute basis. And no consistent Positivist, or Freethinker, or Secularist, no true and logical believer in Demonstration instead of Revelation can accept any sacredness about the Trinity which there is not about the Papacy or our country.

I have heard it sometimes said—Oh! but this is religion! Who is to decide in a criminal court what is religion? That is to accept the theological basis of religion. Is a sincere belief in the Papacy not a religion? Is not the faith of the most patriotic Irishman his religion? Is not the wild raving of Louise Michel a religion to her and the Anarchists who sacrifice their lives with her?

A court of criminal law is not the place to decide whether a man's religion is insulted, or what is his religion, or what religion may, and what religion may not, be insulted.

I quite agree that citizens may be protected by law against outrageous insult and personal injury to their reputation and quiet in the world.

But to talk of giving a man a year's imprisonment for insult to ideas, to thoughts, and that to the thoughts and ideas which if they are sacred to millions are merely popular delusions to millions of other citizens who equally pay taxes and vote the laws—this is setting up a State protection for ideas, and a State persecution for attacking these ideas.

It is ludicrous to suppose the State can protect all ideas. To protect the ideas of a section, even of the majority, is to set up a State religion.

It is all very well to say that this is the opinion of the great majority: that remains to be seen. That is the wretched plea of every persecution. It does not lie with liberals, with freethinkers, to talk of prevalent religions and immense majorities.

Persecution is persecution, however large the majority, and often the more inexcusable the larger the majority.

If they are the immense majority, let them protect their ideas by ideas apart from any question of obtrusion on unwilling eyes and ears. If you require them to be bolstered up by policemen and jailers, I say, you are afraid of them.

For myself, and for ourselves, I repudiate with indignation furthering any cause by brutal outrages on men's dearest beliefs, and coarse lampoons to wound their conscience.

Much more do we repudiate and do we denounce it when it is done to turn a few dirty pence by abominations in the spirit of wanton and unsocial mischief. I say again we denounce this, for a man speaks in public on this matter at great risk, surrounded by eager critics ready to pervert and misrepresent him.

If any man in the Press or elsewhere, referring to my words to-day, shall go forth from this room, where he enters by our free invitation and on sufferance, and shall state that I spoke any word of sympathy with scurrilous lampoon on any religion, Christian or heathen (and there are no worse offenders than our own missionaries), or who shall omit to state that I denounced it with loathing and indignation, I say beforehand that he will commit a wanton and inexcusable calumny.

But I say that, though the difference is great in morals and in ideals, the magistrate dealing with criminal law cannot be allowed to draw a distinction between criticism and satire, satire and caricature; and that to make one kind of caricature blasphemy is to have a State religion and a religious persecution.

It would take me too far to show you that much evil of horrible kinds is not punished by the State. At common law, seduction of the most infamous kind, the desertion of the seduced mother, is not a crime in a civil court; the most horrible insults on the institution of marriage, on the purity of woman, the foulest and most ghastly parodies on the holiest ties of family life are not punishable, provided there be nothing obscene in the caricature. And are men to be imprisoned for one year (a sentence severer than that passed on men who jump on women and beat them to a jelly) for a stupid and witless caricature of an abstract idea which millions of our fellow-citizens think just as completely a bit of history as Jupiter and Odin?

To see judges, Jews, Unitarians, Deists, and Atheists sending men to prison for libels on the Trinity; to see a House of Commons, filled with freethinkers, excluding an avowed secularist, is a startling evidence of the confusion of principle in which this question has drifted.

To tell us "that protection against ribald caricatures insulting to my religion is as much my right as protection against objects which insult my sense of decency," is hypocritical stuff.

Are we protected against Z——'s novels, and O——'s romances and the like?

What protection against ribald caricature insulting to our religion have we or are we likely to have? Or what have hundreds of believers in many creeds? What protection can be given to any religion but that of the majority?

This is but one corner of a great question, but it may carry us far, if we reflect on it till we come to the great principle of all modern civilisation.

1. That the legal methods, the instruments and institutions, by, upon, or whereby force is applied in States in the name of all and by the united resources of all, shall be limited most strictly to things material, about which no doubt can exist, and those external habits and moral observances, about which no sane men feel any doubts or differences.

2. That the persons, methods, interests, and institutions concerned in Education, raising the moral and intellectual level of a people, should never under any pretence be armed or aided by the material weapon of State compulsion.

Freedom, conviction, moral responsibility, and intellectual independence are the essence of all moral and mental development, and no moral or mental development is real which is the result of fear, force, or ambition and self-interest.

State Churches, State religions, State education are all parts of a vicious system—remnants of the Catholic and despotic theories of centuries ago.

However attenuated be these State religions, however vague or elastic they are made, they are none the less evil.

Every system of Religion or scheme of Education must be perverted and poisoned in its source if they are protected by the force of the majority.

There can be little doubt that this act of persecution will prove as fatal to the official form of religion as any single thing in our memory [repudiated by the Court of Appeal in 1917].

For ourselves, I can only say, that we should reject any such protection, as much as we should reject establishment or any State support or control altogether. And if the Primate and the whole Bench of Bishops were to profess Positivism and still seek to remain prelates of an Established Church, we should cast them out as a scandal to our humble but free body.

And if it was proposed to make the denial of Positivism " blasphemy," or to teach the Positive scheme of education by the whole power of the State, we should equally reject it with indignation and disdain.

LECTURE V

(*Newton Hall*, 1893. *Ethical Societies* 1893–1905)

ECONOMIC DUTIES

The life of the Family is the natural introduction to full life, and this family life is transfigured in the light of the maxim *Life belongs to Humanity*. But public life is the central and main form of a complete life, and this also may be transfigured by the same principle.

One of the most marked differences between ancient and modern religion is this: Ancient religion dealt mainly with public, practical, and social life. Christian religion has dealt almost exclusively with private, personal, and emotional life.

The essence of the old polytheistic religion went to stimulate the public qualities, which conduce to the glory of the city, to make warriors, statesmen, artists, citizens having strong and beautiful bodies, the gifts of command, patriotic and heroic tempers. This was emphatically the aim of Roman religion with its Mars and Quirinus and Capitoline Jove; it was the key of Greek religion in a different form, and also of the great theocratic systems that flourished in the Nile and the Euphrates valleys. Personal, spiritual life as we understand it was not considered. Tenderness of heart, sympathy, the sense of sin were neglected. What we call Purity, apart from intemperance and debauchery, was hardly conceivable as a religious idea. The *Republic* of Plato, wherein he, who is often called the most religious of the ancient philosophers, embodied his ideal of rigid virtue, is one of the most impure of books, as we now understand these things in the sense of Paul's letter to the Corinthians—so much so as to be in parts unfit for general reading. In that book, and in the other schemes for a religious and philosophical education, the sole aim is to produce brave, patriotic, cultured, and highly disciplined citizens. The virtue of public patriotism was bought by the sacrifice of what we now understand as personal self-respect and even public decency.

The immense revulsion effected by Christianity proceeded on exactly the opposite plan. Christianity appealed exclusively to the spirit within. It made no serious attempt to regenerate practical life. It assumed vaguely that that would follow as a matter of course. Fatal illusion! The result has been that public life has been regarded as something altogether apart from religion, and has developed an accommodating religion to suit itself.

It is one of the most distinctive aims of the Positive faith to restore a religious aspect to practical life and public life, to effect a religious organisation of practical and public life. And to do this, it applies the same great maxim—*Life belongs to Humanity*—Live for others.

What is *public* life? The answer is—The whole of active life, all life outside the home. In modern speech the term public life has acquired a somewhat narrow sense. When we speak of public men or of a public career, we are understood to refer to *politics*. Much of this political life is unhappily intensely *personal*. Now Positivism looks on all active life outside the home as essentially devoted to the public. The stone-mason, the collier have a public career—fulfil a public office. But, though the ancients were so far right in making public life the essential thing, they took a fearfully narrow view of public life. The ancients restricted public life to a small dominant minority. In a society founded on slave labour it was restricted to the free and to full citizens; the servile and even the alien free residents had no share in it. It was quite distinct from private and domestic duty. Its main object was war; and except in the Roman Empire its sphere was that of a small and self-seeking city. The Positivist view of public life differs entirely from this by referring it directly to Humanity. In the first place, (1) it recognises all adults without exception as citizens, as within the scope of public life. (2) It regards their public life as the continuation and enlargement of their private life. (3) Its whole organisation is for industry—not for war. (4) And it repudiates all ideas of a narrow and dominant Patriotism. We may take each of these points in turn.

I. Positivism deals first with the great bane of all the political conceptions of antiquity—that society exists for classes or privileged families. This primeval vice of social life dates from the age of war and of slavery, the child of war. It was flagrant in Greece and in Rome. Even Aristotle could speak of those who are *φύσει δοῦλοι*, born slaves; and from antiquity comes that maxim of cynical selfishness—*Paucis nascitur humanum genus.* Thus all ancient societies, if within the narrow circle of free citizens they were equal democracies, to all the rest, the great majority of the population of each State, they were the most odious of aristocracies.

Christianity, in the early days of the Gospel, made noble efforts to redress this evil, and practically went far to eliminate slavery, but it certainly was not strong enough to destroy it without the assistance of feudalism. But at length the Church, having powerfully contributed to abolish slavery, and having greatly assisted in mitigating serfdom, fell in with the jealous spirit of feudal class exclusiveness, allied itself with monarchy and aristocracy in their struggle for power, and ultimately, as we see it so often to-day, became the creature of the governing class in its defence of antique privileges.

For ten thousand years we can trace this spirit—first as caste, then as slavery, then as serfdom, then as the distinction between the well-born and the ill-born, until we come down to that inhuman and unworthy formula which is still in possession of the social field to-day—the distinction between "the upper classes" and the "lower classes," which sometimes means the distinction between the idle and the busy, but more generally the distinction between rich and poor.

But there came at length a force which was strong enough to break through even this inveterate prejudice—the Revolution of the eighteenth century. Even that only suggested the idea. It was not able to establish it: it has not yet established it. Borrowing from the noble outburst of the heroic American Republic (itself the late descendant of the Puritan Commonwealth), the French Republic of 1789 proclaimed that all men are free, equal, and independent. It was one of the great moments, one of the turning-points in the history of Humanity.

But this doctrine, though potent and inspiring, was not a little crude. All men may be free from legal slavery; but they are not free from servile oppression, and for many a long day are not likely to be free from it. All are *not* equal: and they never can be in any absolute and general sense. They can be made equal in the eye of the law, which is a very great and a new thing; but in all the essentials of human life they are and will remain unequal. All men are *not* independent: strictly speaking, no man is. Civilisation in one sense increases their interdependence, though it can rob that dependence of a servile and degrading form.

Yet withal, charged as it was with dangerous sophisms, the idea of the freedom and equality of man (and it was mainly freedom from slavery and privilege *by law* that was looked at) was one of the most potent and radical which ever transformed social life. It is destined to grow and enlarge and take unexpected shapes. And Positivism, which is the child of the Revolution, the revealer and educator of the Revolution, puts this crude idea into a systematic form and it proclaims this truth:—

The task of modern society is to incorporate as full and honourable members of it *all* honest citizens alike (without any exception, short of crime)—*all* the workers, and all who have a duty in the world to perform. Society exists for all alike. This is much wider than a mere admission to the franchise, even universal adult suffrage. It means this: That all the benefits, boons, opportunities for which society exists must be offered alike to all citizens. And it is especially the duty of society to see that these things be placed within the reach of the poor, the weak, the hard-worked.

Society exists for the sake of the people. If society fails to give them every social advantage which society exists in order to afford, everything which can be enjoyed by all, in so far it falls short of its first duty; and to appropriate these advantages to some families, some classes, is a perversion of its main and worthiest object.

The reason why society is bound to provide for all is a plain one: that society exists only by and through all. The social incorporation of the people is the first underlying aim of Positivism. It has certainly not yet been accomplished anywhere, in any country, and in any epoch. During the whole period of antiquity and of the Middle Ages, owing to slavery and serfdom, it was obviously impossible. In France the Revolutions of 1789 and 1793 laid it down in principle, but could not work it out. The Revolutions of 1848 and 1870 carried it somewhat further, but they did not accomplish it. The widest franchise and the newest society may fail to secure it. It is far from complete in the youngest and most democratic State of the Far West in America. It never will be complete in any society where a small circle of the more rich and leisured class enjoy a superior order of education, and thereby enjoy the distinction which primarily attaches to special culture and easier habits of life.

The normal society would be one directly organised to secure to the mass of the workers :

1. All essential comforts of material life, including reasonable leisure and ease.

2. Ample opportunities for intellectual and artistic culture in all its forms.

3. Full, solid, free education.

4. Social respect as due to recognised public officials.

Now, this is only possible where (1) there is a common public education, (2) a social and even religious character is impressed on every form of industry, and (3) government rests on public opinion of all. During the great ages of Theology, whether in the Catholic, Polytheistic, or Theocratic types, the aim of the religious organisation was held to be to provide at least the entire free population the means of taking part in the public festivals, worship, and celebrations. In a normal society this would be extended to mean a share in a full scientific, artistic, and philosophic education. Again, a due place will not be reserved to the ordinary forms of human labour, unless they are regarded as essentially types of social and religious duty. Nor could such a spirit of respect be preserved long unimpaired, unless the supreme authority in the State is regarded as ultimately vested in the public opinion of all citizens.

II. This public and practical life must be regarded as continuous with, and concurrent with home life and moral life. That is to say, the practical duties of citizens must be made compatible with full home life, with sufficient leisure, with sufficient means to enter into the life of Family. That form of public, practical, and industrial life which nips and stunts home life is anti-social and retrograde. And the whole question of women's labour turns on that principle.

III. Industry is the direct end of active life—industry in the widest sense—the improvement of the planet, and of man's life on it, including art, enjoyment, appliances of life, the production of all things requisite for a highly cultured existence. But it must be industry purged of its sordidness, its self-interest, its hardness—not the cruel race for wealth which is the degradation of modern industry.

IV. The normal society must repudiate the narrow Patriotism of antiquity, which placed internecine hostility between neighbouring cities —between Rome and Carthage, Athens and

Sparta. Their whole political and religious system of a local and tribal polytheism stimulated war, domination, slavery. They had no conception of a common humanity or of the brotherhood of the human race. And even when the Gospel had introduced the conception of Humanity, it was distorted by absolute doctrines of Christ's Godhead, and the miraculous effect of baptism into His Church, so that the religious duty of destroying the unbeliever became as in the early Crusades a more fearful engine of bloodshed than the rivalry of neighbouring republics; and the cry of "*God's will*" led to the most ruthless wars recorded in history [1883–1918].

The essential result of the rule—that Life belongs to Humanity—is that all work is ennobled. All men labour for society, not really for themselves. All work is in effect a social function: the bricklayer, the seaman, and the collier are doing that without which society could not continue, and the indirect resultants of which it is quite impossible to calculate or trace.

No work of this kind, no good work which is indispensable to society, is really and strictly remunerated. How large a part of our working population receives but such wages as suffice to maintain life. The slave himself must be duly fed, clothed, and housed, and the slave, in ancient times when slavery was the regular industrial basis, was usually far better maintained and nourished than are a large part of the free labourers of modern Europe. We have seen a great industrial struggle maintained with heroic determination to assert the principle of the "*living wage*," by which is roughly meant such a rate as will give the worker the resources of a decent and comfortable existence. The wage, as we know it to-day, means sometimes such a share in the product of labour as will give the worker a tolerably comfortable maintenance, and it very often fails most cruelly even to reach that modest limit. But, as a fact, we know that every really worthy and competent worker gives to his work certain extra zeal and interest, which it is perfectly impossible to estimate by any process. We see it in such conspicuous cases as that of the sick-nurse who enters an infected hospital, the seaman, the engine-driver, the policeman, the soldier. We know that precious lives and valuable property are continually protected by the zealous, instinctive self-devotion of these workers, of a kind that no contract could include, and no money could buy. The same principle holds good, even in less conspicuous forms, in every competent worker. Every worker gives more than he receives. Hardly any wage or salary represents more than the waste, wear and tear, and fair means of living current in the particular employment — enough to keep the worker decently healthy, vigorous, and easy. There is very little of *reward* over and above that even in the best current wages of to-day.

We are all willing to allow this in certain conspicuous examples. A public minister, who, if he be competent, devotes his health, peace, ease, and often life to the public service, receives a salary notoriously less than the income he could obtain by competition in the market. An advocate who becomes a judge or an official usually sacrifices half his income, perhaps two-thirds of it. It would be ludicrous to suppose that members of our Government are *paid* or *rewarded* by their official salaries. Political life, as we all know, means to most men a sacrifice of fortune, of health, of peace of any kind. Every one recognises this in the case of the soldier and the sailor. No one supposes that men can be *rewarded* for giving their lives for their country and their countrymen by a salary of £1 a month. It would be gross ignorance or cynicism which insisted that such men are paid the market rate of their services. It is very easy to say—"Of course they are attracted by the honour and dignity of their profession." We can all see that the sick-nurse who enters an infected hospital, the missionary who takes his life among savages, the soldier, the statesman, the sailor, the fireman, risk their lives out of a noble spirit of devotion, partly stimulated no doubt, in many cases (more especially in that of the statesman), by the honourable recognition they receive from society.

But all honest industries whatever, all lawful employments are also worthy of honour, and, if worthily filled, demand a zeal which cannot be priced. All social work is unappreciable, for its remote effects are infinite. The work of the scavenger, the miner, or the stoker, often has results of supreme importance to society; zealous labour, courage, and self-devotion may avert a fearful calamity: wanton carelessness or folly may at any moment destroy precious things and priceless lives. It is impossible to buy the really conscientious and devoted discharge of any labour which has unlimited social consequences. And all honest labour, when we think it out, has unlimited social consequences. The better spirits accept that which is socially an inadequate remuneration, for they are conscious of a high duty, and feel that their fellow-citizens are conscious of it also. Just as we see in the case of soldiers in an army, who, if worth their salt, and well treated and well led, are not heard to grumble continually about their miserably insufficient pay.

The same principle decides the ancient struggle as to the social prerogative of Birth and of Wealth. From the earliest dawn to civilisation both of these have claimed a peculiar distinction of their own which even in our day neither numbers, nor Christianity, nor education have been strong enough to neutralise. A social and scientific religion proves Birth to be a compound inheritance far too complex to be confined to the narrow line of any single house or name. And as to Wealth, it is found to be the product of numbers which is often concentrated by pure accident, or it may be by some mean natural gift, on the least worthy members of every community. The final and human form of society is the Republican—which makes the sole title to honour or to power the exercise of capacities of great value to the community. Both Birth and Wealth are titles having origins of such wide ramification and so arbitrary and accidentally conferred, that apart from some special service they may represent, they cannot be taken into account at all.

There is very striking novelty introduced into sociology by Comte, one of great importance and wide range. He denies that the ultimate and normal form of social organisation can be either Monarchy, Aristocracy, Plutocracy, or Democracy, if Democracy mean, as it should, the absolute control by the mass of the people for the time being. What then: for no other form of society is ordinarily recognised as possible? Comte invented the term *Sociocracy* to represent that organisation of the State where the keynote of the constitution is the collective interest of the society as a permanent organism. This is a vast extension and great advance on Democracy, pure and simple. It is in vain to grumble about the solecism in the word, a solecism which it shares with Sociology, a term that has conquered its way into the languages of Europe. The term Society is not found in Greek, because the Greek language never rose to the conception of society apart from the *Demos*. Sociocracy (and it is significant that Latin and not Greek supplies the expressive part of the compound) means government in the name of the society as a whole and as a permanent being, and not in the name of any order or class.

Sociocracy allows regard for two things which are neglected in pure Democracy. (1) The legitimate authority of personal capacity; for it conflicts with the arid sophism that all men are equal. Men are not equal, but differ enormously one from another. The test of difference is their respective power to influence and benefit society. (2) The second point is that Sociocracy regards the interests of the society in its permanent form, the generations to come, the future of the community—a very different thing from the interests, much less the claims of the masses at any given hour. They are themselves but too ready to assume that *they* are the society, which they neither created, nor adequately represent. From want of sufficient theoretic training, and under pressure of extreme and urgent needs, they are often willing to put aside every one but themselves. It is natural, but it is not altogether true. The highest interests of England are not quite the same as the interest of this generation of workmen. This is the root fallacy of Marxism.

For such a leavening of the whole society by public opinion, for the welding of all classes into one republican sense of fraternity, for this recognition of the true superiorities of the capable, for this willingness to postpone the desires of the generation that is to the permanent interests of the generations to come, one thing is indispensable, one thing only can give it. This is a common education for all. Without a common education public opinion could not be organised, and would have no solidity, continuity, or energy. Without a common education the mutual respect of all ranks and classes, of all workers would be impossible. No free social intercourse, no true moral equality could be established without it.

Common education is the only possible basis for a true republican life—the root idea of the Positivist scheme of society. One knows that at present the mass of social prejudice rests on a distinction between the order of *gentlemen* and the masses. Socially, all gentlemen are equal. And in our age all are socially " gentlemen " who have a certain education and the habits and qualifications for a share in a given type of social intercourse. A common education will make all men gentlemen, whatever their work, who are willing and able to qualify themselves for cultured social life.

This is not the place to dwell on the Positivist scheme of common education. But it must be noted here that the whole political and social scheme of Positivism is based upon this common education; and all those criticisms of it which are based on the assumption that the present method of public education is the normal and only possible method are necessarily futile and meaningless. Normally, the whole of society would be founded upon this common education—a complete encyclopaedic education freely given to all—to all classes and both sexes, without payment, without any class distinction, given not by the State, not out of the ratepayer's money, but by an independent educating body maintained by voluntary gifts or endowments. When Comte speaks of a priesthood (a term which causes such repulsion), he means a body of educators who will teach all freely and not for hire. When he speaks of a Church (a term which seems to create a panic amongst modern freethinkers), he really means a teaching and training institution entirely independent of any State authority, and having no special privilege or monopoly. Where all are free to teach, and all are free to choose their own teachers, the only difference would be the more or less complete organisation of the teaching institution.

Comte has named such ideal educators *priests*, because he assumes that they will have functions very different from those of college tutors and professors. They will seek, and will acquire a real moral influence, as well as an intellectual influence. They will be occupied with religion quite as much as with science and philosophy. And they will publicly perform ceremonies of consecration, and of commemoration, at birth, marriage, death, and all celebrations, public and private. Hence they are rightly styled a priesthood.

An education such as this must be complete. It must be real training in the range of physical and moral science on a synthetic plan, with a logic and a philosophy adequate to give it unity. Were it not so, the utmost divergence would result, and education would end in being the dissemination of new sophistries.

Such an education must be organised, or it will lead to fresh disunion and disorder of mind. It must be gratuitous. For in the first place to require payment would be to exclude the poor, whilst the main object of the education is to make the poor the equals of the rich, to infuse a common elevation of mind into the masses. We used to hear much both from workmen and from educational reformers as to the paramount value of public education being paid for, and not made a free gift. Could such an education be bought? The very source of all the class distinctions amongst us, in spite of democratic institutions, is simply that the rich are always able to pay for a much higher and much more complete education than the poor. The mass of the people could only pay for a very modest education. As it is, if there were no endowments, no free teaching, no voluntary gifts, the workmen would be wholly unable to pay at all for education.

LECTURE VI

(*Newton Hall*, 1893. *Ethical Societies*, 1895–1900)

THE ECONOMIC PROBLEM

I PASS to consider the economic problem further, and to deal with Industry as it should be.

The picture of industry in the future as painted in the Positivist scheme is an ideal—a type—which rests upon antecedent conditions. These conditions are :

1. A common free education, open to all.
2. A body of men whose sole business it is to counsel, inspire, and moralise society.
3. A regenerated social system — resting on social duty.
4. An accepted religion, practical, social, human ; enforced by public opinion, and by a recognised Church or order of teachers.

It is in vain to point out how the working of such a system would be made impossible by this or that actual condition of habits and opinions in the world. The answer is, that Positivism desires to change those habits and opinions, and does not pretend to hope that the good time can come till they are changed. It is as vain as if it were objected to the early believers in the Gospel taught by Paul that with his view of Charity the amphitheatres never could be filled, and it would become impossible even to buy slaves. The followers of Paul would reply that the main purpose of the Glad Tidings of great Joy was that such slaughter-houses as the Romans enjoyed should be closed, and that such an abomination as slavery should cease. So, Positivists say, their object is, that the Competition mart should be closed and industrial slavery cease—and that by the influence of a purer religion.

The basis of the Positive theory of industry is this—that industry is the natural and permanent form of human activity—the only normal and honourable form of activity. All through antiquity and down to the last few centuries, the only normal and honourable form of public activity was supposed to be war. When war at last was confined to a professional class, idleness and idle sports were held to be the only honourable occupation. The Church encouraged idleness as the spiritual ideal by consecrating the lives of its masses of monks and useless persons of both sexes, who ranged over all forms from that of beggars to voluptuaries and cretins. The Court and aristocracy rather inclined to idle sports which are still considered the only worthy occupation of gentlemen. To this day, when young men of any pretensions talk about their movements, even if they are clerks in the city, or medical students at home, they always tell one another that they are going down to a ball in the counties, or that they are going to kill something. They do not go: but they talk about it for three months. They do not admit that they are doing something useful—as they sometimes are.

Now the first thing is to establish that industry is the only natural and honourable form of activity. Idleness is the anti-social vice. Christianity consecrated idleness, and led to a spiritual animalism which, as the poet says, is the life of one *Venuto al mondo soltanto per far letame*. In the Positive scheme the idle are the parasites of Humanity. Positivism, alone of religions, deals with this by its maxim—*Live for others*, *i.e.* work for Humanity. It does not say love, meditate, suffer—but *work*. The first step towards a wholesome, human, and social religion, is a religion which will consecrate labour.

But all industry is not necessarily *productive*—meaning the making of boots and shoes, engines, and ships. There is an immense amount of energy needed in thought, science, art, education, in many forms of social usefulness which are not *productive*, in the sense of manufacturing anything that can be used; anything visible, but which is eminently social in the sense, that society could not exist without it. The world could get on without boots and shoes, and even without steam-engines, but it could not get on without intellectual, artistic, moral, and spiritual inspirations, and these are things it cannot manufacture for itself. All forms of systematic socialism seem to overlook this, or provide for it in a futile way. In their furious crusade against useless hands in the society they would thrust every man, woman, and child into the same industrial mill. If the State alone is to possess all the instruments of production, every one will be required to produce; and, as no one but the State will possess capital, every one will be forced to labour in that sphere of life to which the State assigns him.

Positivism rejects this arbitrary cast-iron Utopia, partly on the ground that it would oppress free life and necessarily destroy the family life, partly on the ground that it would extinguish all but productive industry. Formal Socialism, apart from the vague improvement of our Labour legislation which is nowadays called Socialism, must do this. Where all industrial occupations are ordered by the State, there can be nothing but productive labour. The State can distribute a million citizens into a thousand factories, and assign his part to every one of the million, with or without formal election. But how can it pick out a Charles Darwin and direct him to give fifty years of his life to study the evolution of Nature, or a Herbert Spencer to devote another fifty years to Synthetic Philosophy, the sale of which would hardly pay for the books he needs. In a Socialist community, Darwin and Spencer, Tennyson, and Ruskin would be treated as idle malingerers and forced to be very indifferent carpenters or poor book-keepers. Neither the State, nor the municipality, nor adult suffrage could create artists, thinkers, teachers, statesmen, or social philanthropists. They can only grow up spontaneously and freely.

If we look through any list of those to whom Humanity is indebted for its real progress, we may observe that at least three-fourths of them have been enabled to live a free life, working out their own ideas without interference. And the indispensable basis for this free and spontaneous life has been capital, or accumulated stock of some kind, either in their own hands, or placed in their hands by others. Not that all of these men have been rich—far from it; some of them have been rich and very many of them have belonged to rich families. But they have been free, because they had a reserve fund either of their own, or placed at their disposal by some one or some body of persons. You do me the honour to come here to hear what I have to say.

If I were to ask half-a-crown apiece from each of you, I should consider myself to be very badly paid, and I doubt if many of you would come again. I am quite certain that neither State nor Council would vote me the means of living in order that I might put forth my thoughts, and I am quite sure that they would not have kept me in idleness all the forty years that I have been studying, thinking, talking, and writing. It comes home to me very painfully that under any system of socialism my life would have been voted one of flagrant idleness.

This brings us to the great issue between the Positivist scheme and that of Communism and Socialism. Comte has eloquently traced all the affinities between Positivism and the nobler forms of Communism. Both repudiate and denounce the existing state of industrial society: the low wages, the cruelty, the waste, the selfishness of the race for wealth and the struggle of competition. Both declare that, if this is to be eternal, it were better for society not to be. Both Positivism and Communism seek a radical solution by reorganising the family, by suppressing the individual selfishness, by regarding the existence of the worker as the very end of society, by claiming for the worker all that a flourishing community can give the mass of the people, by treating capital as the property, in the true sense of the word, of the community that has created it, and by imposing the strongest social conditions on the distribution of capital. These are very real and powerful affinities.

But that which Communism seeks to do in an absolute way, by law and force, Positivism seeks to accomplish in a relative way, by opinion, by moral influence, and a change of feeling and habit—in a word, by a powerful and constant religious conscience. The old, logical, and thorough types of Communism sought to remedy the weakness of family by absorbing families in the State; to improve the condition of the productive workers by excluding all others from the community; to remedy the abuses of capital by abolishing capital; and to redress the bad side of property by depriving mankind even of the good side of it. On the other hand, Positivism would regenerate the family by making it the true basis of life; it purifies capital by making it a responsible public office; and it ennobles property by giving it a uniformly social character, by making the use of property a sacred duty. The difference between the two may be thus summed up. Positivism is a moral and religious socialism: Communism is a material dissolution of society. It is dis-socialism.

The Positive theory as to wealth is this. All wealth is the creation of social co-operation, and is rightly employed only in the interest of society. The share of all who co-operate in the accumulation of wealth is honourable, and the idea that wealth is produced by the inferior for the benefit of the superior—which is still the popular view—is a mere remnant of a system of slavery. But though Positivism so far holds with the Communistic view that the appropriation of wealth is not a moral right, but a legal convention, it still holds firmly by the institution of property, not as a right, but as a rule of social convenience and social progress. Holding by the institution of property, it does so on the ground only of the moralisation of property.

Consider, as if *de novo*, the institution of appropriation of useful things to persons and to families, as if we were starting social life on an island out of the reach of human interference. The appropriation has no mischievous character in itself, any more than that a family should occupy a house, and a house a definite spot on the planet. Human existence implies that amount of appropriation, and civil society implies much more. It is the abuse, not the use, of appropriation which is mischievous. We are too apt to forget that appropriation is the essential condition of social and moral life.

If there were no appropriation there could be no generous use of products—no freedom of life. We should all be really slaves, fed by the State, but powerless morally. We should be free to do nothing but what was ordered by the office, and could give nothing, for we should have nothing to give. Appropriation is essential to any dignity of life—to personal energy as well as to generosity and goodness. What is even more pertinent, it is essential to successful industry. The most extreme Communist never proposed a community of clothes. All men admit the practical convenience, nay, the social and moral necessity for appropriating to man, woman, and child their own coat, gown, hat, boots, and bed. On Communist principles it is an injustice—robbery—for any man to own his own jacket, or his own sheets. On Positivist principles, the jacket or the bed is the joint product of many workers co-ordinated and protected by society; it is the property of society. But society for its own convenience suffers a man to appropriate his own clothes, tools, household goods for the sake of the moral usefulness of such modified kind of property. Every Communist could see the necessity for recognising property in tools, if good work is to be done. But on Communist principles it is quite as wrong to recognise property in tools as in a factory or a farm. It never occurs to them that property in a factory or a farm is even more essential for the production of manufactures and food than the appropriation to the workman of his own tools, hat, or books.

No doubt the modern Socialist treats things of this kind as preposterous applications of his theory. He is not at all logical, or systematic, and treats what he calls nationalising, or communalising the instruments of production in a vague and elastic way. Some propose to nationalise the railways, docks, factories, coal-mines, and so forth; others would nationalise the land; others would carry it as far as steam-engines, ships, warehouses, and so forth. But all this is left perfectly vague, and without anything like a coherent principle. The only sort of reasonable line that some would draw is to include in the nationalisation all fixed or immoveable property, leaving moveables to the rule of appropriation. That is to say, in the United Kingdom some six thousand million sterling is left untouched by the Socialist scheme! There is no real difference between land, factories, mines, engines, stocks and shares, money, tools, clothes, or utensils. All are alike the creation of society, and in strict morality the property of society. It is found to be essential to social life that persons and families should conditionally appropriate their use.

The existence of the family implies appropriation in an intense degree and depends upon it. The fixed home brings out all the moral beauty of property in the things needed for family life. It would degrade human nature to destroy our notions of the home. Yet it means primarily appropriation in an exaggerated form.

No modern Communist ever proposed a community of dwellings, that families should be housed in public barracks, and each person should sleep in a public bunk. No modern Communist calls out for a community of wives and husbands, of children, brothers and sisters.

No modern Communist proposes to do away with the institution of the Family. Plato resolutely did this; and we know the horrible expedients to which he was driven—expedients no longer even mentionable in our society. He may have been followed by a few zealots. But, in truth, this is the essence of the matter. Any Communism which does not destroy the family does nothing permanent—must fail. Family life lives upon appropriation—the home, the hearth, the household goods, the family belongings, the books, the ornaments, transmitted from father to son, from mother to child, carry the sentiment of property to its most passionate and endearing form. And the sentiment of family will continue to foster the desire of property, so that to extinguish property you must begin by abolishing the family, that is—human nature. Plato was quite right: there was no other way.

No people are so keenly alive to all that the home confers, as the mass of the working people, who have so few other things to brighten their lives. The poetry, the romance of the people, is all grouped round this appropriation of cherished things. The home, the decent stock of clothes, the favourite belongings of the mother, the wife, the child, the fire-side arm-chair, the bridal bed, the case of books, the garden round the cottage, the clock, the cups and dishes on the fireplace, the musical instrument, the pictures on the wall—where would these be, say in such a poem as Goldsmith's "Deserted Village," if the very idea of property were a social crime? These things are the joy of the toiler. But to the homeless, the outcast, this appropriation of the products of society may seem an injustice, perhaps an insult. Yet where is the line to be drawn, and on what principle? We are all too apt to judge society by our own measure. What is above what we have ourselves is extravagance—what is below us is penury.

The same reasons which make the appropriation of the comforts and decencies of the home essential to moral life exist for the institution of any property. The household and its contents gives a sense of freedom, of fixity, of means of cultivating the humane instincts—that is when well used: it may be very ill used. Any property, large or small, does the same thing—when well used. To abolish it all, because it is too often badly used, is to deprive all of freedom, stability, and humanity in their daily life. Positivism would very much increase—and not diminish this appropriation of the home by securing to the worker the full property of his home, both in town and country. As Comte says, the populations of our great industrial cities are like armies encamped in moveable huts, not citizens, possessing a stake in their country.

It is an easy transition from the home to the workshop. The smaller shop is fused with the home, and the two are inseparable. Would the condition of the worker gain if the shop were a stall, and the home a cubicle in a common barrack and dormitory? Pass on from the homely shop to the factory. Would industry gain if no man were master in his own business, and every shop were run by an elected foreman? The elected foreman would be the man who promised the highest wages, and offered the shorter hours, and who was the least anxious to lay by a reserve fund. And would the elected foreman be as skilful as the trained capitalist in selling the products and making a market? Serious industry involves long, patient, continuous thought, great experience, and years of training! The simplest trade implies an apprenticeship. It is mere deception to tell the workmen that their elected foreman, or buyer or seller, or traveller, would be competent to conduct the rapid, daring, instinctive strokes of business which make up successful trade, as it would be to tell the young student or city clerk that he could make a steam-engine, manage a power loom, or pilot an ocean liner across the Atlantic. And a single error in judgement or even miscalculation of time might bring the whole factory to a standstill and throw a thousand men out of employment for months.

Much was once hoped from co-operation. It has proved excellent as a club, as a retail shop. But as a normal mode of production it has proved to be a conspicuous failure. After forty years of heroic efforts, the real manufacturing industry of the country is not appreciably touched, and the merest trifle is given to the associated workmen. Co-operative societies are hard and niggardly employers of labour. And the moderate success of a few bootmakers, millers, and painters, who sell to the associated groups and stores, proves nothing as to the power of a body of workmen to succeed in the open market.

The comparison of great joint-stock trading companies is a transparent sophism. A bank, railway, or ship company consists of shareholders, the bulk of whom are capitalists, belonging to, or guided by, the capitalist class. The Board consists exclusively of wealthy capitalists and others who have been trained to business. The whole concern is worked by capitalists, in the interest of capitalists, and in the spirit of capital. Where would a bank be if its concerns were managed by the porters, or even the copying clerks? or a railway and a ship company if the stokers and seamen formed the Board? Habits of managing really complex industries require very subtle qualities. Society would return to barbarism without them, and they are only to be learned by the education of a lifetime. We sometimes hear from the ignorant that the profits of the bloated employer should be distributed to the real workers. The personal profits of the employer—apart from his reserve fund and accumulation—are on an average perhaps hardly more than 5 per cent of what he pays in various forms for labour. Divide that up, and it will give 6d. or 7d. as the rise of the week's wage, 1d. or 2d. on the day's wage, and the loss to the general business profit, of having a committee of workers in place of a professional capitalist, would range from 10 per cent to utter ruin.

Responsibility in a healthy state raises and improves a capable chief, as we all recognise in the captain of a ship, or the general of an army. All of this is destroyed by placing the director under the supervision of an elected committee, who, if they are fairly to represent the great body of the workers, must necessarily know much less of business than he does, and indeed can know almost nothing at all. It is pitiable to see politicians and professors flattering the workmen with assurances that the success of a few tailors or shirt-makers here and there to do a precarious trade of a few hundreds a year after an immense amount of volunteer advertising and patronising, proves the capacity of the workers in any big and complex manufacture to carry on a business of which the turnover is in millions. Clubbing together to buy food and clothing is a very simple process, as old as civilised society.

The industrial future of the world depends on the skill of the managers. The success of the managers depends on their entire freedom and personal responsibility. And their freedom and responsibility depend on appropriation. All this holds good throughout all industry—to the land quite as much as to moveables. Land, a cultivated farm, is just as much a social creation as Capital. The idea that Land is a natural open space, like the sea, is ridiculous. The top of Snowdon or Salisbury Plain may be a natural open space: but, except as open spaces, they both are useless. A cultivated farm has been built up slowly by human labour. The appropriation of the land is even more important for its social use than is the appropriation of moveable wealth. Poetry and romance have taught us the moral and sentimental beauty of the sense of property in the soil. And the narrowness and selfishness which this sentiment too often engenders are easily to be cured by a sound social education and by a religious belief. Land is no doubt special in that it is limited in area, and that it is impossible for all to share in having land. There is little more than an acre per head if the island were divided to our population; and estates of a few acres could not be properly cultivated. But it is essential for the production of food that the land should be occupied permanently by some. Farms of less than 50 to 100 acres, according to soil and situation, would be almost useless for the public interest. That is to say that, if the soil of this island is to be occupied in such a manner as to be beneficial to the people of this country, only one in fifty or one in a hundred could have any fixed interest in it.

The sole question is—what is the best arrangement for the general good of the public? To try and solve such a question by considerations of abstract right is absurd. Take the land in England and Wales at about 37,000,000 acres. Allow six or seven millions of acres for towns, allotments, gardens, and holdings by two million families or so, the remaining 30,000,000 of acres would perhaps produce the best return to the public, if they were occupied by about 100,000 families, not more, in farms averaging 300 acres. No question of tenure, or landlordism, or of owner, farmer, or labourer, need be considered in this connexion. The sole point is that about 100,000 families would have a fixed interest in the soil. The reaction of fixity of tenure, whether that of owner, tenant, or resident labourer is a very real and precious force. If we are to part with all the associations of the farm continued from generation to generation, if the family interest in the particular spot cultivated is to be wiped out, all that is represented to us by the sentiment expressed in Tennyson's *Northern Farmer*, whose conscience in his last hour upheld him that he had done his duty by the land, all that we are told the Irishman, the Scot, or the dalesman feel as to their holding, whatever its size or value, if we are going to sacrifice all that, a great change will result for English life—one not for the better.

Not only moral life but productive efficiency depend upon fixity of tenure as their first condition. And fixity of tenure requires the more or less permanent appropriation of given spots of the soil to particular families. If due use is to be made of the soil, the purely agricultural, *i.e.* pastoral and arable land, cannot well be divided amongst more than about 100,000 families at most. It is not necessary here to discuss the nationalisation of the Land. Under the law of England, the property in the soil belongs to no man: but remains inalienably the property of the State, or Sovereign. It may be desirable to reassert that doctrine in some new and emphatic shape. But under any system of nationalisation or Communism in land, arrangements must be made for the permanent holding of the actual cultivators, whether we call them owners, or tenants, or labourers, whether they hold under a landlord, or the State, or the County Council. There must be fixity of tenure for the farmer, and also for the ploughman.

If there is to be rotation of farmers and ploughmen, as well as of crops and seeds, if the farmer and the labourer are to migrate about the country like Irish harvest tramps, or steam threshing machines, and no farmer is to call any farm his, any more than a lodger in a tenement house who pays a few shillings week by week, if this is to be the normal condition of human life, we shall be going back to the nomad stage. Every system of land cultivation implies some definite *appropriation* of the soil to particular families (whatever be the form of the tenure). If we have that, we have the essential of property. It is a secondary question—what is the technical legal right of the ultimate owner-in-fee. We may make the farmer a mere tax-payer to the State, which is the sole landlord, and which has absolute disposal of every estate and every acre of the soil. But the actual resident farmer, with fixity of tenure, would on communistic principles be the proprietor, and will have all the sentiments of ownership.

True Communism in land implies the mobilisation of families, the production of the food of the nation by migratory casual labourers, a condition of things not wholly unlike the *latifundia* or great estates in the decline of Rome, cultivated by gangs of slaves. The sentiment of property will spring up the moment families are suffered to settle and fix themselves on definite spots of land. And directly the sentiment of property arises, the Communist Utopia is ruined, which would destroy some of the healthiest, purest, most poetic elements in human life, and, at the same time, risk the value of the produce.

Under the Positivist Utopia, the soil would be tilled, as all other industries would be worked, by two orders not by three, *i.e.* by managers (it is immaterial whether we call them landlords or farmers, owners or tenants). They would have a conditional fixity of tenure, the State remaining the legal owner. The others would be the workmen, call them peasants, labourers, or farm servants.

The estates might be of such a size normally as one manager could fairly superintend, not under 300 acres, nor much exceeding 1000 or 1500 acres. Each workman would have guaranteed to him his own house, garden, and plot, so that he would be a free man and protected from arbitrary oppression.

There would be no division between landlord and farmer, between tenant, middleman, and labourer, no idle gentry drawing rents whilst living away, no labourer deprived of any interest in the property of the soil. The political and social power of the landlord would cease to exist, and with it the artificial perpetuation of large estates in families. The odious remains of feudal privilege in the rights and rules of killing wild animals would disappear. There would be in each village and union ample common land for pasture, wood, recreation and games. Free water supply, free libraries, schools, and places of worship. Finally there would exist side by side with the farming system, as in North-Western France, a large number of peasant proprietors, cultivating their own land with their families without any farmer or manager at all. The director of any agricultural industry would take the place of landlord and of farmer. The rural labourer would be at once peasant-proprietor and free labourer for wages. Is not this Utopia as reasonable, as wholesome, as practicable as the Communist Utopia which begins by abolishing ownership in the soil ?

We may now sum up the ideal of Industry in the future as it was conceived by Auguste Comte :

1. Population would be limited almost to the stationary state not only (*a*) by prudence in postponing marriage to a reasonable age, but (*b*) by self-restraint, itself made a religious duty, in keeping the family born in marriage within the limits of comfortable provision for their number.

2. The workers whether in town or country

would be full owners of their own homes: those homes always consisting of at least seven rooms, and naturally in the country including a garden and plot of ground.

3. The wages would be partly fixed and permanent, partly varied according to the employment and the market. But the fixed part would be regularly paid whilst the employment continued and was calculated at £1 per week, whether in town or country labour, and whatever the state of the market. We hear a great deal to-day about the "living wage" as if it were a wonderful discovery of the late struggle. Let us note that in 1856 in France Auguste Comte proposed as a basis of healthy industry, a fixed living wage as a *minimum*, not only in towns but in the country, and exclusive of rent, at £1 per week. This wage, he held, in towns, in an active skilled labour, would amount to one-third of the weekly wage. That is to say, the skilled artisan would be receiving £156 per annum and his house—this, however, is always assuming that the wife and daughter were not working away from home in a factory.

4. The normal hours of labour would be reduced to eight or rather to seven. Here again, I remark, a Utopia which was put forward seventy years ago.

5. The mass of the people would receive a complete free education carried on to the age

of twenty-one, for both sexes. Workmen would be, socially speaking, gentlemen, and, scientifically speaking, philosophers.

6. The people would be freely and abundantly supplied with the public means of air and recreation, with unlimited pure water, with the means of access to collections of art, science, and study, libraries, museums, galleries, churches, and music.

7. All occupations would be treated as public functions and entitled to due respect. The pulpits would not be exclusively occupied with inculcating charity to the poor, but rather with honour to all honourable workers.

8. From pulpit, platform, meeting, club, and workshop it would be constantly insisted as an axiom of religion, of politics, of economics, that the employment of capital was a social duty, and that the management, use, and transmission of capital stood on the same footing as the functions of a general of an army.

9. Thereby the most powerful social restraints would be placed on (*a*) the idleness of the rich; (*b*) on the selfishness and oppression of the rich; (*c*) on the display of wanton luxury and misappropriation of the capital of the community; (*d*) on the reckless abuse of wealth for the mere purpose of amassing a fortune.

10. The people would be felt to be the ultimate court of public opinion, and their voice would be expressed, guided, and sustained by an

organised body of teachers and preachers, working in the spirit of religion and not as a matter of profit — inspiring Industry from top to bottom, from the most wealthy director of the most important concerns down to the humblest hewer of coal in the stifling mine, with the sense that all Labour, all Capital, like all Life, belongs to Humanity, comes from Humanity, and has its only end and purpose in Humanity.

Ah! say our Socialist and Collectivist friends, this is a dream, a Utopia—but how is it to be made real? How? how but by a religion, a systematic inculcation of the religion of social duty, taught us in every hour of existence from the cradle to the grave, sucked in with our mother's milk, surrounding us in every hour of life, and chanted over our weary bones when they are finally laid in the bosom of the earth.

Herein is the root-difference between the Positive Scheme and every form of Communism, Socialism, Co-operation or other Labour Utopia whatever. They touch but one corner of the problem, but one side of life, one sentiment of the human heart, and that not the deepest or the best. These Communisms and phalansteries and schemes of Land Nationalisation are propounded as vast and radical modes of revolutionising life. From the Positive point of view they are only playing with the fringe of the problem. They are thought to be dealing with the question in a grand and generous way. To us it seems a dry, mechanical, and material way. They profess to guarantee rights, to give every worker what is due to his labour, to protect him against selfishness and oppression. They seem to us in this to be taking but a low view of human labour. They appraise the social value of the industrious worker far too low; they estimate good work too cheap. The worker is entitled to far more than they would give him. They give him far less than Society can and ought to guarantee him. They seek (as the teachers of the Gospel sought in their way) to destroy selfishness by appealing to self-interest. They say the world is being turned into a Hell by the selfishness of a few. Therefore let us cure it by giving every one an equal self-interest, by making jealous regard for self-interest not only common but universal.

What to-day mars the fair face of Industry, and turns so much of our modern life into a cruel and ignoble race for Wealth is, not bad land laws or labour laws, much as they may need amendment, not monopoly in land, not property, not the accumulation of wealth; it is not the political power of wealth. It is a far deeper and subtler thing. It is selfishness—selfishness in rich and in poor, in the wages-receiver as well as in the wages-payer, in the husband and the wife, in the parent and in the child, quite as much as in the employer and the landlord, in the foreman as much as in the capitalist, in the apprentice as much as in his master.

And flatterers of the working people dare to tell them that they alone are pure, gentle, and unselfish, and that all will be well, if they take a closer and more systematic view of their own particular interest; that no part of our industrial misery comes from the hardness and brutality of the workman to his fellow-workman, from the cruelty of the man to the boy, of the tradesman to his apprentice, from the jealousy of the unionist towards the labourer. If all the land and all capital were divided up to-morrow in mathematically equal shares to every man, woman, and child in these islands—whilst Selfishness was left behind—in ten short years our present system would be reproduced.

Selfishness is at the root of our industrial evils, and Positivism, alone of all the Utopias, goes to the root of the matter, and seeks to combat selfishness by preaching a religion of unselfishness. And Socialists and Collectivists, whose panacea is to inoculate all with the same selfish poison, smile at a religion of unselfishness and very often at any religion of any kind. Socialism and Communism, as such, have no religion, and do not consider the religious problem as within their sphere. They deal with man solely as a fabric-producing animal, and treat the problem of human life as a mere question how to make certain manufactures.

Positivism faces the entire problem of human nature and proposes a religion, a philosophy, a polity; a new social morality based on social science, and fortified by an organised Church; a system of education, of civic government, of discipline, of worship, of public opinion. When we remember all that was done by the old theocratic religions of Egypt, Judaea, Arabia, Persia, India, China, and Japan to train, civilise, and organise human life; when we know how Sparta and Rome by an iron civic discipline bred up heroic warriors and devoted citizens; when we recall all that Christ and Paul did to purify and transform the bestial depravity of the old world; all that was done by the Church of the Middle Ages to humanise rude fighting men and ignorant half-savage serfs; when we think of all that was done by the Bible and by Puritan religion to make men temperate, courageous, pure, and self-denying; when we think of all that was done by the transient but noble wave of humanitarian feeling which in the last century with vague aspirations inspired the social movement in America, France, England, and the Continent; when we hear in the air to-day, and see in the face of every sincere man and woman striving after a better time the yearning for a nobler religious life which is so striking a feature of our age—we may believe that even so vast a task as the transformation of the human heart and nature in our industrial life is not too vast a task for the Religion of Humanity, the first and last word of which is to impress on every phase of our existence the inward and spiritual sense and the outward and visible sign, that we all do live for Humanity even as Humanity lives for us.

LECTURE VII

THE FUTURE OF THE WORKING CLASSES

(*Newton Hall*, 1893. *Ethical Societies*, 1895–1900)

ONE of the most common objections to the great system of *Regeneration*, known as Positivism, is that it is *unpractical*—some say visionary, Utopian,—a remote and indirect remedy for our present ills.

And then, again, some people find its field too wide and comprehensive for their purpose. Positivism seems to them to be about *omnibus rebus et quibusdam aliis*, and they cannot see why so many different grounds, social, political, religious, philosophical, need be pressed all at once.

This is the real strength of Positivism. The failure of Socialist and religious schemes of Society is due to this, that they are partial attempts to deal with a corner of the problem.

What a mere strip of human nature is it, that the Gospel appeals to—thought, industry, politics, art, all lying aside.

What a petty hole-and-corner affair after all

is the biggest scheme of Communism yet propounded, just dealing with men in their producing qualities, having nothing to say about the past and our relation to it, without a word as to philosophy, art, personal and domestic morality.

The whole *raison d'être* of Positivism lies in this, that it deals with human nature as a whole: it offers a *synthesis* or scheme of general harmony.

As to the objection that it is unpractical.

The fashion is, in this age, to specialise everything, to leave unity and co-ordination to chance.

To-day the cry is for direct roads to results, for political victories, for questions of political freedom, ballot boxes, universal suffrage, household ditto, female franchise, or personal representation.

They say the condition of the agricultural labourer is bad, then abolish all entails. Again, remedies for low wages, reform the Constitution: legislate about hours of labour.

This is the age of short, sharp, clear reforms by Act of Parliament, free trade, cheap press, suffrage, etc., etc., but all these do not produce millenniums.

These objections are not just. Positivism has very much to say about these practical reforms, about Parliament, and Trade Unions, and short hours, and Co-operation, and Free Trade, and the Press and the like. Its own principal interest is reserved for something very much larger and deeper.

In the main, the scheme of Positivism is a Utopia, it is an ideal, its strength lies in its general picture of what human life as a whole may and shall become.

Essentially, the religious promise of Positivism lies in its ideal of the future of the human race.

All great things that ever existed, or that have seriously affected civilisation, have consisted in *ideals*, often, indeed usually, an ideal strangely remote from anything current at the time, and not having on the face of it anything bearing on human life at all.

Take the ideal of Christianity. How strangely vague, unpractical, fantastic, visionary it looked —nay, was.

"Blessed are ye when men shall persecute you," and so forth. "Lay not up for yourselves treasures upon earth."

The Gospel is one long appeal to do things which were wildly ridiculous in the eyes of 999 in any 1000 of the Graeco-Roman world, and which at best only taught in an indirect way certain virtues of gentleness, mercy, purity in the heart. But it contained the magnificent overpowering ideal of Paradise, of a union of the Spirit with an omnipotent Creator, of a future of indescribable bliss by means of the intercession, Humanity and Intercourse, of the Son of this

Creator; and wild as this vision is, as we now know, a thing fictitious and hardly thinkable by the sober reason, by virtue merely of its being a potent ideal, it has transformed the world as we see it. That incoherent picture of a state of bliss has united our world; and for nearly 2000 years it has recast civilisation, changing its form and character, refashioning, altering social life, morality, domestic habits, and the whole condition of public and private life.

Again, it is said that, after the Bible, the *Contrat Social* of Rousseau has had most effect on mankind.

But it was a mere Utopia, it taught hardly anything but a crude, wild dogma of social union and liberty.

So the *Institutes* of Calvin, or the ideal of Monachism, or of Buddhism, of Confucius, of Mahomet, even we may say the same of Homer, of the Roman Republic, of Sparta as ideals of patriotic devotion. They were all ideal Utopias.

Everywhere in history, the great systems of human existence, and the great revelations in human civilisation, have been due to the working of an ideal, or type of life to which the believers were to shape their own sphere. And, even when this ideal was fictitious, narrow, and anti-social, still, when such an ideal comes forth and takes intense hold on the imaginations of men, hits the want of the time and fills the situation, it transforms human life.

We need not confine ourselves to ancient history, which is still exercising influence. Turn to Russian Nihilism: can any scheme be more utterly visionary, more completely an ideal? It settles nothing, creates nothing, suggests nothing. But, by virtue of being an ideal of Freedom, of deliverance from the intolerable pressure of modern social and political bondage, it has gained the devoted adhesion of some hundreds of thousands of men and women of many noble qualities, and it is now convulsing some of the strongest empires in Europe [1885–1917].

What could be less practical than the International Democratic League?

Take any of the Communist theories. What are they but visions of a social future?

The working masses of the Anglo-Saxon race in England and America are much stirred now [1885–1917] by schemes which I will not discuss, but which occupy us and most men who think on the problems of Society and Labour.

One scheme, that of Henry George, is at most a careful plan for one way of holding the land, etc., etc. The promise that it makes for a regeneration of society would be utterly outside its actual teaching, *e.g.* a resettlement of the farming and taxing institutions now in force, were it not that it holds such an ideal—an ideal as I think of a rather crude kind, and of a narrow kind, but still such a picture of the future of human industry in producing, and of wealth, that it completely fascinated numbers of thoughtful men.

Such is the power of ideals, if they are such as really meet any given situation, even though by uttering fantastic and impractical suggestions. Such is the force of a suitable ideal that it can transform the world.

Nothing is so potent as an ideal. The world is ruled by ideals, and it is true that if ever mankind shall excogitate for itself an adequate and complete ideal of the *future of the human race* the course of civilisation will be entirely altered and decided. Such an ideal, I say, the great vision of A. Comte does offer; and not merely is it suitable and meets the occasion, but is as clear and as real and demonstrative as the visions of Christianity and Communism are fictitious, fanciful, and partial.

Of such ideals, as views of human future, there are probably but two others in any way extant. One which has been at work for 1900 years, is less powerful now than ever, embraces less of the sphere of human nature.

The two are the Communist and the Competition ideal. The Communist ideal is a very limited one. Take H. George's scheme. The evils of industrial life are mainly in our city industry. But this will not be much altered by the practical abolition of private land-owning and the abolition of taxation. What would be the social effect? Tea 6d. lb. cheaper, spirits, tobacco, sugar much reduced, and no income tax on the rich. The question is not much affected by this scheme.

The ideal of Competition is the only one seriously in possession of the field. Is there not a growing aversion in all clear minds and generous hearts to this depressing superstition? Promises of happiness are continually believed and falsified. What do they end in? Chaos in our active life, and a growing area of misery.

What they preach to us to-day is perpetual insistence on the doctrine, that everywhere it is the business of man to get the most for himself.

Whilst the official and prevailing religion does little but raise its eyes towards Heaven in a conventional attitude of hope, praying that the Almighty Disposer of Events will bring all things to good in his own good time, repeating in the meanwhile to men on earth: "Lay not up treasures on earth," the practical Gospel of conventional opinion stimulates this assumption on system, by steadily inculcating the rule, that the only way for the world to improve is for every man to mind his own business and to get the most he can for himself!

Thus the ideal of Competition is a perpetual

scramble, becoming more and more trying to the rivals, vast capital heaped up, all the while the workers, the producers of capital becoming a larger body, slightly improved in the main, but under harder conditions of life, and with huge wings or dependants on their army, growing a larger and more hopeless body. Wealth, products, population, business, ever increasing by leaps and bounds, but the interval between luxury and penury, the enjoyers and the toilers, the masters of the world's good things and the makers of the world's good things, becoming ever larger. The men and women and children who make the goods too often live lives unfit for civilised beings. Well then, says Competition, make more goods: and the result is merely, more men, more women, more children, leading lives unfit for civilised beings. What shall be done to help the weak and the helpless, the starving, and the sick? And the answer of Competition is, Leave a man free, for the strong to fight his way to the front! Be sure that if he is doing the best he can for himself, he is doing the best he can for the world!

Under the influence of this cynical and blighting sophism—that real blasphemy if there be such—the wild energy and the splendid qualities of head and character which we see devoted to the multiplication of things useful and good for men, are actually perverted into rendering human life more hard and unlovely. A great genius like Watt, or Arkwright, or Stephenson, or Davy, by miracles of patience and insight and perseverance works out some exquisite invention, whereby it seems moral life is destined to be indefinitely aided and improved. In lieu of the aching muscles of men and animals, a little boiling water shall move tons' weight, and drive huge machines easier than 10,000 slaves in Egypt. In place of the strained fingers of woman and child a living machine shall twist threads a thousandfold for one. A new adaptation of the new genii, steam, shall enable men to rush over sea and land with a speed undreamt of by the men of the past. A chemical discovery shall enable men to work in safety in mines that before were full of death. What a future do these things promise to human life! And what has been the result? Toil, and toil under more severe and more painful conditions, has been heaped on men. By it the fingers of women and children ache worse for it, and a thousand fingers ache where one ached before, and they live in huge camps noxious to life and peace. The air is choked with the smoke and the steam, and resounds with the roar of machinery and wheels and hammers. Cities become black dens of dust and fog, and the face of our island is being covered with iron roads and huge engine sheds and factories and stores. Instead of being a blessing these things all threaten to be a curse. Every contrivance that skill and toil produce for the alleviation of human life seems by some fiend's malediction to end in making human life more terrible, and in widening the area of the suffering [1885].

Our monstrous city here grows huger and blacker and noisier; suburban or circular railways, tramways, and all the devices of science are called in to relieve us of the intolerable pressure of our own activity. And then, as we know, competition effects its inevitable end, and makes all this worse in the end, and leaves our Babel huger and blacker and noisier. The new resources of locomotion, which promise to lessen the fatigues of a vast overgrown city, practically result, as we know, in immensely stimulating the size and population of the already overburdened city. And so the very improvements which seem destined to relieve the worker, themselves are quickly shown to make that condition almost worse, or certainly no better. The sewing-machine bade fair to ease the monotony of the seamstress, and to enable her to earn more by her day's work. But, as if by some inexorable fate, competition converts the sewing-machine into an instrument for making work more monotonous, and mechanical! It tends to reduce prices, whilst it certainly destroys the value of the work. Instead of five million hand-made shirts, each paying the worker sixpence, we have thirty-five million ill-made shirts at twopence each. In lieu of one million toiling seamstresses at ten shillings a week, we have two millions at seven shillings.

There is competition in all its glory!

A rotten shirt sixpence cheaper than a sound shirt, and two millions of overdriven women in place of one million of hard workers on rather better wages.

There is a famous and weird story of a great romancer—how a man was gifted by a supernatural being with a piece of leather which had the miraculous property of fulfilling his every wish, but, at every wish, the skin shrank up, and with it shrank his life, so that with the last corner of the skin, the life of the possessor was destined to end or to be forfeit. I sometimes think that our modern industry is in some such case. As if competition were the malignant power which fulfils the dreams of man's ambition and avarice; but, at every realised wish, at each new triumph of productive skill, another slice is torn off the enjoyable margin of human life. With skill and energy, and the ceaseless race to be rich, and the longing to escape from want, we devise a new resource for each want of our lives, some new combination enables us to make two where we made one, or to do in an hour what used to cost us a day. At each gratified wish, at every triumph of skill and industry, we find our lives oppressed by a new want or new burden, or new difficulties which are the very consequence of this invention, or resource, or combination itself.

Far different is the ideal of Positivism.

The first condition of the working world in the Positivist scheme is, that it is an educated world. When I say educated, I do not mean merely that all the men and women can read and write, or pass the fourth or fifth standard of our School Tests. I mean educated in a high sense—not in the primary or lowest education—not middle but highest education: what we call the education of our colleges and schools, not purely academic. I mean such a scheme of education as was given here—such a scheme as you may get some notion of in reading our *New Calendar*, a training in the Poetry of the world, in the elements of Science and History, and a course of Philosophy and Religion.

Remember, it is the very condition of the Positive system that education shall be general: that bricklayers and carpenters shall receive just such an education as any merchant or manufacturer, of course, bar special technical training. Imagine the revolution in position, when the workers in a great factory or building yard shall have far more leisure for poetry and history and science than their employer, who has to bear with the strain of his anxieties; when they may be able to relieve his cares by giving him and his sons lectures on the poets or on the philosophy of history. Now the base of the Positive school of society is that education shall be common and one: all classes, all occupations, both sexes, having one and the same general cultivation. Culture in those days will be the mark not of the rich but of the poor.

All other systems can look lightly on Education. I do not know what the Gospel offers for Education! Directly nothing! What does Communism? What have Louise Michel and her Nihilists to say about general education? They do not trouble about so common a thing. It may be said—Where is the Education to come from? Well! not from the State. But Positivism is simply a social gospel, having for its object to impress on all, on the rich, on the instructed, on the capable, as on the people, that the great duty in life is the establishment of a high, true, and complete education. Remember, that in Positivism, Education practically takes the place of Religion in theology—is religion in fact. We see even in the slow decay of Christianity, what an enormous amount of energy, of capital, of devotion, of public spirit, is given up to preaching the Gospel. In this city alone, 10,000 churches and chapels are continuously meeting, armies of priests, and ministers, and readers, and Bible teachers, and choristers, etc. are at work. Millions are every year devoted to that cause, and tens of thousands of able and enthusiastic men give up their lives to it.

Now, much as I respect the zeal and public spirit of these men, nine-tenths of all this effort is to my mind mere waste, if not worse. This eternal iteration to trust in the Lord, and calls to meditate on the blood of the Lamb, is to my secular mind little better than calling on Baal—pure waste, except so far as by old association the worshippers may be made better and softer in the process. Well now! under the Positivist system the bulk of this immense force spent on vain invocations and the repetition of mere phrases will be given to Education. Imagine what would be the result of teaching in all the churches and all the chapels, if all the preachers and teachers, the Church Missionary Society, and the professors of the Gospel, were given to the work of Education? What might not be done? Unluckily two-thirds of this energy is at times given to retarding real, *i.e.* Scientific Education.

Education would be in vain unless the hours of labour were shortened. And so it is a fundamental condition of Positivism to make an immense reduction in time of labour, to eight hours, ultimately to seven hours. Eight hours is a full working time for a busy professional man.

An average City man works six or seven, an average barrister or lawyer eight, perhaps nine.

These eight hours are to be obtained in this way. Sleep and food require at least eight or ten; mere relaxation and locomotion another two or three; family two or three; two or three for social public intercourse, study, cultivation, and general improvement of life.

A workman toiling ten or twelve hours per day is *ipso facto* deprived of some of these, and consequently a society under such conditions is in an unhealthy state.

How is this ideal of eight or seven hours to be reached? By insisting on this ideal! How have the hours of workers been reduced from fourteen or fifteen to ten? By the pressure of public opinion, in and outside the working class.

The present theory is that as much time is to be worked as is consistent with the health and efficiency of the worker.

Whilst Competition is in full ascendant, no other consideration will be heard. So long as the Gospel of Struggle to produce and amass, to make the most for self, is the only Religion of the Community, so long, of course, any shortening of hours is impossible beyond the point of attention to health. But when every Capitalist is made to feel that due management of his business, and the well-being of all engaged in it is the very end he is there to fulfil, when every worker, every teacher, every journal, every woman, and every proverb steadily tend to present to all the moral well-being of the community as the first of all ends—then we may be able to shorten work. A great employer will no more seek to extend hours, than a Minister will seek to show what enormous taxation can be raised, or what a big army he can enlist, or what gigantic ironclads he wants. And a capitalist who has injured the moral force of those whom he employs will be condemned by the same opinion which condemns a general who has sacrificed an army to his own ambition or folly.

It is quite probable that reduction of hours may involve a reduction of product. That may be. But since multiplication of products only leads to widening the area of the hard life, let us try if we cannot do better by another plan.

Along with this reduction of hours of labour would come the removal of women and young children from factory work, away from the home. Here again, how is this to be done? Well, to some extent in the same way as women and children have been taken away from mines and other workshops.

The idea of the loss of wages is of course idle. The same amount of wages in the bulk would be had. The scramble for this sum amongst the men, women, and children separately, is only a consequence of the disorganising of the family. With the women set free for home duties, with a free education of the young, with a general cultivation, one can see that the homes would be a new thing.

But there is another side to this. Little would be gained unless the workman, however little of a capitalist, were master in his own house, and owned his home—a place where he could be completely independent.

Now, would this avail, if the wages were inadequate to enable him to live freely ?

Comte has in the question of wages introduced a new and most important condition, viz. that one portion of the wages should be fixed—that is payable during the whole engagement which would no doubt be annual. This to be £1 per week.

Then, that the other portion of the wages should be variable with the profits, involving publicity, and should be about double, *i.e.* £2 per week.

This gives for a city workman £3 per week of wages, in full employment at times of profit. And it must be noticed that this is plus house rent, plus free education, plus air, water, recreation, art, public amusements.

Thus the wages, even out of work, would never fall below £1, together with free rent, a household of seven rooms: and in full times, of £3, or £150 per annum, and a house, of free education, water, etc., and so forth, equal to £200 per annum.

If this is looked on as extravagant under our conditions we must remember (1) that the wages now paid to women and children will go to the men. (2) That the family includes the children, and the old parents, past work, and those who are left without protection—seven persons—and that out of this savings have to be made for the purchase of houses for the children.

Still, looked at in this way the head of a family, having an income up to about £200 per annum, plus a house, plus education, plus public amusement, working seven hours per day, educated as fully as any other citizen, with the whole forces of the State devoted to surrounding his life with health, beauty, knowledge, and public duty, would not be so ill off.

He would have ample time, two hours a day, to give to his own family and children, whose studies he would supervise; ample time to take part in social activity and the political action of his city, and time for self culture and education as well; eight hours labour, eight hours sleep, three for meals and recreation in his family, two for society, and three for study and culture; a house of seven rooms and free access to libraries, museums, temples, lectures, concerts, etc.

Under conditions such as this, the relative position of employers and employed, rich and poor, would be almost reversed.

Instead of the workers living a life of care, toil, and anxiety, it would be the employers and managers who would live far more laboriously, and with continual anxiety, in the full fierce light of public opinion. The life of ease would be comparatively that of the workers. They would have the main advantage of the sense of property in the independence of their houses, and none of the burden and tasks of property. Men, of course, would be always found to undertake the responsibility of direction, just as men are always found to govern, however terrible the task; or to command armies, however severe the risk and the burdens. But in the main, the place of ease would be that of the simple workers who would have as much freedom, and culture, and social respect as any capitalist.

There is a valuable institution of A. Comte's which he calls that of the Industrial Chivalry. Just as in old time, the great swords and heroes of the mediaeval world intervened to protect the weak and to see justice done, so in the new industrial world it will be the part of men, without public functions, possessed of great capital, to intervene to assist the workers at critical times, to maintain them in a just strike, to meet exceptional distress, to prevent local acts of oppression and to supply public services in a crisis. [We see that in this war, 1917.]

What is done by donors of parks, museums, libraries, and colleges, by such persons as Lady Burdett-Coutts, Mr. Peabody, Mr. Carnegie, Sir Titus Salt, gives an earnest of what may be done in that line.

In Greece and Rome the great public amusements were all free gifts—in Athens, due to a sense of social obligation, at Rome, often by political ambition.

If it is asked why should rich men do so, the answer is, as a fact they do both here and in America. In the times of the Middle Ages and of antiquity they did so on a far larger scale, such as Herodes Atticus at Athens.

What would be the motive? Exactly the motive that influenced the knights of old and the great public benefactors of old, sense of public duty, sense of religion, spirit of generosity and social gratitude, honour and devotion. Well, even now all these things are to be found, but in a somewhat irregular way. But under a social and religious system which inculcates all this, as the most obvious and plain of social duties, we shall see it indefinitely extended.

Economists no doubt will say, All this is very fine talking, the thing is how is it to be done? Well, no Acts of Parliament that men are to have eight hours a day of work and eight shillings a day of wages will effect it. What we look to is this. Devote to the implanting in the mind of man, woman, and child, rich and poor, worker or ruler, the governing truth that wealth, power, force, is a complex thing to which all contribute, and that it has to be used for the common benefit of all. Make the manager of every business and the owner of every property feel that the control of his business or property is as much a public office as the command of a ship of the line or a judgeship, and has to be exercised under the control of public opinion; that for every act of the administration he is accountable to the public. Make him feel that, not the accumulation of more capital, but the well-being of all concerned is the thing; that to accumulate capital at the cost of ruining the health or the moral character of those employed is as disgraceful as losing a ship and drowning the crew in an attempt to make a quick voyage. Let every business man, whether banker or merchant or manufacturer or shop-keeper, feel that he is just as much accountable to public opinion for the conduct of his trade as a Prime Minister is accountable for the protection of this country or the peace of the realm. Make all this part of morality, of education, of religion, pressed on men from the first school, and perpetually urged on them by the talk of their neighbours, and preached to them in churches, reiterated on them personally in sacraments, and rehearsed over their graves—make it as much the habit of their lives as courage in battle was the habit of their lives to the companions of Leonidas, or as knightly duty was the habit of men in the true chivalrous age. Make social obligation fill in men's minds the place now occupied by competition, saving their own souls, and rising in life. Substitute for all these ideals and standards the one plain rule of living for Humanity, even as Humanity lives for us, and we may see the result we look for. If all the energy which men now throw into the accumulation of products, and the improvement of their own relative position, were systematically and religiously devoted to a social and not a personal result, we can hardly doubt that the end would be easily attained. Once let it be understood that the preservation and not the unlimited extension of our actual system, whether in material resources, in wealth, in population, in local area, once let it be felt that change is not the sole test of success—and we may see even stranger things than this effected.

This scheme of Positivism, therefore, if it be an ideal, is a sober ideal—sober as compared with the startling, and I may say paradoxical, ideal of Christianity, or of Buddhism, or even of chivalry or of competition.

What so paradoxical and extravagant as the

gospel of Plutonomy—"to cure all the evils of selfishness by stimulating self-interest"?

What of the Gospel of Christ—"cure all the evils of worldly evil by thinking nothing about the world"? and so on.

How far larger and broader is this ideal of ours! The ideal of the Gospel shutting its eyes to industry, and the instinct of production; Political Economy shutting its eyes to the instinct of affection, and knowledge, and beauty; Communism shutting its eyes to all this and fixing them exclusively on the manufacturing instincts of men.

It is a curious reflection if we work it out, how very small a part of the whole social problem would be solved by the widest species of Communism, even if it answered all the expectations of it. The favourite scheme of Communism now before us, that of socialising the land, only touches the agricultural part of the question; and even if it realised all its promises would only relieve us of taxation by making rent the sole tax.

But take the most thorough system of Communism or Collectivism now before the world. I know of none that goes farther than this, that the whole of the profits go to the workers. Well, suppose the profits went not in the least to direction. Suppose that communities of workmen succeeded in making as much as capitalists. Well, these total profits would not average all round 10 per cent on the entire gross wages paid. Two shillings in the pound on the wages: *i.e.* wages of £50 a year would be raised to £55. The *Co-operative Annual Diary* shows innumerable instances of failure and loss. The Rochdale Cotton Mill shows success; but, in twenty years, it has made rather over £100,000 profit, equalling £5000 a year. Suppose every farthing of that divided amongst the 500 or 600 workers, it would only average £10 in the year—four shillings a week. Now is that four shillings per week, eightpence per day, to make the entire difference in human life?

I rest this not on any figures whatever. But I will say this. The most favourable calculation cannot make a total profit exceed one-fifth of the total paid in wages. Well, one-fifth is but four shillings in the pound, *i.e.* the man who receives £50 a year is now to receive £60.

But all things remaining untouched, is this £10 per year to make such an enormous difference?

The truth is, that wildly as the economists overrate the gain to mankind of any material improvement and multiplication of capital, the Communists of all schools equally exaggerate the importance to civilisation of any conceivable rearrangement of the merely producing faculties of man and of the division or communising of capital. The older schools of Communism—all honour to them!—saw this and they all propounded a complete reconstruction of society—little as it was of rational that they had to say about the family life, or about philosophy or science, or art or politics or religion. Still, they propounded great ideals, in appearance just touching on these things.

Where are these schemes now? Not one of them is so much as remembered except by students. The most enthusiastic Collectivist or Socialist on the Continent could tell you nothing about Cabet and Fourier, or Owen.

But when we come to the present day we have the Communist party divided up into schools which differ about everything, but no one of whom has a word to say except about the manner in which they propose to get rid of capital and capitalists.

It is far too narrow and petty a result in its consequences to justify so great a revolution.

Communism, like the Gospel, is a creed for the future of mankind which has manifestly lost its vitality, its elasticity, its creative energy. Both are fading away into more and more incoherent echoes of their old selves. The salt has lost its savour. The field is clear for two great theories or schemes of life. The one is in possession no doubt of the official forces, in possession of the wealth and the social authority, and is deeply grounded on self-seeking instincts and passions.

It is the scheme of competition, or mutual

rivalry and struggle, every man's hand against every man, aye, and every woman and every child—and we see its works.

It is smitten with the paralysis of conscience. The good feelings and the good sense of mankind are rising up in judgement against it. The earth is weary of it; the voice of the weak and the poor and the overtasked masses is rising to witness against it. The ear of the just and clear spirits everywhere is open to their cry.

On the other hand stands the only other scheme or rule of life that has a future before it. That is the scheme of Positivism, substituting everywhere social co-operation for mutual rivalry, unselfish standards of conduct in place of selfish standards, resting on science, on history, and the law of evolution in all things, appealing to men everywhere not in the name of envy, destruction, and hate, but invoking the deep social passion of good fellowship, and generosity, and reverence: opposing interest by the word duty, religion to replace utility: holding up to every man from the cradle to the grave the image of that eternal Humanity from which he derives all that he has, and to which all that he can give is but justly due.

LECTURE VIII

THE GOSPEL OF INDUSTRY

(*Newton Hall and Societies*—1885–1900)

What is the essential feature of modern as compared with ancient civilisation? Obviously that it is industrial and not military. In the words of Auguste Comte: Three great epochs are (1) the Military, (2) Defensive War, (3) the Industrial.

(1) and (2) have their respective social and religious organisation, *i.e.* the Græco-Roman and the system of the Middle Ages.

Our want is, that we have no moral and religious institutions properly adapted to an industrial life.

Now a movement of any kind, religious, social, or political, has no meaning at all unless it can deal with the industrial conditions of modern society.

Positivism goes straight to that problem. Its motto is: *The organisation of industry is the essential problem of human life.*

Look at the condition of Europe [1885–1918]. It is one of acute industrial crisis, as it has been for a century. Note the anarchical condition of France all through the last years of the nineteenth century.

The Commune of March 1871 was a complex movement. At the bottom of it was the protest of the people of Paris against the exploitation of the poor by the rich. Many years have passed; and the question is no nearer solution or settlement than it was—no nearer than it was in 1870, or 1848, or 1830.

Germany was honeycombed with Socialist societies, only kept down by the bayonet; Austria is as bad as Russia. Italy is in no better state. Spain was lately in the throes of an anarchist rebellion.

In Russia the question is rather more political than industrial. But in essence it is industrial there too [1885–1917].

In England our Irish question is largely an industrial one.

In America we have the newest system of Socialism.

The result is this. Socialism and Communism, though more incoherent than ever, though leading now to that wretched state of disease loosely spoken of as Anarchism or Nihilism, is still as active and irrepressible as ever; still thunders in the ears of capital, of the employer everywhere, the imperishable problem of industry and the claims of the poor.

And what answer is there to all this? No one can say that Socialism or Communism is clearer, more coherent, more logical, gaining in intellectual strength; rather the reverse. But are the answers to it gaining in strength and acceptance?

Is the stupid, helpless cant, roughly called Political Economy (*i.e.* the maximum of non-interference with industry, moral, social, or political; in effect, to leave the stronger to have his own way), is that making any progress? On the contrary, the purblind dogmatists of the last generation hardly venture to defend their own prejudices. Certainly no clear and sympathetic intelligence capable of grasping the modern social problem any longer pretends to find in *laisser-faire*, or the dogma of "fight it out," any real answer to the dilemma which Socialism and Communism present and force on us all.

Has Christianity in any form any answer to the problem? It never had. Christianity indeed took centuries before it had any effect, even on slavery.

Justinian's code of law, after the official establishment of Christianity for two centuries, treats slavery as a normal institution and codifies the complex laws of slavery as if it were no less eternal than the law of marriage. Christianity never had any real effect on industry, until after many centuries of life it developed into Western Catholicism, and the action of the Church, and Feudalism.

And now that all the institutions and discipline of that Church are gone, and remain only in disconnected fragments, what prospect is there of Christianity really dealing with the great industrial problem?

It has nothing to say, except that queer bit of affectation called Christian Socialism which merely means a sentimental leaning to Socialism from the point of view of the Sermon on the Mount. But real Socialists reject Christianity; and real Christians reject Socialism; and Christian Socialism has not added one thought, one precept, one suggestion to the problem of man's life. I have deep respect for the pure morality and intense spirituality of the Sermon on the Mount, nor do I deny its profound effect in softening the heart; but its sphere is personal life not public life; and when it says, "Lay not up for yourselves treasures on earth, take no thought for your life, take no thought for the morrow, etc. etc.," its effect is simply disturbing, paralysing, anti-social.

Quietism like this may have some ennobling effect on the individual soul and may purify the heart. But it can teach men nothing of duty in the associated work of life. The thing we want is to learn how we may in common, usefully and prudently, lay up treasure on earth. The problem of life is to take sound and right thought for our life, and for the life of others around us. Our true religious duty is simply to take thought for the morrow—wisely, truly, nobly, in a social spirit, and in a practical and real way.

How different are the maxims of Comte :

"Know, in order to foresee, and do that in order to provide."

"Act through affection, and think in order to act."

Thus everywhere in Positivism action, work, product of some kind, is the end of the whole synthesis or scheme of Humanity. The end progress—improvement. Hence, if Socialism or anything else is to bring about any real improvement in man's industrial life, it will have to put aside the teaching of Christ and act on the direct contrary, throwing aside the entire mystical, superhuman, hysterical side of the Gospel altogether. Christian Socialism is a mere idle bit of affectation, as unreal as a modern tournament, a mediaeval bazaar, or a Greek ball ; a playing with a great matter by people with no heart in it, or with no head in it. How different is the attitude of Positivism to it. The healthy recasting of industrial life is *the work* ; religion, morality, society, science, philosophy, government exist as institutions, not for their own sake but simply to bring about a healthy, wise, right condition of active industry. We learn in order to foresee, and both in order to provide.

Affection is the principle of action, and thought is the instrument of action.

" Action—action—everywhere ! "

Briefly, in a few words, what is the Positivist key to the problem ?

It is this : Human nature is a very complex, but quite organic thing. That is, it has several ideas, many instincts and forces, and yet all work together, act and react like the organs and tissues of a living body. Thus, human nature must be treated as a whole on all its parts.

Christianity and every other mysticism which appeals to the heart but neglects the energies, is sublimely indifferent to science, is *ex hypothesi* disqualified for dealing with human nature.

Socialism which deals directly with action and action alone, regards society as a mere producing machine, and has nothing to say as to the affections, and is just as sublimely indifferent to science as the Gospel itself, is also disqualified *ex hypothesi*.

The true gospel of Industry must be a scheme of industrial activity, on the lines of science and sociology, in accordance with history, and inspired with a deep and energetic religious spirit of duty.

The creed of Positivism, in a word, is to make

industry the true sphere of religious duty; that religious duty being to make all life unselfish, by living for Humanity as the only source of man's happiness.

Our solution is Moral Socialism, or Social Economy. Positivism stands so completely midway between the systems of sound Economy and Socialism that it is difficult to say whether it belongs more to one than to the other.

The strength of the economic solution is that it realises the enormous power of institutions, property, independent energy, distribution of functions, and social spontaneity, things as old as the history of human civilisation, that it has analysed the precise conditions of social co-operation in production, that it rests so far as it goes on observed facts, on history and sociology.

The weakness of Economy is that it is utterly unable to give any moral tone to work, or to satisfy the incessant cries of the workers, men, women, or children; to devise the smallest real improvement in modern industry or to alleviate its horrible evils. It often makes them worse.

The strength of the Socialist solution is that it acknowledges all this; it professes to deal with the evils; and, come what will, it is resolutely bent on making a change.

The weakness of Socialism is that it has never really refuted any one of the scientific conclusions of Economy, as a matter of scientific observation, that it has no scientific scheme of its own, or rather no scheme at all. After fifty years Socialism remains a mere protest, just as completely as Political Economy remains after a hundred years a mere set of observations. The world can be set right quite as little by observations *per se* as it can by protests *per se*. Now Positivism says: The protest of Socialism is one of eternal force, the aspirations of it to reform the social organisation of life are of infinite value and truth. And so the observations of Political Economy are of solid truth, only they remain impotent, and may often be most pernicious, unless they are moralised and organised by a true doctrine of life.

Positivism may be said to favour the Socialist solution, only that it holds on to the great economic institutions and economic laws, so far as history and science establish them.

So it may be said to favour the economic solution: only it seeks the same end as the Socialists, and is inspired by the same idea as the Socialists, the social unity and common co-operation of the human race.

Both Economy and Socialism have the same weakness: both are partial, deal with at most one-third of the problem. Economy practically regards man as a producing animal. So in fact does Socialism. Now, man is a reasoning and a loving animal as well, has fifty energies and fifty wants which neither Economy nor Socialism account for.

The question is not in essence the organising of human industry but of human nature.

The science of the economists is perfectly true as far as it goes; but as it stands for a law of practical activity, it might hand human life over to a veritable pandemonium.

The social enthusiasm of the Socialists is a precious force; but unless it is based on science and adjusted to the rest of human instincts it can end in nothing but anarchy.

To put the problem in a few words, it is this: The existing uses and modes of capital are full of horrible misery to those who produce it.

The answer of Political Economy is: "Never mind; we can't help that."

The answer of Socialism is: "Abolish all property in capital."

The answer of Positivism is: "The modes and uses of capital must be utterly transformed, the key of the whole question lies in the origin and use of capital."

These questions have to be answered:

1. Is capital the product of individual labour?

2. Is its appropriation a natural right of the producer?

3. Is its appropriation useful to the community?

4. Is it also necessary?

In the system of rights these questions are all answered in an absolute way.

Economists say a man has a right to his product; and it is useful and necessary that property should be accepted. The Socialist declines to go into questions of usefulness, etc., and looks only to rights.

The whole social philosophy of Positivism establishes that capital is the product of social not of individual labour. So far it wholly adopts the Socialist view of the social origin of all wealth and product. But Positivism goes much further.

Positivism shows the social origin of all power: intellect, moral, material, artistic power. In fact, it eliminates individual activity altogether, proving that an individual is an abstraction. There is no such thing in reality. A dangerous and criminal lunatic is the nearest approach in Europe to an individual (and of course his whole life is dependent on society and he is only an individual subjectively). In the mind's eye the whole conception of Humanity implies the social origin of every power or resource or faculty possessed by men. Thus the conception of Humanity, the development of history and the fundamental truths of social philosophy, on which Positivism rests as a whole, carries the Socialist postulate of social combination beyond the wildest dream of any Socialist, and it does that in a real and scientific way, and at the same time it roots the great Socialist postulate in the spirit, with a completeness and gives it a lofty title to men's respect such as no Socialist theory ever pretended to give it.

But it does not follow that because capital is social, no qualified appropriation is to be allowed as a matter of convenience and under the control of public opinion and religious stimulus.

It does not follow that, because capital is not the right of any particular producer it is absolutely the right of all the rest.

Because property is entirely a matter of sufferance of the community, it does not follow that there are not deep and permanent reasons for admitting its appropriation, on sufferance.

Now Positivism wholly rejecting any idea of rights to property, or any absolute legitimacy of property in any kind, finds in the practice of appropriation all sorts of moral and intellectual values: so that it becomes in fact, apart from any sort of right, the very basis of any high civilisation.

All Socialist schools proceed on the assumption that all industry is necessarily of the materially productive sort, that industry is exclusively occupied with our material life. And the Economic schools to a great degree follow their lead. But an immense amount of industry of the most valuable kind is not productive of material value.

For example, thought, art, science, inventions, political activity, social usefulness. If we think of all the useful work which is done by those who never make anything that the public can eat, or drink, or wear, or use, we shall see that it includes almost everything that constitutes high civilisation. But this is only possible on a basis of appropriation to individuals.

Freedom is only possible in that way. The communistic arrangement of society would destroy the requisite freedom of action.

But the same thing is true of reproductive industry. The skilful and successful direction of any joint work implies a degree of concentration and central responsibility only to be found in the institution of property.

The communistic solution in Property has the same fallacy as the ultra-democratic solution in Government. Just as the vices of tyrannical and selfish rule drove men to the absolute doctrine of mincing up Power and distributing it to all, so the vicious and selfish abuse of wealth drove men to the doctrine of partitioning Property amongst all. But the democratic answer is not more true for Property than it is for Government.

The answer is the same for both. Both in the use of Wealth and in the use of Power amend the conditions under which they are held, make the spirit of social duty regenerate both, and keep them in their task by an ever-active public opinion.

This at present seems impossible to the Economists and also to the Socialists. The solution of both is alike material. Both ignore any true moralising influence. Economists are willing to go on without any such influence. Socialists seek to obtain their result by material and political agencies.

I think the entire body of doctrines on industry may be all reduced to these two laws :

(1) Man's whole active existence depends on Humanity ; and should be devoted to Humanity.

(2) Freedom, personal responsibility, and concentration are essential to that devotion.

The institution of property is only one form of that responsibility and concentration of function.

Every kind of activity has to be treated as a social office. The employment of wealth is just as much a social function as the governing the nation. But then, every kind of labour is also a social function. The Prime Minister, the manufacturer, the bricklayer are all alike employed in the service of the commonwealth. Their offices are different, more or less conspicuous, more or less difficult ; but all are honourable, and all demand the highest devotion in the actual holder.

Now so far from diminishing appropriation by

families, Positivism would very much increase it by insisting on the fixity of tenure of their homes, at least by every normal family whether in town or country.

Comte insisted that the great condition of healthy moral life for the worker was the sense of fixity and independence, resulting from property in their own homes and residences, both in town and country. We all know how the best influences of family are associated with specific property in the things of the home. The tendency of the Socialist view is towards the barrack view of the home. That of the Positivist is towards the yeoman or peasant-proprietor type of the home. Looking at the conditions of such huge encampments as London, and even Paris, as they are now, there would be a very large number of workmen in both cities to whom the fixing in one residence is practically impossible, inconsistent with the migratory nature of their employments. But the Paris and London of to-day are morbid results of a wild industrial scramble. They are as certain to be limited as Rome or Constantinople have been. Cities like Lincoln, Norwich, York, or Edinburgh are much more like the normal types of a true city.

We shall find that the problems of industry, one after another, can be solved if we keep in view these two principles :

(1) That our industrial life is to be organised

from top to bottom with a view to the greatest general benefit of the community.

(2) That this general benefit is to be secured, not by artificial and legal restrictions, but by education, religion, and the constant pressure of public opinion.

Take the problem of the cultivation of the soil—the proposal to divide up the soil amongst an infinity of peasant proprietors, or to reserve it to the State and to prevent any appropriation by arbitrary and stringent legislation. Both these have in view the rights of the actual holders; both assume a complete *statu quo* in moral and social obligation: neither pretend to say that it is the best for cultivation, that it is an absolute rule.

Now the Positivist solution is to accept the institution of property in the soil as old as civilisation itself: and also that of employers and employed. Wherever there is association of skill, there there must be distribution of duty; and wherever there is this, there there must be some directing authority.

No doubt there are soils, climates, and local conditions such as make the system of peasant proprietors, each owner of a small patch cultivating his own land, very suitable, and one associated with fine qualities and traditions. But it cruelly sacrifices the family: the women necessarily are bred to a life of outdoor labour. No peasant really cultivates his own soil. It is always cultivated by the family: to a very great extent by women and children, with the help of casual, pauperised, and destitute helpers, whose condition is generally little better than slavery, and far worse than that of hired labourers of England. Such are found in Belgium, France, Italy, and Ireland wherever the system of the small cultivator is rigorously carried out.

Hence we say, allowing for exceptions and local conditions, and admitting the usefulness of peasant properties alongside of others, the exclusive system of small culture is really a semi-barbarous one: it is now retrograde; it would stereotype a low civilisation. It sacrifices the family, it stunts the education of the children, brutalises the women by imposing on them severe outdoor labour, and tends to foster some of the worst and most anti-social vices of property. Those who know the peasants of France "at home" in spite of their many merits, will hardly deny this result.

Hence the solution of Positivism would be: Let us have properties of such a size as one owner can personally direct himself, and no larger. Comte even put this at something more than 1000 acres. I need not say this is no arbitrary or legal limit, but as an illustration. It is what is called in the great arable countries a "large farm," occupying say thirty persons as labourers, about as much as one of our great Norfolk or Lothian farmers, with the highest intelligence and adequate capital, can now work by his own personal management.

Observe that this implies, of course, two classes on every agricultural estate—two, if not three—the owner and manager, and the wage-receiving resident labourers.

Only, with a difference, the farmer has become owner (there is no landlord: that is a feudal survival), or the owner has turned farmer; also the labourer owns his own residence and garden, and hence is himself a sort of peasant proprietor; also he receives the same education of a general kind as the owner. Not only has the owner no political, legal, or manorial privileges, but the ultimate political power rests with the labourer.

There is no "idle class," no quasi-military, or aristocratic class. The estate is not hereditary, for to bequeath it to an incompetent son would be an act reprobated by public opinion. There is no ignorant class, for all are alike educated. There is no utterly dependent and subject class, for the labourer is as much owner in his own home as the manager is in his estate.

Is not this picture as attractive as that of the Socialist? And on the whole is it not easier to raise society by moral means, as it has been raised from the stage of war and slavery into that of industry and freedom, than to break society into fragments and recast the shattered dust of it in new cast-iron moulds ?

Pari passu the other problems of industry can be solved. The great town industries will be put on similar footing.

Again in manufactures there must be a considerable concentration of wealth. Normally, works would be not so large but that one man could superintend say 500 workers.

Restrictions would be put on the work of women and children, far more real and careful than any we know, not by the rude and inefficient method of law, but by moral agencies and the force of public opinion.

Then comes the reduction of the hours of labour to seven. And this makes possible a state of high general education.

If all the effort and energy and intelligence now directed on the principle of everybody getting the best he can for himself were directed on the other plan of everybody working his best for Humanity, the revolution in life would be great—indeed, amply sufficient to remove all the ills which Socialists and Nihilists assail.

Why is the substitution of one belief for another so wild and extravagant a hope ? It is not nearly so vast and difficult a recasting of the human habits and nature as took place from the corrupt and cruel polytheism of antiquity to the spiritual earnestness of Christianity in its great days. The change is not nearly so great as when the great settled theocracies were established in Egypt, or India, or Central Asia, superseding the tribal conflicts and wandering condition of the old groups.

The change is not so great as the change from the rigid fetters of the feudal times to the life and freedom of modern civilisation.

History can show us at least on ten great typical epochs changes from one form of life to another as deep and as great as anything dreamed of by Positivism.

The task before our times is not so great, not so difficult or so complicated, as the task of social regeneration that Humanity has passed through before. And it is no idle dreaming to fancy that it may happen again. It needs only a faith in the great resources of our race.

No doubt it is impossible without religion. But very few things—no good things—are possible without religion. And when we think of all that religion really means, we shall see that there is no social regeneration which it is incapable to effect: for religion is simply a complete set of doctrinal truth, with a code of practical rules of life, centred in a dominant sense of devotion to the Power that rules our lives.

If there be such a thing possible again for man, then the re-ordering of human industry will not be a task too vast for his strength.

LECTURE IX

(*Newton Hall*, 1893. *Steinway Hall*, 1907)

COMTE AND MILL—I

Of the various criticisms and examinations to which Auguste Comte has been subjected, by far the most important is that of J. Stuart Mill in the 27th vol. of the *Westminster Review*, republished as a work 8vo in 1865.[1] It is the source from which most subsequent criticisms have been drawn, that which has in the main coloured public opinion. It is indeed the only examination which combines full knowledge of the work criticised with philosophic and scientific competence. For though John Morley, Professor Edward Caird, and Professor Fiske may understand Comte's scheme as well as Mill, they have none of them Mill's lifelong experience of the logic of the sciences or his signal philosophic power. On the other hand, Mr. Herbert Spencer, Mr. Huxley, Mr. Mark Pattison, Mr. Goldwin

[1] *Auguste Comte and Positivism*, by John Stuart Mill, London, 1865, here cited as *Positivism*.

Smith, Dr. Martineau, and the theologians generally, have but a very limited and superficial understanding of the Positivist scheme of thought. George H. Lewes, George Eliot, Littré, Miss Martineau, are partial adherents rather than critics.

The real effect of Mill's book has been curiously misunderstood. It has served as the armoury whence the casual light skirmishers of literature have drawn their weapons of attack. But these latter have entirely put aside the great and crucial points of agreement between Mill and Comte. A large part of Comte's most original philosophic theories were accepted by Mill in whole or in part. As to some very important sides of the scheme, Mill was opposed. And a good many points of detail he met with indignation and even ridicule. These are the points which are remembered and repeated by the literary wits, who never seem to have heard of the essential points of agreement. In truth, Mill was an imperfect disciple of Comte, but a disciple who was deeply offended and disgusted by certain of Comte's later deductions.

From first to last Mill made immense concessions to Comte. He substantially accepted the Positive Philosophy; he accepted the general idea of a human and social religion; and he accepted the outline of a practical sociology. Mill, of course, was not a Comtist—in the sense of accepting Comte's scheme *en bloc.* Neither are we. There were many minor differences about which too much has been made. And there was certainly one grand difference which entirely separates the two minds. Comte's ideal is social organisation; Mill's ideal is individual development. Neither would exclude the ideal of the other. But what Comte put second Mill put first. Comte looked to the elevation of the person through the reaction of society; Mill looked to the progress of society through the improvement of the individual, and the improvement of the individual through freedom and self-help. And when it came to the crucial question — Is human life capable of being organised by a systematic religion? Mill answered, No! where Comte answered, Yes! The difference is indeed great. But it did not prevent the two men holding the same ideal of human life, the same scheme of philosophy, and the same type of religion.

I wish now to draw attention to the cardinal points of agreement first. These have been studiously ignored. It is also plain to us that Mill much overrated and overstated the dogmatic claims made by Comte. He took quite literally Utopias and hyperbolic dogmas which Comte conceived as illustrations of his meanings, though Comte was often carried away into giving them an extravagant air of authority and precision.

And finally, it is quite possible to be a convinced Positivist whilst declining to accept a great many of Comte's most definite assertions. I cannot speak of Mill without gratitude and honour; for we must always recall his early appreciation of Comte's work in the *Logic* (1843); his long correspondence and his generous contributions to his support. Nor can I personally forget my own friendship with and admiration for Mill as a man and a teacher. He will be regarded in the future, I believe, as an early and partial colleague of Comte.

Let us take the points of agreement between Comte and Mill, bearing in mind that they are vital and cardinal matters. Dealing first with philosophy, we find:

I. Mill speaks with enthusiasm of Comte's general conception of a possible science of sociology. In his *Logic*, as early as 1843, Mill spoke of Comte as having alone seen the true basis of a science of social phenomena on a sound historical method. The conception and the name of Sociology have since been accepted by Mr. Herbert Spencer and by all competent philosophic minds. Now the general conception of sociology as a science, analogous and superior to biology, is in itself, if we consider it, an intellectual step quite as important as the conception of the solar system, or the law of gravitation—indeed much more so. It is really the most important single step ever taken in the whole course of human thought. And Mill, whilst denying that Comte has created sociology as a science—a claim which Comte himself never made, but expressly repudiated—Mill maintains that Comte has made sociology possible (end of Part I. *Positivism*, p. 124). And he justly regards this as a great achievement.

Curiously enough, Mill seems to persist in the paradoxical assertion in his *Logic* (end of chap. xi. vol. ii. p. 525), that Comte made the fundamental logical error of having no teleology, that is no *end* in view, as the proper and worthy object of human civilisation, but considered his task ended when he had indicated the actual tendency of human progress. Mill insists that there must be a dominant aim or standard in human life, and that there can be but one ultimate principle of conduct. To a Positivist such a criticism seems utterly unintelligible. That it might have been made in 1843 is intelligible enough. But the whole course of Comte's subsequent writings, the *Polity* from cover to cover, is occupied with expounding such an ultimate principle of conduct. Comte died before his work on morals was complete. But it is plain that his entire conception of philosophy and of society turned upon a dominant moral aim. And Mill himself censures him for the degree in which he was morality-intoxicated, and for his excessive passion for this single aim of all individual and social life.

II. Mill calls "the law of the three states" the backbone of his philosophy, "the key to his other generalisations." In the *Logic* (ii. p. 514) Mill speaks of this law with unmeasured approval as having a high degree of scientific evidence, and as throwing a flood of light on history; and twenty years later in the *Positivism* (pp. 9-20), he uses far stronger terms to express his admiration of it. Mill goes on to explain the misconceptions of critics like Mr. Huxley and others who try to make a point that the three stages are sometimes found simultaneously in the same mind. Mill shows that, as Comte had observed, this very often occurs, but in relation to different matters and different sciences. An astronomer or a physicist adopts positive theories of his own science, but treats moral and social affairs on a theological basis. In a word, Mill is quite as strenuous a supporter of the law of the three stages as Lewes or Littré.

III. In the third place, Mill most emphatically approves of Comte's classification of the sciences in the serial order of their decrease of generality and increase of complexity. In his *Positivism* (pp. 33-45), he thoroughly discusses the whole question, with a view to the famous criticism of Herbert Spencer. Mill supports Comte's view and rejects that of Spencer. And Mill has been supported by G. H. Lewes and by Littré, and apparently by Professor Bain.

IV. Next, Mill enthusiastically adopts Comte's Synthesis, or Philosophy, of the Sciences, "that wonderful systematisation of the philosophy of all the sciences, which, if he had done nothing else, would have stamped him, in all minds competent to appreciate it, as one of the principal thinkers of the age" (*Positivism*, p. 53). Mill goes on to qualify this language by asserting that Comte had given no method of proof. "He supplies no test of proof" (p. 55). We are inclined to think that Mill himself did much to systematise the methods of proof in a form that Comte specifically approved, and in a manner quite consistent with Positive canons. And those who carefully consider all that Dr. Bridges and G. H. Lewes have written on this subject will hardly think that Mill has seriously qualified his acceptance of the Synthesis of the Sciences.

V. Mill, from the first, as Professor Bain tells us, enthusiastically adopted Comte's dominant idea of the partition of sociology into the theory of statics and the theory of dynamics, an idea which has been adopted by Herbert Spencer, by Littré, by Lewes, by Bain, as well as by Mill. But this cardinal classification of the elements of sociology, with its own luminous terminology, has passed into the commonplaces of the science.

VI. Next, Mr. Mill accepts the dominant law of human evolution, Comte's theory that progress is determined by intellectual advance. He defends this view against the criticisms of Herbert Spencer and others, aptly pointing out that if the boiler and engine supply the motive power of the steamship, it is the helmsman and captain who direct its course.

VII. Mill also adopts Comte's conception of moral progress, and the relation to it of intellectual progress. He maintains Comte's view as against Buckle, who is disposed to doubt the reality of moral progress.

VIII. When he comes to the philosophy of history, Mill uses language of the warmest admiration. "The survey," he says, "fills two large volumes, above a third of the work, in all of which there is scarcely a sentence that does not add an idea." He calls it Comte's greatest achievement except his review of the sciences. Well, but the review of the sciences is the essential purpose of the other four volumes of the *Philosophie*. Mr. Mill wishes he could give "even a faint conception of the extraordinary merits of this historical analysis." He finds "no fundamental errors in Comte's general conception of history," and a singular freedom from the exaggerations common in such speculations. He speaks of Comte's "profound and comprehensive view of the progress of human society."

The points where Mill demurs to Comte's view of history are few and subordinate. Now this in itself is a striking fact. That, in a field so vast and complex as the entire course of human civilisation, a critic so cool, dispassionate, and yet so independent as Mill could give his assent to an immense body of historical judgements and analyses, extending, be it remembered, over 1600 pages, is evidence that the matter had passed into the region of science, and indeed of a science already in a high degree of development. This striking fact shows that more had been done than merely "to make sociology possible."

IX. Mill accepts with admiration the idea and general scheme of the *Positivist Calendar* or series of great benefactors of mankind, the list of 558 worthies of all ages and all branches. This, again, is an example of extraordinary convergence of ideas, dealing as it does with actual names and concrete history. His list includes, says Mill, " every important name in the scientific movement, in art, in the religions and philosophies and the really great politicians, in all states of society.

X. Finally, Mill accepts Comte's own comparison of his philosophic work to that of Descartes and Leibnitz. His last word is that Comte was as great as either of these two, if not greater. And, though Mill considers that Descartes and Leibnitz both committed great blunders and extravagances, he admits that the trio form a group of similar minds. I am not aware that many Positivists wish to place Comte on a higher rank of mental power than Descartes, though with Mill they may think that Comte's historic position enabled him to do more than was possible to Descartes. But how can Positivists regard as hostile a critic who compares Comte favourably with Descartes and Leibnitz ? Rather we would say that a philosopher who accepts Comte's Synthesis of the Sciences, his scheme and analysis of sociology, his philosophy of history, his leading doctrines and methods, and finally claims him as the most comprehensive of modern thinkers, is for all intents and purposes an adherent of the Positive Philosophy, even if he had reserves and differences far greater and more numerous than those of Mill.

We will now turn to the religious and social scheme of Comte and compare Mill's mode of regarding that. I shall follow the *Letter* of Dr. Bridges to Mill, 1866, which is a model of controversial method, and I shall use it freely without any further or other reference.

I. The initial and supreme difficulty of all consists in the idea of a human, terrestrial, and non-theological religion at all. Now Mill accepts this cardinal idea, and warmly defends it (*Positivism*, p. 135). He shows what are the conditions of religion: (*a*) A belief, claiming authority over the whole of human life; (*b*) a sentiment, powerful enough to give it authority over human conduct; (*c*) that this should be crystallised round a concrete object. All of these conditions, says Mill, are fulfilled by the religion of Humanity. And he joins Comte "in contemning, as equally irrational and mean, the conception of human nature as incapable of giving its love and devoting its existence to any object which cannot afford in exchange an eternity of personal enjoyment" (p. 135). This is precisely the ground on which theological and literary critics of Positivism exhaust their indignation or their sarcasm.

II. Next comes the question whether the idea of Humanity was an adequate centre of religion. On this Mill is most emphatic. "No one before has realised all the majesty of which that idea is susceptible." He adds: "Not only was Comte justified in the attempt to develop his philosophy into a religion, and had he realised the essential conditions of a religion, but all other religions are made better in proportion as, in their practical result, they are brought to coincide with that which he aimed at constructing." Nothing can unsay these remarkable words. No criticism, no qualifications can seriously affect this judgement. This was undoubtedly Mill's practical religion, as it seems to be that of Spencer, Huxley, and that of thousands who in language are ever ready to repudiate Comte and everything connected with Positivism.

III. Mill accepts the cultivation of *altruism* and the subordination to it of *egoism* as the basis of moral discipline and the end of religion.

Egoism, he admits, is bound and should be taught always to give way to the well-understood interests of enlarged altruism. This is a summary of the Positive view. The excessive and ascetic repression of personal enjoyment which Mill wrongly attributes to Comte is quite a misunderstanding; and no competent student of Comte would admit Mill's language to be an accurate statement.

IV. Mill accepts the general idea of moral discipline—indeed, he extends it to mean ascetic discipline, and he uses that phrase and looks forward to a time when "the young will be systematically disciplined in self-mortification." There is nothing that I know of in Comte so ascetic and Spartan as this. And how the man who advocates it can charge Comte with asceticism, with being "morality-intoxicated," and with sacrificing everything to morality, it is indeed difficult to understand.

V. Mill accepts the general notion of the social nature of labour, the social origin and duty of capital, and the relative social obligations of capitalists and labourers, managers and workers, to each other and to the social organism as a whole. In a word, he heartily accepts Comte's general system of industrial organisation. And the sketch he gives (*Positivism*, pp. 147-149) may be accepted as an adequate summary of the Positivist social doctrine. This in itself is an immense part of the reorganisation of a society admitted by both to have an industrial basis and an industrial aim.

VI. Mill accepts the principle that a *cult* is essential to religion—and by *cult* he means a "set of systematic observances intended to cultivate and maintain the religious sentiment." Mill seems entirely to sanction the general idea of Comte (pp. 149-155) as to the necessity for some *cult*, and also as to the way in which Comte considers it must be met. Mill's strictures relate solely to the details, the mode, and the form in which Comte proposes to work out the idea. We need hardly go into that here—all the more that we have never seen our way to carry out these systematic observances, and thereby give the best proof that we do not look on them as ordinances imperatively binding on Positivists, or as indispensable to the religion of Humanity.

VII. Mill accepts the general principle of a spiritual power, at least so far as it implies the ultimate authority of scientific guides on social matters, when the requisite agreement in social science shall have been attained. But Mill's essential proviso is — that this intellectual authority shall always remain spontaneous and shall not be organised into a body, from which he apprehends incalculable evils.

VIII. Mill is quite prepared to see education vested in such an order of man. "That education should be practically directed by the philosophic class, when there is a philosophic class who have made good their claim to the place in opinion hitherto filled by the clergy, would be natural and indispensable" (*Positivism*, p. 99). Mill's objection again is to these educators being organised. This, however, is a matter of degree. When there is a class who may be compared as a class to the clergy, some sort of association seems a natural consequence. We in this hall have never insisted on any particular degree of organisation.

IX. Mill accepts the general principle of the need for a social aim in all intellectual pursuits, though he holds that Comte carried this to a dangerous point. If that were so, Mill goes no little way with him when he says—"No respect is due to any employment of the intellect which does not tend to the good of mankind" (p. 172). "Whoever devotes powers of thought which could render to Humanity services it urgently needs, to speculations and studies it could dispense with, is liable to the discredit attaching to the well-grounded suspicion of caring little for Humanity." For my part, I am not prepared to put any bar on the freedom of inquiry that goes much beyond this point. Mill is indignant with the rigid limits which he represents Comte as putting on the freedom of thought, limits which Mill seems to me greatly to exaggerate. If those restrictions were really part of Comte's scheme, we must be said to carry out that scheme very ill. Mill's merely bookish criticism of Comte is often best corrected by looking at the practice of those who have dedicated their lives to carry out Comte's ideal. How ludicrous would it be to ascribe to M. Laffitte, the successor of Comte in Paris, and his colleagues in the work of public education "a real hatred for scientific and purely intellectual pursuits"! (*Positivism*, p. 176). How absurd would it be to ascribe such a hatred to myself and my friends here! Where does any rational Positivist show this obscurantist tendency? What a purely literary and verbal objection is this!

X. One of the practices of Comte which have been most criticised is what he calls his *hygiène cérébrale*, or abstinence from promiscuous reading and even from the pursuit of new knowledge. In the case of a thinker, with a mind and a philosophic object like his, Mill seems willing to justify it in the case of Comte, whilst pointing out all its dangers. Certainly no follower of

Comte has ever thought of trying the régime himself and none is likely to do so. The only Englishman who has attempted it is Mr. Herbert Spencer, who very closely follows Comte in abstaining from gathering in new material whilst absorbed in his task of systematising the material he has amassed. It is quite certain that the world would never have had the *Positive Polity* without Comte's *hygiène cérébrale*, though we can see the force of Mill's argument about its extreme dangers.

XI. There are many minor points of social organisation where Mill heartily supports Comte's ideal—such as the need to put the maxims of health on a social rather than a personal basis, on the social grounds for limitation of the population, on the morality and even social beauty possible to the religious treatment of the institution of domestic service, and many more things of the kind.

It comes then to this: Mill accepts in its general scheme the Positive *Philosophy* as a scheme and synthesis of man's knowledge. And for the *Polity*, or social and religious reorganisation of society, Mill accepts (1) the idea and the possibility (what Dr. Bridges calls the "legitimacy" of a religion of Humanity); (2) the principle of altruism as the basis of life, and the need for a systematic training in altruism; (3) the social organisation of industry; (4) the importance and conditions of a practical *cult*; (5) the social authority of trained social philosophers, provided they do not form a corporation; (6) a great many new and characteristic canons of practical conduct.

I will now deal with the objections of Mill *seriatim.* But on this two preliminary provisoes are to be noted. First, Mill attributes to Comte's scheme an imperative character which is, I think, an exaggeration of Comte's meaning, and which is certainly not accepted by Comte's followers either in France or here. Mill's is an entirely bookish criticism of Comte, whilst Comte's scheme is, after sixty years, still a living and working institution in the house where he lived and died. And secondly, Mill's strictures may be in many points well founded, but do not affect the social construction as a whole. They may impugn Comte's reasoning, but they are not conclusive against a form of Positivism which takes no account of these details at all. Mill was no poet and had little sympathy with poetic Utopias. In the record of the relations between him and Carlyle we see how much he misunderstood Carlyle, and how Carlyle misunderstood him. Mill's precise, rigid, and somewhat matter-of-fact mind was often mystified by Comte's hyperbolas, hyperbolas which I freely admit are not seldom too much for me to follow.

It is not a thing on which I care much to

insist. But Mill has fallen into some palpable errors of Comte's meaning. Many of these are noticed in Dr. Bridges' pamphlet and may be studied there. Mill makes the truly ludicrous assertion that Comte does not seem to have been aware of the existence of such things as wit or humour (*Positivism*, p. 154; Bridges, p. 56). The truth is that Comte had unbounded admiration of both. He has put into the *Calendar* almost every wit and humorist of ancient or modern times, Aristophanes, Aesop, Menander, Lucian, Plautus, Terence, Horace, Juvenal, Boccaccio, Chaucer, Rabelais, Swift, Defoe, Lesage, and Sterne. Why are these held up to the honour of mankind except as being immortal wits and humorists? As for Aristophanes, Cervantes, Fielding, Goldsmith, and Scott, Comte is always expressing for them unmeasured admiration and delight. Why did he put in the *Positivist Library* the *Arabian Nights*, Aristophanes' *Comedies*, the *Fabliaux du Moyen Age*, *Don Quixote*, *Gil Blas*, *Tom Jones*, the *Vicar of Wakefield*, the *Antiquary*, and the entire works of Molière, if he never knew that wit or humour existed?

Comte was himself the author of some of the most brilliant epigrams extant, as when he said: "Our physicians are too often mere veterinary surgeons"; "No truth is *absolute* truth save this truth only"; "Atheists are the most irrational of all theologians." Comte's own conversation, I can testify, was a succession of striking *mots*. He was, of course, of a very serious, perhaps a severe temperament. But the man who was never weary of *Don Quixote*, of hearing the *Barber of Seville*, and the *Marriage of Figaro*, of reading *Tom Jones* and *Gil Blas*, was not insensible to wit or humour. Like all religious and social reformers, Comte was utterly indifferent to the ridicule of the ignorant, the vulgar, and the fastidious. He had unbounded courage; and if he did not adopt the style of either Voltaire or Carlyle, it is not recorded that this playful humour was exhibited either by Jesus Christ, or Buddha, or St. Bernard. They also did and said many things at which the mob and the critics laughed without measure. It was not from defect of humour but from excess of courage.

Dr. Bridges (p. 56) has well pointed out the singular misrepresentation of Mill (*Positivism*, p. 189) that Comte detested the Greeks and had travestied Greek history, for which he shows no interest. As a fact, Comte has spoken with unbounded admiration of the great epochs of Greek heroism—Thermopylae, Salamis, the age of Pericles, and the conquest of Alexander. All leading Greek statesmen from Lycurgus to Polybius—seventeen in all—are in the *Calendar* together with seventy-three Greek thinkers. In the *Library*, are Herodotus, Thucydides, Plutarch, Arrian, four out of six ancient historians. There are twice as many Greek names in the *Calendar* as Roman, and more Greek than any other names, except French, with whom it is about equal. No doubt Comte placed the Romans as a great people far above the Greeks, and there Comte is right and Mill was wrong. But to say that Comte despised the civilising mission of Greece is not so much a mistake as a misrepresentation.

Again, Dr. Bridges has shown, how curiously Mill misunderstood Comte's language about disease being not so much a specific thing in itself as the disturbance of the systematic action of the organism. Here, as Dr. Bridges shows, Comte was really stating what is now an accepted theory of modern pathology. Mill indeed mistranslates and misconceives Comte's term *unité*, which is with him rather *harmony*, organic correspondence, not *unity* in the English sense. This is a perfectly common and correct use of the term *unité*, as Littré shows in his *Dictionary*. With Comte, *unité* corresponds with *ensemble*, and means the organic co-ordination of parts and functions.

Dr. Bridges again has pointed out that Mill is quite wrong in attributing to Comte any reliance on *phrenology* as ordinarily understood. So far from giving his approval to phrenology, Comte expressly repudiated it. It is a mere misconception to treat Comte's psychology as a phrenology of any kind (Mill, pp. 65, 185; Bridges, p. 62).

It is a distinct misrepresentation to assert (*Positivism*, p. 122) that in Comte's scheme "no representative system, or other popular organisation, is ever contemplated." Well, but in the *Polity* Comte proposes an assembly to vote the finances, elected triennially by universal suffrage, three deputies for each department. And as to "other popular organisation," has not Comte insisted on the paramount influence of the people to be exercised by the constant supervision and activity of the people in the way of clubs and discussion of all public affairs.

What Mill has said about the *Positivist Library* as a selection of 100 books and the holocaust of all other books is a preposterous and wanton burlesque which is quite unworthy of Mill, and which has unluckily passed into modern literary opinion. The *Positivist Library* consists of 270, not 100 works (even bound up together they are 150, not 100, volumes). The 270 works are contained in our ordinary libraries in about 500 volumes. This is a very fair library. The *Library* was a selection of books intended, as Comte said, "to guide the reading of the people"; it was to serve as a type of the books most useful for general and habitual study. It was avowedly provisional; and there was not a word in it about proscribing other books. The jest of Mill's (for it was little more than a clumsy jest) has been repeated in a thousand forms by booksellers' hacks and the jesters of the journals. Men like the late Mark Pattison and Andrew Lang have given it general circulation, though the statement is positively untrue, and although even such miscellaneous men of letters as they are have probably never read more than half of these very 270 works, and could not read or understand at least twenty or thirty of these books even if they tried. I could hardly name three men in England who are competent to master the whole of this *Library*, including all the science and all the mathematics it admits.

I am willing to admit that Comte was over-confident. We can now see that he was carried away to really extravagant illusions, as when he thought in 1854 that the era of war was ended. But what great social visionary has not had such noble illusions? It would not disturb me to admit that Comte indulged in Utopias and propounded things which do seem to us absurdities. And I am free to admit that he recommended what seem to me indefensible and even dangerous forms of moral discipline.

I say this as a Positivist—I am bound as a Positivist to say it. For it is in accordance with one of Comte's most formal declarations: "I have always been aware that the full execution of the final construction would belong to my successors. What was reserved for me was to lay its immediate basis, and to characterise its spirit after having conceived its plan. In a word, it was for me to institute the Positive religion, it was not for me to constitute it." This is at the close of his *Polity* (vol. iv. p. 205), written three years only before his death.

After this formal and final declaration it would be superstition and the weakness of fanaticism to look on the *Polity* of Comte as final, as complete, as claiming authority in all its parts. There may be persons who take this narrow view, but we in this hall have never done so. M. Laffitte has never done so. I say it deliberately: Comte had better not have lived, and the Positive system had better not have been heard of, if a verbal inspiration is to be attributed to all the writings of Auguste Comte, as Pharisees treated the letter of Moses' law, and as fanatical Puritans treated the Bible.

Comte said that he had "instituted the Positive religion: he could not constitute it," exactly as Mill said that "if Comte had not created the science (of sociology), he had at least made its creation possible." As Dr. Bridges has shown (p. 50), many of Comte's estimates and suggestions which Mr. Mill takes as laws of the Pentateuch or the Koran were expressly stated by Comte to be illustrations intended to fix attention. It is perhaps true that Comte, in the fervour of his vision of the future, slid into language of positive prescription, and very probably he often failed to observe his own rule, and used imperative language which could not be justified in his own programme.

Mill has no doubt drawn attention to some real defects in Comte's scheme or his mode of stating it.

I take up first the point of which Mill makes so much, and where he has been followed by Huxley and others, that Comte rejected any Psychology, that is he denied the legitimacy of any study of the laws of Mind. This is a misconception, founded on a verbal confusion, into which it is extraordinary that Mill could have fallen. Any one who reads Comte's essay on Broussais (*Pol.* iv. Appendix 6) will see that by *Psychologie* Comte means the pretended intuitive introspection of Cousin, which Mill rejects quite as much as Comte. *Psychologie* had acquired in France seventy years ago that narrow sense. Of course Comte himself professed a Psychology or analysis and systematisation of the laws of Mind as an essential branch of science. Professor Beesly, in translating the *Polity* (vol. iii. p. 39), very properly uses the word *Psychology* as equivalent to what Comte calls the laws of Mind. Comte means by *Psychologie* the divorce of mental science from rational biology, and reliance on introspection as an instrument of observation. Both Littré and G. H. Lewes, perhaps on this matter authorities superior to Mill, have entirely cleared Comte of the preposterous charge of neglecting Psychology in our modern sense; and both rather incline to Comte's view rather than Mill's, though both find shortcomings in Comte's. I shall not go into the difficult metaphysical question whether more has not been made by introspective methods than either Comte or Broussais expected, nor whether Comte was right in the place which he assigned to Psychology in the general scheme of Philosophy. The matter has been thoroughly discussed by G. H. Lewes in his *Psychology*, and for my part I am inclined to agree with Lewes. But the question is quite subordinate and may well wait the final constitution of Sociology.

Again, Mill insists on the need for a distinct system of Logic, which he says that Comte rejects, treating Mathematics as itself Logic. And so Littré in his work on Comte (Part iii. chap. v.) to much the same effect. Unquestionably Comte recognised a system of Logic, in the sense of principles of reasoning and an organon of proof. Comte took much interest in, and approved of, Mill's *Logic*, which no one could regard as being based on an opposing doctrine. My own view is this. I am inclined to doubt the sufficiency of Comte's latest view that

Mathematics really constituted and represented Logic. But Comte's *Synthèse Subjective* is unfinished and we can hardly judge what Comte intended. Comte's final view is one very difficult to grasp, and the first thing is to be satisfied with what Comte meant by *Mathematics*. It certainly seems to me that towards the close of his career Comte was tending towards an obscure form of mysticism on the subject. I am not aware that any one in this hall has pretended to adopt all that is contained in the *Synthèse*, and I am certain that no one of us has ever professed it. It is also quite possible that Comte underrated the value and legitimacy of what Mill understood by Logic, and that Mill at least as much overrated the degree to which Logic could be treated as a substantive branch of education detached from an encyclopaedic training in the sciences.

Mill insisted on an independent science or study of Political Economy. Here again the dispute is largely one of names. Comte perfectly recognised the legitimacy of economic laws as a part of Sociology. He often grouped these laws and carried on protracted investigations into them. Mill, as much as Comte, repudiated the barren method of the old economists who thought that political economy was an independent science —some of them think it a mathematical science with concrete laws that are deduced from the constitution of human nature and are paramount like the law of gravitation. Mill's whole treatise on Political Economy is an inquiry conducted as a branch of Sociology. It is quite a minor point to what degree can economic laws be detached from the rest of Sociology and treated in separate treatises. Comte always spoke of Adam Smith as one of the greatest of philosophers and one of the precursors of Positive Sociology. When the late Professor Cairnes made a trenchant criticism of Comte's view of Political Economy, Mill did not agree with Cairnes, as I know from his own lips at the time. All of these are minor matters still under debate. It is true that error on any one of such points would be fatal to any claim for absolute infallibility or final scientific accuracy. But no such claim is made for Comte, and he certainly never made it himself. Details of this kind can have little bearing on the sum total of Comte's work.

Let us grant that Comte did put too little value on the method of introspection for discovering the laws of Mind, that he was wrong in not giving a more distinct place to the laws of Mind, in not recognizing a formal body of Logic, that he was wrong in not allowing a more independent efficacy to the study of economic laws—these are all questions of degree. I am myself inclined to think that not only Mill but Littré, G. Lewes, and Spencer, if not Caird, have pointed out qualifications and provisoes on each of these heads which may very probably be ultimately accepted as sound. Yet, notwithstanding, the great work of Auguste Comte, the foundation of a religion of human duty based on a scientific relation of Man to Humanity is not only not shaken, but is perfectly unaffected by these points, any or all of them together, however they be decided. The framework and principles of the Positive Philosophy as a whole, accepted by Mill, by Lewes, by Littré, stand unaffected. The conception of Humanity as the centre and ideal of human life stands unaffected. The general condition of human duty on the basis of science stands wholly untouched. And in this hall these things are the essential doctrines which alone we have sought to enforce.

APPENDIX

John Stuart Mill

(*Auguste Comte and Positivism*, p. 135.)

"The power which may be acquired over the mind by the idea of the general interest of the human race, both as a source of emotion and as a motive to conduct, many have perceived; but we know not if any one before M. Comte realised so fully as he has done all the majesty of which that idea is susceptible. It ascends into the unknown recesses of the past, embraces the manifold present, and descends into the indefinite and unforeseeable future. Forming a collective Existence without assignable beginning or end, it appeals to that feeling of the Infinite, which is deeply rooted in human nature, and which seems necessary to the imposingness of all our highest conceptions."

He adds: "Not only was Comte justified in the attempt to develop his philosophy into a religion, but all other religions are made better as they coincide with his aim."

LECTURE X

(*Newton Hall*, 1893. *Steinway Hall*, 1907)

COMTE AND MILL—II

I CONCLUDE my review of Mr. Mill's important book on *Positivism*, which sums up nearly all the objections which have been raised by serious students of Comte from the non-theological standpoint. I have done so not in any controversial spirit but to compare the two theories of life and thought, and when we put all controversy aside we can deal constructively with the Positivist synthesis. As we have seen in my last lecture, Mr. Mill accepts all the fundamental points of the Positive Philosophy. He accepts the general idea of the religion of Humanity as a practicable and an elevated type of religion. He accepts very much in the moral scheme of Comte. He exaggerates many minor differences. And he utterly misunderstands and misrepresents certain other points of Comte's scheme.

Let us now deal with those objections of Mill which are not at all misunderstandings or minor differences but deep-seated antagonisms of mind and nature, affecting the entire Positivist scheme for remodelling human life on a basis of the religion of human duty. They have been formulated by Mill, but have been repeated in various forms and have permeated modern thought in this country.

I. Mill objects that morality holds an extravagant place in the Positivist scheme, nay, that it is the sole motive of action tolerated, and that it takes an ascetic form. Mill, using an expression of Novalis, calls Comte "a morality-intoxicated man." I do not find the charge in this queer phrase a very atrocious one, even if it were true. It is nothing indeed but a rather clumsy jest. Mill says that *vivre pour autrui* means—Cease to love yourself at all, or to care for self in any form. Comte, he says, requires all believers to be saints—and damns them if they are not.

To any one who has assimilated Positivism this sounds as a wild parody. Comte may have used in places language of somewhat severe kind —great moralists usually do—but his express statement of his ethical analysis and his specific language as to conduct are quite unmistakable. Comte's moral standard is essentially that of Mill, though perhaps far more relative and genial. Personally, Comte was an ascetic: but he exacted from others no imperative rule of asceticism.

Take his wonderfully luminous analysis of human nature, where Comte fully admitted that seven out of ten dominant instincts are personal and concern self. He fully admitted that these seven personal instincts are more energetic than the three social instincts. And he states the moral problem to be—to enable the social propensities, not to extirpate, not to crush, not to dominate, but to control and educate the seven personal instincts. And throughout his whole system he continually dwells on the egoistic functions with their imperious claims becoming the basis and condition of the development of the altruistic or social feelings. His whole theory of the family rests on this conception, whereby the nutritive instinct, the sexual, the maternal, the destructive, the constructive, the love of ruling, the love of approbation are beautifully and mysteriously educated up into a "life for others" which begins in life for self.

"Life for others" in its full sense does *not* imply any literal sacrifice of self. It means control, spiritualise, develop self. It does not mean mortify self in every act and movement. It is far less prone to mortification than the Christian theory of morality, or any ascetic theory. It means bring the egoistic passions into working correspondence and co-operation with the altruistic emotions. These latter may be weaker, but they are more equable, continuous, and satisfying. They leave no exhaustion behind. They are liable to no gusts and spasms of irregular intensity followed by remorse and satiety. *Live for others* means—Have a social and not a personal standard of duty. It means what Mill admits to be the normal standard of duty—"Egoism must be taught always to give way to the well-understood interests of enlarged altruism."

That is what I understand the ethical system of Positivism to be. There is no suppression or extirpation in it at all. The ethical system of Positivism is one of cultivation, education, elevation. All forms of domestic, social, public enjoyment which stimulate the altruistic and not the egoistic passions form a moral force. All of this is part of human duty. Morality is not, for all that Mill says, the last word in Positivism. Humanity is the last word and central idea. "Imperfect as our nature is, yet social sympathy has an intrinsic charm *which would make it* paramount,—but for the imperious necessities by which the instincts of self-preservation are stimulated. So urgent are they, *that the greater part of life is necessarily occupied with actions of a self-regarding kind*, before which Reason, Imagination, and even Feeling, *have to give way*." In face of this ("General View," *Polity*, I. p. 289), how can it be said that Comte sought to crush, starve, deaden the natural instincts of self?

Neither in his own life, nor in his specific instructions, nor in the lives and teachings of his friends and successors is there any such crushing and starving of self, except such as was heartily approved and practised by Mill himself. Comte certainly in the close of his life, in his extreme solitude and preoccupation, maintained a system of extraordinary self-denial and scorn of all delights that could interfere with his laborious days; and in this Mill warmly commends him as required by his work. Mill's own life and teaching was as sober, as self-regulated, as much under the uniform spell of duty as that of Comte. The *Polity* is full of evidence that the ideal of Comte is not a life of self-torture, of mere self-sacrifice, but that it is inspired with the same ideal as that of Mill. The happiness of man is no mystical self-abnegation, but centres round the consciousness that man is the creature and servant of Humanity.

In the second volume of the *Polity* Comte propounds a Utopia where, the physical wants being entirely relieved, human nature could develop itself in spontaneous ways; and this he thinks would take the form of a continual resort to Art, and appeals to the Imagination in all its forms. The *Polity* is full of ideals in which the social enjoyment of Art is the central key. When we turn to the *Calendar* we find Homer, Aristophanes, Pheidias, Virgil, Horace, Plautus, Shakespeare,

Raphael, Ariosto, Molière, Fielding, Scott—the poets, the romancers — Calderon, Mozart — the painters, sculptors, musicians, and humorists. And so in the *Library* we find the comedians, the novelists, the lyrists, the Benvenuto Cellinis and the *Arabian Nights*, and so forth. What does this mean ? How comes it that these wild, gay, and even boisterous spirits are held up to our eternal admiration, and that these pictures of beauty, of wit, enjoyment, and of humour are presented to our daily study, if the Positivist scheme is one of inhuman asceticism and no one but a saint is regarded as worthy to live ? What would mean Comte's own devotion to the Opera, where he kept his stall, and that of Laffitte to the theatre, where he is a frequent visitor—what mean so many anticipations of the grace and joy of the future if it be true that Comte sought to crush out of human nature every fibre that did not stir man to some definite act of self-sacrifice ? "The greater part of life is necessarily occupied with actions of a self-regarding kind," says Comte. So thoroughly did he realise that the extirpation and even the sterilising of the normal and basic instincts of Humanity was an unnatural paradox, and that the problem was to elevate, purify, and utilise the selfish by the influence of the unselfish instincts.

Live for others does not mean—Die to self. It means a life of sympathy—happiness sought in a social ideal. The morality of Comte in effect is the same as that of Mill; their characters were similar, their lives in some ways parallel. Both of them exacted from themselves far more than they sought to exact from others, and both asked from others a great but not an extravagant unselfishness of life. Consider the words with which Comte closes his "General View of the Religion of Humanity" (*Polity*, i. 318): "The grand object of human existence is the constant *improvement* of the *natural order* that surrounds us: of our material condition first; subsequently of our physical, intellectual, and moral nature. And the highest of these objects is moral progress, whether in the individual, in the family, or in society. It is on this that human happiness, whether in private or public life, principally depends." How moderate and balanced is this view of human nature and its destiny! How can any one see in this a fanatical asceticism?

The grand object is the improvement of the natural order, first of our *material* condition. The highest object is moral progress: it is not the sole object. Human happiness depends *principally* on moral progress—not exclusively. How then can it be said that morality is the sole aim of Comte, that everything but moral self-sacrifice is condemned, and that what is not a moral duty is a sin? Comte has said nothing of the kind. He has said that though the greater part of our life is necessarily occupied with our self, and though the improvement of our material condition is our first object, still moral progress is the highest object, and on it human happiness principally depends. Has any professed moralist in ancient or modern times ever said less than this, or more fully acknowledged the paramount necessities of the egoistic basis of life ? To me the moralist to whom this seems most nearly to approach is the wisest of the ancients, the immortal Aristotle, who also placed happiness mainly in moral progress, though he could not deny the antecedent necessities of our material condition underlying all moral and intellectual life.

II. A large part of Mill's treatise is occupied with complaints of the over-regulation and moral and mental tyranny which he considers would be the lot of the human race under the direction of the spiritual authority as conceived by Comte. Undoubtedly Comte did imagine a spiritual authority which was to educate, guide, and spiritualise society in the future. That has been the claim and intention of every religious reformer, and the language that he uses is naturally that of looking to a regeneration of society by the scheme proposed. I am myself quite willing to think that if the mass of Comte's illustrations, suggestions, and ideals are to be taken as Levitical prescriptions, it would amount to a system of tyranny which I for one would never accept or countenance. Even if Comte has used language of excessive positiveness, and I think he not seldom does this, it would be nothing like the arbitrary and cruel formalism of the words of Christ in the Gospel—to leave father and mother and follow Him—or the tyranny of the Koran, the rules imposed by Buddha, Confucius, by Calvinism, Quakerism, and Puritanism. There is nothing in the *Polity*, even if all the suggestions were taken with Pharisaical literalness, to approach the dogmatism of Moses, Mahomet, Calvin, Knox, and even modern Socialism.

But this is a practical question—not a literary controversy. I am not standing here to justify every sentence in Comte's writings, or to pretend for him the authority claimed over practical life for Christ, Mahomet, Calvin, and Knox. I am pleading for the Positive religion of Humanity, as understood and practised by us in this hall, under the direction of Comte's successor in Paris. It is our conduct, as we mean it to be received, and not Comte's words that are now under review. The *Polity*, however high we put our reverence for Comte's genius and authority, is no book of Leviticus or Koran for us. We practice no Pharisaical subservience to all that we find in it. This is a practical matter. A new scheme of life is not to be adequately grasped or estimated by reading four or five volumes. It has to be understood in practice. The practice of M. Laffitte, who lived in intimacy with Comte since his youth, and who adopted the entire Positivist scheme just sixty years ago, is conclusive on this matter. He has never pretended to practise, nor has he called on others to adopt any mechanical following of minute rules of life in the *Polity*. He has not shown this hatred to scientific inquiry, this contempt for intellectual activity, this narrow view of knowledge, this aversion to books and all the other ritual observances which Mill declares that Comte imposed on all his followers. The charge against us is that we are quite worldly. We live in no phalansteries—we are not given to mint and anise—we are not slaves of a book as Jesuits whose motto is *perinde ac cadaver*. Mill and his friends may fancy they have scored blots in Comte's books—and they are welcome to a literary triumph if they please. They do not touch us in Newton Hall.

Whatever may have been Comte's precise words in different places, they are all governed to my mind by this emphatic declaration already quoted—that his task was to lay the basis and not to fulfil the final construction. "He could only institute the Positive religion, it was not for him to constitute it." That is his final, formal, definitive declaration. Had he made any other claim, I for one should repudiate it. If he used words inconsistent with this, I cannot help it. I am not here to maintain Comte's consistency of language. I am here to profess the Positive religion as instituted, that is, as sketched and conceived by Comte, but as certainly not constituted, that is, *prescribed* by Comte, as Moses constituted the Mosaic dispensation, and as Mahomet constituted the Mussulman dispensation. I will have nothing to do with it, and that because it would be treason to the first principles of Positivism.

III. Mill makes a most determined onslaught on Comte's supposed restrictions of intellectual freedom and his hostile attitude towards scientific discovery. I will say at once that for myself I have no criticism to make on Mill's own attitude and practice; and if Comte taught such a system of obscurantism, as that he had acquired a real hatred of scientific and purely intellectual pursuits, and that even *proof* should not be demanded, I most heartily abjure it and all its works. Comte has in this matter used language which I feel it difficult to reconcile with a religion of demonstration and a religion based upon the development of scientific certainty. But even if Comte has used expressions difficult to reconcile with his systematic conception of Positivism, Mill's use of these expressions and the monstrous parody of Comte's meaning is a far worse exaggeration.

Mill himself has gone a very long way in

requiring the social spirit to be dominant in all intellectual exercise, and also in expecting a great and legitimate influence from trained social philosophers. "No respect is due to any employment of the intellect which does not tend to the good of mankind." These brave and wise words are not Comte's but Mill's (*Positivism*, p. 172). "It is precisely on a level with any idle amusement" (*ibid.*). "Whoever devotes powers of thought which could render to Humanity services it urgently needs, to speculations and studies which it could dispense with, is liable to the discredit attaching to a well-grounded suspicion of caring little for Humanity" (*ibid.*). I ask nothing more than this as a definition of the Positivist doctrine. If I am asked to go further than this, I am not prepared to do so.

To assert, as Mill does, that Comte desired to put a limit to the further development of the sciences, that in this matter we are to submit to the authority of previous generations, this is far worse than exaggeration—it is flagrant misrepresentation. If Comte acquired a real hatred of science, how came he to prescribe (what is no doubt a Utopian impossibility) a complete scientific training for all of both sexes and all occupations? Why did he devote the last years of his life to abstract science? Why did he expressly state that all the sciences other than Mathematics required to be reconstituted, and that he was satisfied with nothing except his theory of Mathematics as far as it went?

Take Comte's own words in the "General View" (*Polity*, i. 257): "To (the Reason) we look for the revelation of the fundamental order which guides our life in obedience to the natural laws of the phenomena around us. . . . Concentrated on its high office, and thus preserved from useless digression, the intellect will yet find *a boundless field for its operations* in the study of all the natural laws by which human destinies are affected, and especially of those which relate to the constitution of man or of society." . . . "Practical questions must ever continue to preponderate, as before, over questions of theory; but this condition, so far from being adverse to speculative power, concentrates it upon the most difficult of all problems, the discovery of moral and social laws, our knowledge of *which will never be fully adequate* to our practical requirements" (p. 259). How can any one dare to tell the world that this picture of the future of the intellect with a boundless field for its operations, "which it would never be adequate to cover," was drawn by a man who had acquired "a real hatred for science and for purely intellectual pursuits"?

I confess that I feel it very difficult to excuse Mill for this misrepresentation or to forgive him for giving way to a wanton satire. This was no literary Bedouin who said this, but the philosopher who wrote and who acted on the maxim, "*No* respect is due to *any* employment of the intellect which does not tend to the good of mankind." Unfortunately this wild parody of a moral maxim, expressed rather more strongly than his own, has passed into current literature. It has been repeated by all the idlers in the literary market-place, and by the professional jesters who are called critics. No other charge has so deeply injured Comte, and none is more difficult to track out and hunt down. But this, like the rest, is a practical matter, so far as Positivism is concerned. Let us grant that Comte has used inconsistent or extravagant language. Assume that, in his burning zeal to see intellectual energy which now runs to seed in mere futility or mercenary servitude, he overrated it if it were devoted to the advancement of human civilisation, the best proof is the practice of those who have given their lives to Positivism. Is Pierre Laffitte, who has officially been appointed to the chair of the History of the Sciences, the pupil, friend, and successor of Comte, is he the enemy of science; does he hate intellectual activity; is he a finality man, an obscurantist, a Jesuitical opponent of all intellectual freedom? Are we in this hall such obscurantists? Do we try to put science in a vice and hate all independent intellectual activity? It is too absurd!

IV. A large part of Mill's criticism of Comte

turns upon Comte's aim at Unity, as Mill calls it, his passion, as he says, for uniformity, and in contrast with that we have Mill's passion for individual diversity, which is the theme of his book on *Liberty*. Now much of this antagonism arises out of a misconception of language, a mistranslation in fact. Mill takes Comte's *unité* to be equivalent to *identity of type*. I understand *unité* to mean, harmony, *i.e.* organic co-operation of the organs of a complex organism. Turn to Littré (*Dictionary, sub voce*). *Unité*, of course, means the property of the first number, one-ness: it also means identity, or uniformity of measure; it is also opposed to plurality. That is how the word *unity* is used in English. But in French it also means correspondence, keeping, tone, as consecutive conduct, coherence, correlation of parts. Voltaire says *unité* is the first quality of a romance. He does not mean uniformity, identity of type, but *coherence*. Marmontel calls *unité* in manners to consist in its just correspondence with real character—being true to oneself. It is a term of art—the *unity* of a picture means the tone, or balance of the composition; *unité de lumière* means in a picture due harmony in the values of light and shade. The dramatic *unities* are certain rules of proportion of time, place, and action. There is nothing in all this of identity, much less of uniformity, of conformity to a fixed pattern. Mill assumes that where Comte asks for *unité* he means conformity to a single pattern. It is perfectly clear that by *unité* Comte means harmonious and normal adjustment of action to organisation—as the poet says, *To thy own self be true.* That is exactly Comte's *unité* of life, coherence of conduct in correspondence with the nature.

Mill is astonished and even scandalised that Comte should assume *unité* to be a good thing, and the end of religion. Understood as *uniformity*, it would be indeed a narrow and degrading type. But understood as *coherence*, adjustment of function to organ, and of organ to organism, it is obviously the aim of all philosophic and religious teaching. Coherence of organisation is compatible with the furthest limit of individual variety and individuality. All philosophy, all religion, all systematic thought and work, intellectual or social, aim at producing some harmony. Aristotle begins his *Ethics* thus: "Every art and every science, and likewise every action and every purpose, aim at some good. Hence *the good* is said to be that at which all things aim." Just so Mr. Herbert Spencer calls his great work *Synthetic Philosophy*, *i.e.* the philosophy which gives harmony, *i.e. unité*, to all separate studies, and brings out their relations and correspondence. Comte was a writer upon *system.* He called his whole system a *synthesis* or harmony of thought and of life. Of course, therefore, he regards *unité* as *the good* in Aristotle's language. But he means by it, not uniformity or identity of result, but the adjustment of thought and act into harmony, first, with the organic constitution of the individual man, and secondly, with the sum of Nature and Humanity around the individual. If Comte meant by *unité* a uniformity other than this, for my part I entirely repudiate it.

Comte, as I say, is a writer on system, as Mr. Herbert Spencer is, as every preacher of every religion or philosophy is. His whole object is to show that life, thought, society may be made more coherent, more harmoniously adjusted to facts, more systematic, if you like to say so, by a right scientific ideal or type. To complain of Comte constantly appealing to harmonious functional activity is like complaining of a preacher of the Gospel that he assumes the saving of souls to be a good thing. There will always perhaps be some who prefer incoherence and irregularity of thought and life, just as there are always some who like to take their chance of being damned. But this harmonious adjustment of self to man's true mission is quite compatible with individual effort, with incentives to free action and the necessity for personal development on the lines of the individual nature.

The basis of the whole Positivist scheme is

the harmony between (1) individual development, and (2) social convergence. Take the declaration in the "General View" (*Polity*, i. 294): "Separation of temporal from spiritual power is as necessary for *free individual activity* as it is for social co-operation. Humanity is characterised by the *independence* as well as by the *convergence of the individuals* or families of which she is composed. The latter condition, convergence, is that which secures order; but the former, *independence*, is no less essential to progress. Both are *alike urgent.*" And he goes on to show how in ancient times "the independence of the individual was habitually sacrificed to the convergence of the body politic," and that true progress will only be possible when the independence of the individual is permanently guaranteed by an education which shall assert the liberty and dignity of man as the organ of Humanity. Comte does not reiterate, so much as does Mill, the need for personal independence, because the problem of social organisation seems to him to be more urgent and difficult. But he fully recognises the fundamental need of human freedom as the condition of morality, and makes it an indispensable basis of life.

This question of Comte's supposed "unity," or suppression of all individual spontaneity, is again, as we have seen before, a matter of practical experience. Whatever may have been

Comte's words as to the paramount value of *unité*, and whatever the French word means, is there after sixty years the slightest symptom of this paralysis of spontaneous life in the individuals who listen to Mr. Laffitte in Paris, or who meet in this hall? Are we such mental and moral slaves? Are we bound down to one cast-iron type? Is absolute uniformity our besetting sin? Is not the *Calendar*, with its names held up to eternal honour, full of the memory of the great free spirits of the world—such men as Isaiah, Æschylus, Lucretius, Socrates, Tacitus, Themistocles, Demosthenes, the Gracchi, Paul, Lanfranc, Bernard, George Fox, the Cid, Raleigh, Rabelais, Defoe, Burns, Byron, Shelley, Goethe, Molière, the two Bacons, Diderot, Condorcet, Hume, Turgot, Cromwell, Washington? And in the same spirit the *Library* is full of the books which illustrate the force of human character and the incalculable energy of the personal will. It was in this spirit that Comte attached so high a value to the poetic revolt of Goethe and Byron. "They taught the Protestant nations," he says, "the true freedom of the mind"—"the moral grandeur of man when freed from the chimeras that oppress him, was foreseen by Goethe, and still more clearly by Byron" (*Polity*, i. 239, 274). This is not the language of a man to whom a new spiritual despotism was the one thing needful to revive on earth.

V. Lastly, there remains Mill's incessant complaint of any spiritual organisation whatever—the burden of the most emphatic part of his book. Here we come at last to the grand fundamental point at issue between Mill and Comte, and between the individualist school and the socialistic school. The whole matter resolves itself into this—shall society be regenerated by an organised effort, or shall its future be left to spontaneous and individual movement? Mill quite admits the need for systematic education. He also admits that a philosophic class is indispensable for education. "That education should be practically directed by the philosophic class . . . would be natural and indispensable" (*Positivism*, p. 99). That is a very strong thing to say and a large admission. That such a class should not merely teach physical science and the like, but should have great influence over practical life, is also admitted by Mill. What Mill protests against is—"that all education should be in the hands of a centralised authority." Well, no one can protest against such a thing more than we do ourselves. And if Comte ever proposed to suppress complete freedom of opinion, of teaching, of public expression on any subject whatever, scientific, moral, or social, we should resolutely decline to follow him. That education should "all be framed on the same model, and directed to the perpetuation of the same type" could not be more repugnant to Mill than it is to us. Comte has perpetually insisted on the social importance of maintaining the utmost liberty for all free thought and free teaching, even if a central spiritual authority were completely organised.

What do we mean by being organised? It is surely a matter of degree. How could education be "practically directed by a philosophic class" if each teacher is bound to remain an isolated unit, without any intellectual agreement with his fellow-teachers? How is a class to arise, how is it to be trained, how could it educate, how could it succeed to the influence now possessed by the priesthood if it is to have no organisation? No one has more vigorously opposed the principle of academies, and scientific societies, and State Churches, and State schools than has Comte himself. He held that all such bodies tended to hamper the free action of intellectual and spiritual growth. What he did look for was the spontaneous aggregation of a body of men entirely independent, quite powerless to control or put pressure on any one, but which would gradually acquire a moral and social influence by virtue of their knowledge, their disinterestedness, their devotion to the public good, and their blameless example of life.

Consider what this "philosophic class" would be as conceived in Comte's ideal. It would be entirely without any State authority, force, or lawful claim of any kind. It would have no monopoly. It would have no wealth, no privileges, and nothing to offer. It could neither confer anything which men would desire nor receive anything which men could give. It could neither compel nor bribe any one to accept its guidance or to listen to its teaching. It would possess neither the legal rights of a State Church, with the aid of the temporal arm, nor the spiritual thunders of a theological commission. It would have neither prison nor outlawry to threaten. It would have no Heaven or atonement to promise. It would be surrounded by perfectly free teachers, who might without interference from the State or the magistrate form, if they pleased, other free communities. *Ex hypothesi*, all teaching, preaching, moral and intellectual guidance of every kind is to be entirely free. And such conceivable Church is compelled to rely solely on its own moral weight and intellectual usefulness. This is not a promising field for a spiritual despotism; and the dread of such a despotism is really a survival of the old Protestant horror of a Catholic Church armed with real spiritual terrors, possessing supernatural claims and powers, and effectively backed by the secular arm of a despotic State.

And yet Mr. Mill is aghast at the prospect of any intellectual or social organisation on any terms. But it is impossible to argue a question so general and so completely "in the air" above any actual experience of facts. It is a question which every one must decide for himself on his own general tendency of mind. Mr. Mill stands forward as the apostle of individual freedom, on behalf of which he wrote, spoke, and acted so bravely and consistently. But one cannot help reflecting how far, in the sixty years which have passed since the work of "*Liberty*," which he regarded as his most enduring achievement, the doctrines of that work have passed away from public opinion, and how strikingly the set of the world has been towards socialist and not individualist ideals. As Professor Ingram in his history of Political Economy points out, the whole current of thought in these sixty years has been towards Comte's estimate of economic science and not towards Mill's. Mill, I say, is the apostle of individual freedom. Comte's ideal is the double and harmonious interaction of individual freedom and of social co-operation. As Dr. Bridges has so well put it in the last sentence of his *Letter to Mill*, "there are two inseparable aspects of the social problem: union of efforts, individuality of efforts. The first is for us, in the present generation at least, the more important and the more difficult. And, once realised, this involves the other far more surely than the other this. One word sums up the whole. You seek nobleness of life through liberty. We think that the highest liberty is that which comes unsought through nobleness of life."

Mill's whole intellectual career was devoted to the cause of Liberty and in his *Autobiography* he gives us a most touching account of how his work on that subject and with that title, was the joint product of himself and his wife, and how he believes that on that account it is likely to survive longer than anything else which he has written. We assuredly do not undervalue the principle of liberty in the sense of free development of the individual mind and nature. But we value no less the other indispensable side of human good and happiness — the convergence of efforts, the ordering of life, the organisation of society. This is the urgent problem of the hour. The vast wilderness of intellectual discovery and the stores of knowledge accumulated beyond all expectation and management seem to cry out for some clue or *synthesis* to reduce it to shape, to give place to the "mighty maze." The conflict of classes and interest in the modern revolution of practical and political life cries out for some moral power to restrain the strong, to protect the weak, to conciliate antipathies, and to calm passions. The sense of aimlessness and uncertainty in our thoughts and habits that has come to so many in the break-up of old beliefs and the decay of Churches and forms of worship seem to yearn for a central idea, a social government—a spiritual order of governnment—a religion in fact.

What was the religion of Mill? We should find it difficult to say. His interesting *Autobiography* tells us nothing of this cardinal point in a great teacher's life history. The posthumous *Essays on Religion*, written at various epochs and not altogether consistent with each other, reveal Mill as a somewhat uneasy sceptic who had ceased to believe any creed, and yet would be glad to think that some creed were possible. He seems to think that on the balance of probabilities and impossibilities, moral and physical, there is a fair presumption in favour of the theory of Theism, provided the attributes of creation are very carefully limited, qualified, and loosely held, that the theory offered some moral advantages, though it might have no scientific assurance. But this hardly fulfils Mill's own first condition of a religion—that it must have a creed "claiming authority over the whole of human life." Mill's Theism seems too much to resemble what the French philosophic humorist called *Le Grand Peut-être*.

It is a very fair question to ask of a philosopher who elaborately criticises a new conception of religion by another philosopher—What is his own religion? Mill's practical religion—for I think few students of the whole of his work and teaching will say that his theoretical Theism amounted to a creed "claiming authority over the whole of his life"—his practical religion was (no ignoble one) a belief in individual effort. Is this religion of his making way? Has it made way in the years which have elapsed since the height of his influence and popularity? Is this faith of his felt by many to be the one key to the tangled problem? Hardly so. It seems rather to be melting away along with that which was its social expression—the old economic dogmatism. The hesitation, the negativism—almost the despair of this good, generous, acute spirit, as men look back on his brave and laborious life, seem to me to be producing a reaction on men's minds. The world for the last fifty years has been groping rather towards synthesis, towards social Utopias much more than towards individualist ideals. And there is a feeling that Mill's nature was too critical, dry, and dispersive, and his mind wanting in co-ordinating genius entirely to fill the void and command the future of modern thought. Men are feeling that this mournful, negative, and discouraging cry of No organisation! is a barren thing. We see how Mill's criticism of Comte may have given us useful warnings on minor subordinate matters, that he may often have proved Comte to be over-sanguine, over-eager, dangerously confident, sometimes wrong, now and then inconsistent, visionary, paradoxical.

But this work of Comte is to be seen not only in eight or ten volumes, but in the spirit and ideas which he has given to those whom he has left behind him, in the teaching and habits of the friends he had, in the life of the little community which he just lived to found. Those who look into that can hardly doubt that the acute and trenchant criticism to which Mill has subjected the books of Comte has done nothing to shake the force of that religion of Humanity which Mill recognised no less than Comte in practice, of which Mill's life, no less than Comte's, was in fact a noble example and product.

It is a thought which may make us here serious and anxious enough that, in our own small and humble way, we are ourselves, each of us, the justification of the scheme for a religion of Humanity, and the proof of its "legitimacy" and possibility rests with the living testimony of our lives and example. It is a thought to make us humble and anxious, that if the generations to come are to see that Comte's work and teaching has been other than a vain thing, it must be that those who have accepted that teaching manifest in their lives that it is a real religion whereby men and women may live and die, and whereby there is a hope of bringing light and peace into the dark turmoil of this latter age.

LECTURE XI

(*Newton Hall*, 1892)

THE MORALS OF TRADE

THE more widespread, the more common, form of our social activity is not government, but industry. And so, if political duty be of a nobler rank, our economic duty, as workers, producers, and heirs of the capital of ages, is far the most familiar form of all our public life.

Now, as the keynote of Positivist conception of Political Duty is the substitution of Duty for Right, so the keynote of our conception of Economic Morality is to substitute the general welfare of society as the industrial motive—in lieu of personal gain. Just as the contrast between *Right* and *Duty* is the contrast between what I can get from the public and what I can do for the public, so the contrast between Political Economy and Social Economy is that between individual gain and public service. It is the fashion to treat this as fantastic and impossible. The cynical view—and in this Politician, Economist, and Socialist agree—is this: Men will only serve their own interest; and to place Industry on anything but self-interest is utterly chimerical.

I am more hopeful. Now, notice that some of the most conspicuous functions in life—the most important—are not placed on a basis of interest, but of public duty. To treat them as based on interest, as being bought and paid for, is universally looked on as something degrading and unworthy—too cynical to be seriously imputed to honourable men. Take statesmen, generals, and great public servants. No one seriously thinks that their labours are bought and sold. To avoid living politicians, take George Washington, Wellington, Nelson, Cobden, Peel—does any one venture to say that they worked, fought, and lived for hire? Or Mill, Darwin, Macaulay, or Tennyson? They all received public rewards, honours, and profit of some kind. But no one ventures to say that we owe them nothing because they were duly paid. Take our ordinary language as to soldiers or sailors, who fight our country's battles. No man dares to say that they were hired to fight, and to die. Does a shilling a day pay that? Or the ministers of every creed, the curate on £60, the Catholic priest in a western Irish county, the Free Kirk minister in the Highlands, and the Baptist missionary in a crowded city. No one says they are hired and duly paid for. Or men who teach—ourselves in this hall. We are not hired. Well, then! If whole classes of men are supposed to labour for motives other than self-interest, why is it utterly chimerical that the bulk of industry may be so organised?

But it may be said, Yes, but statesmen and public servants labour for honour, peerages, fame, etc. Soldiers die for patriotism; and poets, and preachers, for the love of their art or religious motives, etc. Even we in Newton Hall may be said to have what is so much despised—some queer philanthropic motive. Just so. But we do not propose to eliminate all motives of social esteem. We do not propose to put factory labour on a higher level than that of Members of Parliament or Poets Laureate. We only say that something like the same considerations *may* be thought to apply.

It is found that men are, and always have been, ready to labour in the public service upon public and not purely personal grounds. The government of the State, the defence of our country, and the teaching of morality and religion have always been invested with a certain special quality, by military and theological ideas and recognised forms of society. They have never succeeded in making peaceful industry honourable in the same way. They have never tried to invest it with a social character. They have accepted the old brutal contempt of the fighting man for the labouring man, the old indifference of the mystic with his thoughts set on a life to come who disdains the practical improvement of the human race on this planet. This is the justification for our calling for a new order, a new order in the social life and in the spiritual domain. For the old order still obstinately encourages the military, aristocratic, and theological scorn of Labour.

Now we seek to found an era of Peace—and of Industry—to raise the triumphs of honest and artistic toil to a point of honour far above the triumphs of war, and to show that rational, progressive, social industry is the natural form of human activity. The Captains of Industry are greater than the Captains of the battlefield, and the soldiers of Labour are nobler patriots than the soldiers of the Sword. They have no lust of victory and destruction. Everything turns on the Inauguration of Peace and practical energy in improving the life of Humanity. When that is found to be Patriotism, Religion, and Loyalty—all in one—we may look to see the life of honest labour raised to a point of dignity such as was never yet reached by soldier or by mystic. It is our fault if War still retains a halo which Industry has not. The glory of Labour is to save, to help, to construct, to enlarge peace, beauty, happiness.

What is it that has so long given dignity and

public recognition to the labours of statesman and soldier? The manifest fact that they did not labour or die for themselves—the plain evidence that their pay was a mere accessory, that they were really maintaining or defending the accumulated inheritance of centuries and working for generations to come. It was obvious that they were carrying on the labour of the past, and were handing on labour to the future. In the case of statesmen and soldiers, largely in that of the poet, philosopher, or artist, it was impossible not to see the country, the past, and the future in their work—and this gave it dignity and placed them in an honourable class. Well, but the past of the country—nay, of human society—of the past and the future—is just as real in the case of simple industry, though it may not be so obvious. The men who are making a railway, a ship, a house are just as truly labouring for country, for the public, building on the past—laying up a store for the future. Nay, this is true of the man who is digging coal, or sowing corn, or driving an engine. Civilised life could not go on without their labour. Their labour would be impossible without all that had been done in the past—machines, inventions, organisation, prepared ground, appliances, etc. And their labour will be shamefully wasted unless it leaves much prepared for the future. All that we have to do is to make this familiar, to teach it as the foundation of common knowledge, to make it a part of our religion—in order to rise to the social recognition of the dignity of labour. Shall every linesman or drummer-boy or cabin-boy who ever fought in a battle for our country wear a medal, and be treated as a hero, whilst the printer who sets up some immortal work, or the mason who helps to build some national monument, shall be treated as a man who was amply paid by sixpence an hour? It is said the soldier and the sailor risked their life and limb. Does not the engine-driver, and the policeman, the miner, the sailor in a trading freight ship risk his life and limb; does not every workman more or less risk all he has—his wealth, rest, and manhood? I trow more lives are lost to-day (1892) in civil industry than on battlefields.

Another profound suggestion of Comte. Not only is every form of civil industry a prolonged act of patriotism—worthy to rank with "*the Services*," as they are called—but what we call the pay of the labourer is not really the equivalent of his service, it is what he is legitimately entitled to in order that the service may be performed. "All real honest labour," says Comte, "is gratuitous." You cannot buy it. All really good work is so thorough, and involves such a multitude of fine extra cares, that no money equivalent can be imagined.

If we look at it closely we shall see that no

really high-class work is in strict sense bought. All good work requires constant minute attention, zeal, sudden inspirations of self-sacrifice and heroism, which no money can buy, and which could not be included in any contract. In war no one would doubt this, or even in a ship. You could not buy the soldier or the sailor's act of heroism in an emergency—no, nor the miner's nor the engine-driver's, and so on. One moment of hesitation, of sleepiness, or of carelessness, and work—even everyday work—would be spoilt. Take the case of a nurse-girl with an infant. Is £1 per month and poor food the honest equivalent of her watchful, motherly care—day and night—when one minute's carelessness might mean death ? And so we might go on. Mason, miner, engineer, gardener, ploughman, printer, or tailor all put their love into their work—if they are true men, with an earnest zeal and minute thoroughness which no money could buy and which no vigilant supervision could enforce or detect. What a cur would the man be who suggested that when a soldier rushed into the breach, or saved a comrade's life at the risk of his own, his real motive was to earn one shilling per day, or the man who said that if Tennyson polished his verses and fashioned a rhyme over and over again, he did it to get more five-shilling volumes sold. No ! All true labour is or ought to be gratuitous. It is done only with the help of the past and for the sake of the future. It is the service of society which society should honour, and wages paid are but the bare means of enabling the worker to do his service—often the very scanty and inadequate means of doing it.

Thus the scientific, sociologic, moral view of Industry extends to *all* honest Industry the same idea which is familiar and accepted in the service of the State, in war and some of the higher and more conspicuous acts of life—viz. that all kinds of industry are social functions with these qualities :

1. They are all for the general use of society.

2. They are all dependent on some existing social machinery.

3. They all have to be conducive to some future social end.

4. The money payments they receive are in no true sense their equivalent.

The object of Positivism is to make universal the spirit in which the highest functions are treated at present. It would be disgraceful in the general of an army or the captain of a ship so to order a campaign or voyage that he should feather his own nest. Why should it be chimerical to extend this same public opinion to Captains of Industry ? The capital is no more really theirs than the army is the property of the general or the ship of the captain. In case of disaster the captain is the last man to leave his ship. Why in case of commercial disaster is the capitalist to be the first to get out of the concern and to leave the workmen and the paid employees to bear the loss ? It is due to a narrow and unreal tone of social opinion which holds the general of an army responsible for his men, but treats the capitalist as the irresponsible and absolute owner of his own capital and of the whole concern or business he directs.

Our religious and social standards were formed unhappily under the influence of Catholicism and Feudalism, and Catholicism and Feudalism both founded their ethical code under the rule of—

1. War and military habits.
2. Slavery or serfdom.
3. Chivalrous contempt of labour.
4. Superstitious indifference to human civilisation and progress on this earth.

Unhappily, no new religious and social code has taken the place of the Ecclesiastical and Feudal Code which still silently encourages military and feudal ideas. The problem is to found a religious and social code which is adequate for a régime of Peace, industry, and equality. And there is nothing chimerical, if the Gospel taught the learned Greek and the masterful Roman that the soul of his least slave was as valuable in the sight of God as his own—there is nothing Utopian in the expectation that a new

Social Gospel may teach the men of science of to-day and the rich capitalist of to-day that their knowledge and their wealth are both social products, entrusted to them in the sole interest of society—actual and future.

The capitalist under the influence of this teaching will come to feel that his first charge is the welfare of the soldiers under his command, and that to bring them to disaster is as disgraceful as for a captain to lose a ship by his own recklessness, or a general to have his army forced to surrender. No one asks the capitalist to practise monkish austerities or a fantastic self-denial, any more than the captain is expected to mess in the forecastle or to go aloft to the masthead; nor is the general expected to carry his own knapsack or take his turn with the spade in the trenches. But it is obvious that totally different rules are applied in judging the general or in judging the manufacturer. Now, they ought to be the same rules. And the whole condition of Industry would be transformed if those who manage the social capital of mankind were expected to behave as those do who direct the armies and ships of the commonwealth.

This social point of view has to be pressed first and mainly on the *Capitalist*—but it is also just as necessary for the workman. In the very natural reaction against the selfish view of *Capital*, the workmen, and still more the workman's teachers and friends, insist that the common product is all *his*—that he has produced it and that he may consume it. Management, they say,—well, five per cent for management, or take the management in turns, or hire a manager by the month, etc.—just as if the conduct of a great factory or a steamship company were as simple a thing as driving a cart.

This theory of the labourer's self-interest is just as false and as immoral as that of the capitalist's self-interest, and for the same reason. Neither workman nor employer alone, neither capitalist nor labourer by themselves, made the product—and the labourer quite as little as the manager. In a greater or less degree—always to some large degree—Society produced the indispensable conditions, without which nothing could be made. In a factory, the workmen (hands, as they are called) did not make the building, did not make the machinery, nor the raw material, nor the market where it is sold, nor the civilised country where it is made. And the men who made the factory, the machinery, the ships, etc., did not invent the organisation, nor the machines, nor the ships, etc., nor the complex arrangements of civilised life. And so we might go on *ad infinitum*. It is always *wheels within wheels* and one man's labour dovetailing into that of another. And as to "management," in nine out of ten cases management means the creation of the whole work. Take a coal mine. Who first discovered the seam, who found the £20,000 to make the shaft, etc.? Were Napoleon's battles won by his soldiers? They did not think so. When in 1870 the French were defeated in scores of battles by Germans, why was it? The French were not man for man greatly inferior to the Germans and they had better guns. It was "organisation"—command. On one side a great commander, on the other a diseased and bewildered despot. Why didn't Napoleon III. hire a good general? The case of industrial organisation is just the same. The intellectual guidance is often *all in all.*

When we have made scientific demonstration familiar to all and part of their fundamental moral and religious duties, the whole range of industrial activity will be penetrated with the sense:

1. That all industrial products depend partly on thorough conscientious work by each worker —work that no money can buy.

2. Partly, on intellectual guidance, the proportion of which none can estimate, but which may be nine-tenths.

3. That the product belongs neither to one nor to the other.

4. Because a proportion (never quite to be determined) belongs to existing society.

5. Another part to antecedent society.

6. And a large part of the result is morally due to posterity—if we make posterity at all.

The regeneration of modern social and industrial life depends on a sense of this being the familiar idea of *all*—from the directors of the Bank of England down to the dustman—all are alike servants of the public—all are working with the means given them by society for the general benefit of society, actual or to come.

The first result of this new Social Creed would be that the directors of all industrial undertakings should provide against any production which might lead to reaction and collapse. At present the sole test is the personal interest of the capitalist. No prudent man will risk a panic in his own trade which might involve his own capital. But no capitalist abstains from making his own fortune because so doing might glut the markets of India, or ruin the American producer, or lead to a collapse in a distant coal-mine. From the social point of view, the duty of the capitalist is to avoid any glut in any market which may lead to widespread distress and disturbance, and avoid any over-production, even though it double his own fortune. Far more than that—the true business of the Captain of Industry is to produce such things in such proportion and in such form as may be most conducive to the welfare of the community, not blindly to follow what are called the "laws of supply and demand." We do not

mean that men are to set up for any prophetical insight into the wants of society, but are not artificially to stimulate some demand of the hour—which must tend to a reaction.

It is quite true that shorter hours, higher wages, more holidays, and avoidance of all competition in cutting down prices, cost, and quality, and more humane modes of conducting all industry may lead—infallibly will lead—even with the utmost caution and care—to a very considerable diminution in consumable products. Things will have to cost more, and the gross product will be distinctly smaller (1892).

But what is the remedy? That far greater caution should be exercised as to what is produced—that the production of idle luxuries for the few shall be largely diminished, and the production of necessary comforts for the many shall be increased. There will have to be fewer embroidered satins, less of lace, diamonds, race-horses, and hot-house fruit; more bread, more woollens, better houses, and brighter homes (1892–1918).

I said just now that *wages* did not form and could not form any real equivalent to the worker for the industry and sacrifices he makes, for the *life* he puts into good work—that wages were, socially regarded, only the means of living whilst the work was going on. Is there, then, no compensation to the worker for all the sacrifices of conscientious labour? None perhaps that can be reckoned in £ s. d. But to those who work for society, Society owes a great deal. First and foremost comes a liberal education—not an education up to the sixth standard carried at furthest up to the age of fifteen—but a thorough scientific general education in science, philosophy, history, and art, including languages and literature, carried on systematically up to adult age, and more or less extended during leisure through life. And this education has to be free, and to include artistic training, libraries, museums, concerts, clubs, temples, festivals, worship. What increase of wages could be equal to the universal diffusion of thorough education?

But systematic education implies greatly increased leisure—to acquire it and to make use of it. Hence the first condition of the economic ideal is shorter hours. No life can be healthy, free, easy, refined, with hours of ten or twelve per diem. Comte's Utopia is a day of seven hours, say, from eight to four, with an hour's interval. That is practically now the limit of higher professional work, leaving twelve hours for sleep, meals, mere rest; then seven of serious work, two for exercise, air, and change of place—three for mental and moral improvement.

Again as to wages. In Comte's view the permanent wages would be one-third fixed wages, two-thirds fluctuating, the total about three pounds per week (this was in Paris, 1850). Women's labour out of the home would be withdrawn. Useless labour being abandoned, labour would be directed entirely to general utility.

Next comes a permanent home guaranteed in ownership. Put these conditions together: Complete freedom from responsibility and anxiety, and a permanent home in property; thorough scientific and artistic education; social opportunities for improvement in culture, art, and recreation free; day of seven working hours; wages £150 per annum; complete social equality guaranteed by political power and common education.

This forms a Utopia *equal* to that of any Socialist (1892). And it is compatible with all existing social institutions. In spirit, in purpose, and I think in effect, it is Socialistic. I am not aware that any Socialist looks to attain more than this—if so much. But it avoids the social dissolution which we can hardly expect to come about, even if ultimately successful, without a series of bloody struggles leaving undying memories of hatred. It avoids the risk of placing the control of our common industrial undertakings at the mercy of the most ambitious, violent, and ignorant of the community. And, above all, it avoids the selfishness which Socialism in most of its forms teaches—the selfishness of the worker invoked to cast out the devil of selfishness in the Capitalist, and the selfish appeal to the worker of to-day to ignore the Society of the Past and the Society of the Future, the selfishness of trying to regenerate the social organism by invoking rights instead of raising morality.

LECTURE XII

THE MORALS OF THE INTELLECT

(*Newton Hall*, 1892)

THE very term I use will surprise and scandalise very different classes of hearers.

1. The most advanced Socialist does not insist on any social control over any intellectual function.

2. It is a commonplace with all engaged in intellectual occupations that they require as a condition precedent absolute independence from any control, not merely legal but social.

Notwithstanding this we maintain :

I. That not only no kind of Socialist society but no society at all organised on a social basis : *i.e.* no purely moral and religious Socialism (as Positivism is) could exist for a generation if it left intellectual force entirely out of account, and quite free.

II. That intellectual force would be a curse to mankind, and a wretched and futile thing, if it were regarded as wholly free from the considerations of social duty which are constantly claimed for political and economic force.

How fatal a mistake it was in those dogmatic Socialists of old, who left intellectual force out of their account. It was a sure test of their extreme narrowness, their pedantry, and want of any living touch with society. They were mere idealogues: their influence is now gone. But it is a proof of the absence of any philosophic grasp in all the modern forms of Socialism, that they offer nothing tangible on intellectual force. This they leave free, either regarding it as unimportant or having nothing to suggest about it.

But how great an error is this! Intellectual force is at the back of all other force ultimately.

It is a mere fallacy to talk of even bayonets as force irrespective of opinion. There is no force pure and simple except muscle; and that, in an age of arms, machinery, and civilisation, is trifling. Even in modern war, the muscular force of one soldier is nearly equal to another's. At any rate, no single muscular force exceeds that of two men. We are not in the Homeric age of Achilles and Hector. The only force is the mind of those who act together. Those who can make or unmake that opinion control the force.

The weak spot of all Socialist theories is that they are materialistic in so far as they alter legal arrangements; but have no general philosophy of life, no ethics, no religion to affect opinion. It is necessary, not only to form opinions but to keep them active by constant exhortation.

This is just the strong point of the Positivist scheme—that it recognises that:

(*a*) Progress is due to intellectual advance,

(*b*) Intellectual advance requires a systematic basis in philosophy.

Socialism, without philosophy and an organised scheme of teaching, is a mere experiment and would not last a year [Russia, 1917–18].

This fact points to the necessity for bringing intellectual force of all kinds within the same influences as apply to political power or wealth. For ages the only attempt was to bring political power under control. In our own and the last generation it has been seen that nothing could be done until the power of wealth and capital was brought under control also. Positivists stand alone, or at any rate, alone amongst social reformers (theology admits it) in requiring Intellect—all spiritual force—to be brought within the same influence. Till that is done, nothing is done.

When we say intellectual or spiritual force we mean all forms of energy other than material—art, science, philosophy, as well as moral and spiritual influence proper. All form civilisation and all should contribute to civilisation.

This rests on two grounds—

I. All manifestations of intellectual force obtain the larger part of their force from society.

II. All react on society so deeply and so quickly that, whilst they are outside the social synthesis (whatever it may be), everything is unstable and open to individual caprice.

I. We hear much of the proud individuality of the thinker of genius, but it is an empty boast. The most original and creative minds are doubtless those of the great philosophers who have transformed the course of human thought. But how completely even they are dependent on their predecessors, their own age, and their intellectual parents. Take the greatest of all—Aristotle, Descartes, Bacon, Hume. There never have been more creative and original minds. Yet we know that Aristotle would have been impossible without Thales, Anaxagoras, Archytas, Socrates, to say nothing of Plato; Francis Bacon without Copernicus and Montaigne and Bruno; Descartes without Francis Bacon, Kepler, and Galileo; Hume without Hobbes, Locke, and so forth.

The whole history of Philosophy as a system of evolution would be unmeaning but for this, that is: filiation in thought. Comte always spoke of himself as evolving the ideas of his forerunners. Poets seem the most spontaneous, personal, and original; and so they are in form. But how impossible it would have been to make the *Iliad* in the age of Virgil, or the *Æneid* in that of Homer, or to suppose Dante the author of *Paradise Lost*, or Milton the author of the *Divina Commedia*, or *In Memoriam* in the age of Pope, or *Faust* in the age of Louis XIV. The history of mankind offers no example of original, transcendent and incomparable genius equal to the Tragedies of Aeschylus and the Plays of Shakespeare, yet who can imagine the Tragedies of Aeschylus produced in any other place or age except the Athens of Themistocles and Pericles, or the Plays of Shakespeare in any place or age but the England of Elizabeth. The language they speak, the ideas they paint, the images they use, are all the common property of their age partly, and still more of the ages before them.

Precisely the same filiation is true of science. Galileo would be impossible without Copernicus, Tycho, Kepler ; Newton without Galileo ; Bichat without Harvey. The history of all the Arts, from painting to music, bears out the same thing. All intellectual force is the expression of the age and the results of the past.

There is therefore no right in the claim of genius that it is an independent individual gift, and the Carlylean view of the Heaven-sent creator of ideas is opposed to all rational views of history. And yet the power of genius is undoubtedly great, and if exerted in an anti-social spirit would be subversive of society. All the just condemnation which we are ready to heap on the selfish use of wealth or political force is quite as applicable to the selfish use of any intellectual superiority whatever—for precisely the same reasons and in the same way. And this applies to art as much as to science. The corrupting tale, the inhuman picture, the seductive or anti-social poem, may be quite as injurious to its age as the ambitious statesman or the tyrannical employer.

The degrading nonsense of some *petits maîtres* about "Art for Art" is as shallow as it is mischievous. There is no more sense in Art for Art than there is in the maxim Wealth for Wealth, Riches for the Rich and Pleasure for the Pleasant, Power for the Powerful—or enjoyment for those who can enjoy. In fact, that is the literal meaning of Art for Art. No more mean and silly view of any human quality was ever put forth. Why not food for the sake of food, or turtle soup for the pot-bellies, and good wine for the strong heads? If it means that Art is to have no higher aim than self, the pleasure which the exercise of its faculty gives to the possessor, it deserves no more respect than gluttony or any form of debauchery. All true and honourable Art implies the ennobling of human life by clothing the actual in the form of beauty. If Art were to imply nothing beyond the gratification of the artist, it would deserve no honour more than any form of selfish gratification.

If Art for Art means only that Art is not to be the slave of society, cannot work in chains, we all know that, and this is true of science, philosophy, government, and wealth. But all stand on the same footing. All must be free equally with an ever-present consciousness of social obligation. Whether it be science, research, authority, wealth, or art — all must acknowledge the same duty, the same dependence of their own powers, the same end of their activity—whilst all must alike be free to act on their own responsibility. But Art for Art, if it means entire freedom from any social responsibility, absolute right in the artist to please himself (and in practice it comes to this), is as utterly absurd and as grossly immoral as would be a cry of Money for Money, Enjoyment for the sake of Enjoyment, or Empire for the sake of Domination. All such doctrines are alike untrue, degrading, anti-human, and paradoxical.

This brings us to the fundamental condition that when we speak of social responsibility we do not mean the material control of law, the power of any legal authority to intervene or the right of any outside person or body to dictate the conditions of intellectual activity or to prescribe for it any course of action.

In the melancholy collapse of all moral and

spiritual influences over daily life, it is the habit of our age to invoke material and legal control. And if anything in the nature of social control is proposed, no one seems able to imagine it can be anything but legal and material superintendence. Thus Governments have been found oppressive and deaf to the wants of the masses and the demands of public opinion.

Their suggested remedy is "Place all political authority in the hands of a direct decision by the whole body of persons affected": to which they now add, all the women as well as all the men, and why not add all the children. Our essential remedy is—impress the rulers and ruled alike with a new social morality. Leave the rulers, when duly regenerated, with a free hand, but place the exercise of their power under the continuous influence of an active and educated public opinion.

So again with wealth. Dreadful sufferings are found due to the selfish and irresponsible use of Capital. And the Socialist remedy is to place Capital under the direct management of the whole body of workers—whereas our remedy is, Reform both capitalists and workers with a new sense of social obligation.

And lastly, in the case of intellectual activity, the only need for any sort of control or influence is that which we propose—a moral and spiritual control. And it is at once assumed that we are asking the State to dictate to men of special intellectual powers how their faculties are to be exerted. Nothing of the kind. We are quite consistent, whether in the sphere of Government or of Capital, or of Science or of Art, we repudiate any further attempt to reform Society by law; we reject the attempt to abolish social institutions; we would retain the ancient social institutions, government, and governing authorities, private appropriation of Capital, even distinct orders in the industrial as in the political economy; we propose even to retain the institution of a Church—only we seek to educate anew, to moralise and to socialise, to humanise government, capital, Church, alike. We would throw them all alike under a real social responsibility, and maintain that by an organised public opinion. And in the same way, and in the most essential thing of all we propose to moralise, to humanise all intellectual activity.

But if there be any one of these—Government, Industry, Church, Intellect, which it is peculiarly impossible to control by law or to subject to any kind of material direction, of them all, the one the most utterly impossible so to control, is the exercise of intellectual force. To attempt anything in that direction would be to violate that fundamental doctrine of the whole Positive scheme—the most unbounded freedom of opinion. Thought must be free, whatever else is controlled by law, free, that is, from any legal restraint but that of conscience and public opinion. One sees in the miserable Vivisection controversy how futile have proved attempts to deal with a purely moral and social problem by legislation —indeed, how much the cause of humanity has suffered by short-sighted appeals to legislation.

There would indeed be little need of any legislation or angry controversy if the principles of a religion of Humanity had been recognised throughout this business by all. If all men of science had recognised the moral and social obligations of all research, had been as carefully educated on the moral and human side as they have been on the purely intellectual, if they had freely consented to admit that society had every reason to expect from them the utmost humanity and respect for all the brute helpmates and friends of humanity, if they had from the first given as many guarantees of their moral conscientiousness and moral science as they have given of their biological zeal and physical science, we should have heard little of this business. One sees how vain legislation must be, if there be an absence of a social conscience burning quite as brightly in the soul of the man of science as his passion for research. Unfortunately a few zealots in research have claimed an absolute liberty not only from legislative and judicial control, but even from any moral control either from their own conscience or from public opinion.

Absolute freedom of Intellect from all control of conscience and public opinion can never be conceded without putting the whole fabric of society at the mercy of individual caprice, vanity, or ambition. We do not propose that the State should dictate to any man how his faculties are to be employed, or that the law should punish either any exercise or any non-exercise of any intellectual faculty. But we do maintain that Society can never be in a condition, either wholesome or stable, until the exercise of every intellectual faculty is felt to be as much a matter of conscience and social duty as the direction of the nation's policy, or the command of the nation's armies and fleets, and is the subject of systematic review by public opinion as being animated by a social and religious spirit.

And now, at the close of this course on Society as reformed by Positive Morals—wherein I feel to myself that I have only touched the very fringe and surface of this vast and profound theme—I wish to recall your thoughts to what I said at the beginning and have been saying more or less all through—that Positive Morals professes to be merely an extension and development—not a conflict or contradiction—of Christian or any theological or practical morality

—rather a new method, or revival of an old method, not a complete reversal.

In the first place, so far as personal and domestic morals are concerned, the Positive Scheme seeks only to develop and extend and give a new social meaning to the personal and domestic morality, as taught by the Churches and familiar to the conscience of civilised humanity.

It is rather in the field of public morality that it seeks to act—the neglected field—the abandoned field—and almost for the first time to introduce the sense of social duty into the exercise of industrial activity and intellectual and artistic activity.

But there is another feature which specially marks off Positive morals. It is that it seeks a positive method—not a negative method. It looks to stimulus not to restraint. Its instrument is education, not penalty. The ideal is to inspire noble sentiments, not to threaten practical evils. Its sanctions are all inspiring, not terrifying. It teaches the beauty of holiness and of goodness, not the agony of hell fire. It has no hell. Its heaven is a good conscience. Its method is to cultivate the heart, not to use the sense of self-interest.

Compare the Ten Commandments with the Positive maxims. The Ten are negative, coercive, minatory, the Positivist are positive, hortatory, inspiring. All the ten, except the fifth

(Honour thy Father and Mother) are minatory. All the Positivist are positive, hortatory. These are:

Live for others. Live openly.

Order and progress—

Learn, in order to foresee; and foresee, in order to provide.

Act from affection, and think in order to act.

Reorganise by the systematic cult of Humanity.

Be conciliate in act: in principle be firm.

Wealth is social and should be used for social ends.

Devotion of the strong for the weak: the weak owe the strong respect.

The intellect should be the servant not the slave of the heart.

All these are positive—inculcate duty—they do not forbid offences. And so on throughout.

Positive Morals in fact form one side of Religion, whereas current Morals are one side of law. The essence of Positive Morals is the moral and social inspiration of the affections by a systematic training begun in the cradle and continued to the grave, the keynote of which is cultivate, stimulate, train, practise, develop the spirit of:

1. Attachment.
2. Reverence.
3. Sympathy.

In the Jewish theocracy, in all theocracies

and in all formal and absolute societies, Puritan or Polytheistic, Morality is essentially negative. Thou shalt not eat pork. Thou shalt not work on the seventh day. Thou shalt not commit adultery. Thou shalt not blaspheme. Thou shalt not break some rule of caste.

And in modern society—the practical rules of morality are all of this negative kind. Provided you break no law, violate no social usage, and defy no convention of your order, you are a strictly moral person, and you may be miserly or extravagant, grasping, unkind, cold, unsociable, conceited, self-engrossed, cynical, and irreverent. That does not constitute immorality. You live decently with your wife, do not persecute your children, do not commit sharp practice, subscribe to the local charities, pay your taxes and your pew in church, and you are a good man. Any little blots on your inner conscience you will settle with your Maker at the Day of Judgement. That is your religion: your morality is unexceptionable. Such is the current morality.

Now the claim of Positivism is this: that you can never get further than this on the negative method. We propose to try the positive methods, *i.e.* to train the affections continually, to appeal to attachment, reverence, sympathy. That, no doubt, is the aim of Religion, and it is quite fair as a criticism that Positive Morality is incomplete without Religion, and in fact invisibly shades off into Religion. That is quite true, and I said so before. There is nothing new in this. What was Christianity, as introduced by Paul, except an effort to supplant a purely negative scheme of morality by a positive morality based on and incorporated into Religion? The old Graeco-Roman morals in the first century amounted to this—"Obey the laws, and serve the Commonwealth bravely."

The claim of Paul was to rouse the whole nature with a new inspiration—the love of God and the hope of Heaven—and it succeeded up to a certain point and for a given time.

And the same was the case in a far higher degree during the great age of the Mediaeval Church, of St. Bernard and St. Francis and St. Dominic. Moral conduct was then for a time inspired and saturated with a religion which, in a visionary and indirect way, consisted in appeals to the affections, to love of an ideal goodness by dwelling on the thought of Divine Pity, Mercy and Love, and on the intercession of superhuman tenderness in the Virgin Mother of God. All this the remorseless criticism of six centuries has eaten away, and with it the very idea of basing Morality on any mere cultivation of the Heart.

Comte has often declared that the essential purpose of Positivism was to revive the aim of the Mediaeval Church on a scientific and purely human basis; and this has been grossly misunderstood. He has been taken to mean a crude restoration of the hierarchical machinery of the Church and the sacerdotal despotism of the Papal system. Nothing could be further from his thought. How can the principle of entire freedom of opinion consist with clerical despotism? How could the condition of universal scientific demonstration consist with Papal infallibility? No! the essential and inner parallelism between the Positive and the Catholic scheme is this—that both, for the only time we may say in the history of mankind, seek to regenerate human society by a systematic training of the affections.

The key of Positive morals is the direct cultivation of the heart—not by indirect means, but by direct, not by any visionary and ecstatic machinery, but by perfectly practical common sense and real means—not with absolute, superhuman, and fictitious ideals, but with the perfectly real, relative, and entirely earthly fact of a collective Humanity, in which all our sense of attachment, reverence, and sympathy can be centred and transfigured.

In saying this, of course, we admit that morals cannot suffice for conduct by itself; it can only give us rational motives for conduct and scientific guides to conduct. But Morals does not by itself supply any incentive and inspiration to conduct in the stress of passion and interest.

For this, it must look to Religion, which will unite in one end science, morality, art, government, law, industry, and private life, inspiring all with a common synthesis and a common enthusiasm.

It is no defect in Positive Morality that it does not pretend to suffice for human conduct without the wider and more powerful inspiration of Religion. If it did, on Positive principles Ethics would suffice; and there would be no need of Religion at all, and that is the view, the erroneous view, we believe, of our friends in the various Ethical movements. But this character of Positive Morality is shared by Christian Morality in its highest manifestations, which declared itself to be nothing but the entrance to the temple of Religion. So will it be with Positive Morality. It will be only the outer court of the temple of Religion—the Religion of Humanity. Only the Religion will be entirely earthly, essentially based on science, always open to demonstration, wholly practical; human, sympathetic, relative, and real.

The Cause to which my life has been devoted, and which this book seeks to illustrate and explain, is not simply a theory of Society, but is also a practical scheme for the regeneration of Society in the future. That is, it has a twofold character, being a Social Philosophy and a Social Polity. In the first Part of the book, I endeavour to sketch some of the essential doctrines on which we conceive a normal Society should be based. In the second Part, which follows, I give some examples of the way in which a group of men and women convinced by these doctrines sought to work them out in their lives. Mr. Mill's memorable work ON LIBERTY, 1859, *contained only his theory of the fundamental doctrine on which Society should be built. Would that he or his eminent followers had given us a working model of the practical application of his doctrine to actual life. It has not been done.*

I shall now, very humbly and with much misgiving, place on record some of the pieces, not hitherto published, in which, as leader of the Positivist body in England, I endeavoured to trace the working of an infant Society on the ideas of the "Positive Philosophy" and the "Positive Polity" of Auguste Comte.

F. H.

BATH, 16*th July* 1918.
1 *Dante* 129.

PART II

INAUGURAL ADDRESS

(*The Opening of Newton Hall*, 1881)

It is with a very deep and lively sense of humbleness and of mistrust of self that I offer myself in this place to-day as the mouthpiece of those who have agreed to form here a centre for their thought and work.

It is the first time that we of our English Positivist group assemble to take possession by ourselves of that place of meeting which we have long sought. It is an occasion, therefore, on which the whole weight of the task that we have taken on ourselves comes home to us, and when we have to look forward to what we have before us. It is a responsibility in which we all have a share, a responsibility which I, whose lot it is to put in words these thoughts of to-day, necessarily feel in a special degree.

But there is another source of self-mistrust and of hesitation which presses upon me to-day with even greater force. It is that I have in this place immediately to follow the teacher and leader whom we have lately had amongst us, and who has given us a series of brilliant and memorable discourses drawn from the immense resources of his learning and wisdom. Our movement is necessarily destined to wait on the development of that in Paris, inasmuch as it will, I fear, be long before we can look for any teacher here who can speak with any part of the authority and force that belongs to every word of M. Pierre Laffitte.

Since the death of A. Comte, now twenty-four years ago, he has continued to carry on the work of organising and directing the Positivist movement, with the zeal, power, and success that we know. Only those who have followed the history of this movement and studied the work of its director can at all imagine the great qualities which it has called out in him—courage, perseverance, goodness, forgetfulness of self—the immense range of learning, the profound grasp of ideas, the philosophic elevation—the wonderful mental fertility united with a goodness and simplicity of nature, a peculiar tenderness of sympathy and healthiness of moral sense, a richness of social enthusiasm, of which it is most difficult to convey an idea to those who have not previously felt its charm and its power. Many of us have heard the luminous and penetrating force with which he handles in his public addresses questions the most difficult and most diverse; indeed an audience representative of English culture has been able to get some idea of the stores of learning and of thought, the mastery of principle, the wit, the grace, the subtlety, the goodness of the nature which for forty years Pierre Laffitte has freely devoted to the cause of his life. Of his surpassing merit as a teacher, not we only, but the public, have fair means of judging.

But I, who for nearly three weeks have been living in daily and hourly intercourse with him in the intimacy of my own house, I am glad to find an occasion for saying that it is his great qualities of nature and character which have impressed me even more than his great qualities of knowledge and intellect. What filled me day by day with new admiration and respect, has been the exquisite and childlike innocence of heart, the freshness and delicacy of sympathy, and religious fervour of social self-devotion, the beautiful magnanimity of nature, with long-suffering endurance, patience, perseverance. And not less than with this native goodness of heart, have I been struck day by day with his wisdom of general judgement, the sagacity and penetration in giving counsel, the extreme care with which he comes to an important resolution, the intensely human, social, and healthy way in which he works out every religious, moral, and practical problem about which his judgement is appealed to. In Pierre Laffitte we have a leader who, more than all other men in Europe living or dead, has been for forty years steeped in the best and most vital principles of Auguste Comte; who represents him and carries on the living spirit of the Master with whom for thirteen years he lived in daily intercourse; who has become imbued with the essence of the religion, the philosophy and the practice of Positivism, as hardly any man of modern times is ever imbued with any system at all, philosophical or religious; and who is quite as worthy of being the successor and continuer of Comte on grounds of heart and character as on grounds of thought and brain.

So that if it is a natural source of disappointment to us all to feel that our meetings here have lost the centre and strength that they recently have had, and if, in particular, I must feel embarrassed at being called to fill, even casually and temporarily, a place which only last Sunday was so very differently filled, the very thought of M. Laffitte's visit, both to me and to us all, has its great consolation and encouragement. We are acting under his direction and advice. He has now, by personal contact with Positivists here, drawn close the bonds of unity between the French and English groups, he has strengthened our regard and confidence in himself, he has ascertained the actual position of affairs here and has had some experience of our wants and opportunities. We feel that we have his judgement to refer to; he can come again amongst us for any special purpose that may arise, and I believe that he does propose in any case to repeat his visit next year. He has given us, publicly as well as privately, a body of practical ideas and of governing principle, applying to the whole series of questions. As we have all heard, he has taken up in the most definite way the position of the responsible director of a working Religion and that religion the religion of Humanity.

To him Positivism means the systematic regeneration of individuals and of society alike by a series of forces that shall act on feeling, intelligence, and conduct. It is no lecturer or professor of science to whom we have been listening: but to the energetic director of a real and actual church, with a system of culture, with a body of doctrine and with a method of action. It is true that it is in its germ; and that a great deal of its action is at present only indicated as possible, and that it does not in the least pretend to be an exclusive body of professing members, a sect, bent on separating themselves from the world, and saving their own souls. In some ways it is more like a social and political party than a sect which seeks to modify men around it; but then our party implies really religious objects, and religious means of action. It is as the leader of a real religious movement, though that movement be strictly confined to human and demonstrable things that M. Laffitte takes up his position. He remains for us the immediate head and guide of our action. As we have heard, he has authorised the committee which he has named to act for him and in his name so far as may be necessary, and in the meantime to do their best to carry out the Positivist faith into practice.

We have seen him on two occasions celebrate two of those solemn rites which Auguste Comte regarded as welding our private and public life, and which he called sacraments, and he showed us the essentially social, practical, and even physical realities on which these phases of our human existence are based. M. Laffitte has become to us now, not only a teacher whom we have heard of and whose writings we have studied, but a living friend and practical leader. It occurs to me that I should do what is most useful if I were to-day to recall some of the definite ideas and suggestions which he has given us in private conversation as well as in his public discourses. Many of those who saw him did not by any means hear the whole of his public addresses; and very few indeed heard all that he communicated in the general course of conversation.

M. Laffitte himself very pointedly referred to the remarkable fact that our movement has practically established a real Western sentiment, a community of thought and feeling, quite unlimited by national barriers. As he said, he, a Frenchman, speaking no English, knowing Paris only not London, in the name of a movement which embraced men of many nations, was addressing people of his own faith in London, and actually administering the rites of sacrament.

Note the importance of this *Occidental* character. We may be sure that any spiritual and moral movement whatever which limits itself, or which is limited, to *national* bounds has no true vitality, or elevation in it.

The thought, science, oral standard, and social sympathies are not *national* but *Western, i.e.* the advanced nations of the West form one people for this purpose. Political and practical relations are local and national confined by language and political divisions. But all the intellectual and spiritual relations of modern civilisation are common to all the advanced communities of Western Europe.

A movement which does not deal with these is really outside of the highest intellectual and spiritual relation of modern civilisation.

See the profound barrenness and helplessness of Protestantism owing to this. Imagine any science, or any philosophy which deliberately addressed itself to one nation. A *National* and *local* note is fatal to the claims of the higher spiritual movements.

The sole guarantee of reality and vitality in

any spiritual or religious movement is this—that it is perfectly indifferent to, we may say, practically unconscious of the local and national limits.

The great safeguard of Positivism is to hold on to this general Western character. The civilisation of the West has such various local types that they correct each other.

A religious movement confined to England would almost certainly slip back in a generation into some sort of imitation of one of the local English types of religion, or it would acquire the character of a national and political party, or in some other way fall into a sectarian, or local phase.

The fact that our movement is practically common to Europe makes us feel that its human, social, and essentially religious character is ever before our eyes, that it is not likely to stiffen into one of the party movements of the day, or become a local peculiarity. When for instance, our organ in France warmly supports the protest which we in England have felt necessary to make against selfish national ambition in Asia or in South Africa ; when, again, we call on our French comrades, as we are about to do, to consider the consequences of selfish national ambition in North Africa, then we see the religion of Humanity seeking to influence the public opinion of the West across all the outbursts of national egoism and race prejudice.

Every movement which could ever pretend to a religious character in the higher sense of the word, has been extra-national and supra-national, human, spiritual. The followers of Christ were a feeble variety of local Judaism, till the great Paul taught them that Grace was for all nations and all races, that the Gentiles were as open to it as Jews and more, and that God had made of one blood all nations of men for to dwell on the earth.

The religion of the Middle Ages was at least (in principle) Catholic, and its strength still is that it is practically independent of national limits whilst Protestantism is everywhere afflicted with the hide-bound narrowness of purely national and indeed quite local and even class limitations. All that was good and great in the New Birth of thought and life in Europe of the fifteenth and sixteenth centuries was European, not national. And so all that was good and great in the emancipation and new morality of the eighteenth century was European and not national. It began, in fact, in England and in Holland as much as in France. So too we may say that if Humanity is ever to become the recognised centre of our thoughts and acts it must be presented to us as a force before which national and local varieties have no force or meaning.

We may go farther. We may say, in the converse, that so soon as any social and practical movement shows itself superior to limits of nationality and peculiarities of race and local government and provincial prejudices, so soon as it takes its place firmly as a part of the life of Western civilisation, it is certain to prove a real force with a future before it; for nothing but a spirit of true elevation and noble humanity can raise us above the pressure that is exerted over us by the differences in language, political union, national habit, and race history. If we can conquer that, we shall win more hereafter.

It will be one of our most valued and anxious aims, that in this place, in all we do, we shall to the utmost strengthen the bonds between ourselves and our fellow-believers in the rest of Europe, and through Europe in the rest of the world. A belief in Humanity would be a poor thing if it were not at the outset human, world-wide, general.

Next to the character of Occidental generality which M. Laffitte has given to this movement there is nothing on which he so much insists as the complex and many-sided nature of the Positivist movement. He reminds us, in every act and word, by his example as much as by his teaching, that what we call the Positivist movement consists of a great number of different things no one of which can be neglected, and each of which can be itself broken up into a number of other subjects and duties. *All* of these are essential. Positivism consists in the due combination of them *all*. Its work, in fact, its substantive existence as a faith consists in the due recourse to these together, in the mutual assistance they give to each other.

Now these are:

1. An intellectual basis, a body of principles solidly taught and grouped together, a mass of real scientific knowledge.

2. A system of moral education, a personal training in feeling and duties, a direct appeal to the nobler emotions.

3. A practical scheme of society and politics, leading to a new future for the commonwealth of nations.

Positivism is hence at once:

1. An education in scientific truth.
2. A moral discipline in conduct and worship.
3. A political programme or movement.

It is impossible, as we have so often said, to limit Positivism to any one of these—all are alike characteristic. Hence it cannot be compared with any of the current phases of religion. How compare with Christianity, either in the Calvinistic or the Catholic type, a movement which is just as earnest about the international relations of European States and about the true classification of the sciences, as it is about any creed or any worship? How compare with any of the philosophies or metaphysics or materialistics a movement which cares far more about the progress of the working classes towards comfort, education, and power than it does about the origin of species, or the geometry of four dimensions? And yet, again, how compare with any of the socialisms or social Utopias of this age a socialism (as in one sense Positivism undoubtedly is) which seeks to base the Future on the laws of the Past, which looks to see society regenerated by means of a common religion and through the organised teaching of an authorised class or order of teachers and moral and intellectual leaders?

How is it possible to compare Positivism with any Theological Religion? It is a Philosophy; it is Socialism; and none of these sides can be dispensed with or forgotten or even postponed. All are alike important—all must be co-ordinated. For Positivism is an effort to bring about the synthesis or harmonious ordering of modern civilisation as a whole—to put the reordering of thought and education, the purification of our moral life, and the settlement of our society on just and happy terms—on one common scheme or plan, and that plan is the direction of all alike, —science, morality, society—by the light of our duty to Humanity, or knowledge of Humanity, and our dependence on Humanity.

Either of these three great sides of the vast task imply very much, and may be subdivided into several—*e.g.* (1) The intellectual basis implies a conception, and practical acquaintance with the cardinal ideas of the great sciences, and more, with the underlying key of these, in the governing philosophy, the classification of the sciences, the analysis of our cosmological, sociological, and moral laws. Therein lies the whole question of popular education, the training of the young, the training of the people, but also the whole question of the training of the trainers: *e.g.* the education of those who are to teach. Let us not forget, it has been the continual warning of M. Laffitte, that we have got to collect together and leave behind us a body of persons thoroughly imbued with the cardinal doctrines, especially with the logic of Philosophy (as Comte called it in the widest sense of the term). Now this is a thing which will not come of itself. It needs severe study, meditation, and habits of abstract thought. It is the side of the Positivist synthesis on which we in England are perhaps the most weak, and where we have the fewest competent students. When I remember the enormous pains which Comte himself took in working out the abstract laws of mathematical and general reasoning, the relations of the great mathematical processes, the first philosophy or general canons of philosophy, the central analysis, the scheme of moral science (indeed all that which is embodied in the tables so familiar to us (other than the concrete Calendar)); when I see the pains that M. Laffitte has for twenty years taken, and is still taking, to form a competent body of workers to carry on this tradition, I am in dread lest (so far as we are concerned) a great deal of this may be lost.

There is much of the most precious part of the teaching of Comte which is not reduced to books at all—*e.g. Morals*.

This exists at present almost exclusively in tradition, possessed by M. Laffitte. It is of great importance that this should not be lost. And it will be lost if our whole energies and time are given to any immediate and direct popularisation of Positivism, whether it take the form of political propaganda or of popular exposition of the Positivist truths.

I am far from saying that this is the exclusive or even the most urgent want of our movement. But we must never forget this—that the permanence and experience of the Positivist synthesis, ultimately depends on its finding a body of persons capable of combining the traditions of its philosophical basis. I have been speaking only of the various sides presented by the first department of Positivism, the *intellectual*. Turn to the second, the *moral*, the moral training, the systematic appeal to the emotions of attachment, veneration, benevolence.

Here is included that which is usually called *worship*. But what is called worship is only a small part of this one side. It is all very well for the theological bodies to reduce religion to formal adoration of a Creator (either privately or publicly) and to call the religious life the habit of meditation on the supposed will of the Creator. But that is a crude and starved way of looking at religion. We entirely reject the notion that religion can be *reduced* to any moral education at all, to any simple action on the heart or the sentiments of awe and gratitude. We think religion implies a sound philosophy, a complete education and a healthy society.

But taking *moral education* as a whole, how very much does it contain that is not in the least included in any mere scheme of *worship*. Moral education in its fullness implies the discipline of the young from birth to manhood, the influence of the home and the training of the mother, the training of the father, the gradual initiation of the young to citizenship, to society; it implies the subordination of self to family, of family to the community, of community to the State, of the State to the West, of the West to the human race, of the human race, as it exists, to Humanity in the past and the future. All this is a part of the moral training of the individual and the race, and it includes the whole of these processes—call them sacraments, or public ceremonies, or celebrations and commemorations.

In all this, Worship technically is but one

instrument, one very valuable, an indispensable method of training the character—but not the whole of moral education, nor even the main part of it. What is *worship*, public or private prayer (as understood in Churches and Chapels)? Looked at in a real not in a mystical way, worship, prayer is a process of directly stimulaing certain natural and noble emotions, the emotions of reverence, of sympathy, of benevolence, by presenting to them a worthy object of adoration; either in the silence of private abstraction or by the force of kindred association with fellow-worshippers. A great and indispensable resource for moral exaltation, but after all one which takes many forms, and one out of many means of moral purification. In the mystical and fictitious schemes of theology this stimulus to the emotions is apt to pass for the whole of religion, or the substance of religion; other things (it is thought) will follow—goodness of disposition, purity of life, charity, courage, truth, wisdom, and sympathy—if we only pray often enough and hard enough. Unluckily we know that this blessed result does not follow. Tenderness, charity, purity do not at all necessarily ensue; sympathy is often crushed out in the process; pride, prejudice, and pharisaism are directly stimulated instead of mercy and love and unselfishness. And wisdom and truth are driven out with ignominy and violence.

Well, let us never forget, says M. Laffitte, that any attempt to concentrate our scheme of action on a mere revival of formal worship, nay, any attempt to reduce even moral training to formal worship, will end with Positivists in precisely the same narrowness and Pharisaism that it has brought on theologians. The moral nature is only to be trained by lifelong work—the work of the individual, of the family in which he is bred, of the mother who bore him, of the father who begat him, and his brothers and his sisters after the flesh, or in fact by the society in which he lives, and by the Church or moral teaching which is responsible for his training; and if Positivists came to think that all this life-long toil could be superseded by ejaculating at set intervals a few invocations to the noblest types of moral goodness, by protesting our desire to live up to this goodness, by calling on the name of Humanity, and chanting the greatness of Humanity—if, I say, Positivists came to think that this, *per se*, will give them the moral regeneration which it is the dream of Positivism to see a reality on earth, then I say they are preparing for themselves a miserable and cruel disappointment, which will lead them ere long to a barren, conventional, and self-righteous formalism.

In the vehement and picturesque language of M. Laffitte—If I am asked to regard as the centre and symbol of Positivist religion the meeting to invoke Humanity and to utter protestations of devotion to Humanity, whilst those who are prepared to make these invocations and protestations are so few and the means whereby their feeling can be duly appealed to are so inadequate and scanty, whilst all the while so much remains to be done, so much to be taught, so much to be known, before even we who have given the best years of our lives to the thought, and can honestly say that we *know* all that Humanity means, or know how properly to devote ourselves to Humanity, whilst the community that is to serve Humanity yet needs such a mass of forming and organising and the very formers and organisers of it have themselves to be formed and organised—if, he says, I am to be told to give myself mainly to worship under such conditions, and in such a time, then I have heard him say repeatedly, I would prefer to go and join the congregation of some Christian Church where at least the tradition of a mighty past visibly rests on the service, where the resources of art, and numbers, and historic association are adequate profoundly to appeal to the emotions, where at any rate there is not a deliberate adoption of mere formulas, and where an effort of the imagination can enable me to recall what the Christian Church once has been in its noblest day, and what in the future the much vaster

Church of Humanity will one day be able to manifest.

That, I think, is the spirit in which we here are prepared to work. Without in the least undervaluing the great part which worship, or at least, to use a wider term, the formal expression of feeling, must always have, without in the least avoiding it or silently ignoring it, we do feel that the formal expression of feeling, at least in its public form, is of necessity a thing which must gradually evolve itself out of the society which craves such expression. It cannot be prematurely stimulated, or forced upon that society, for it has to follow on from knowledge, and practice and work, and discipline, and community of action and life, and thus no legerdemain can enable us to make it a *substitute* for knowledge and life and practice, no, nor a royal road to knowledge and life and practice, and above all, that inasmuch as the religion of Humanity is something radically different in kind from the religions of Moses, or Christ, or Buddha, or Mahomet, we must be cautious, very cautious, how far we allow ourselves to slip into a mere parody of what is called worship in Churches and Chapels, substitute Humanity for God, and Comte for Christ.

I think, I may say, that those who have established a movement in this place have no intention at any rate of doing that. This room is meant (let us hope that we may prove, all of us, equal to our resolutions)—this room is meant for *work*. We feel, in all its force, the vast arrears of work that await us. We are under no illusions as to all that we have to do. We desire to learn, to know, to act, to live, to feel—but we do not think all this can be satisfied by any easy method. Those who by curiosity, or accident, may stray into this room, and expect or wish to find us going through some unfamiliar ceremonial, and uttering some strange invocations, I think will be a little disappointed. Small as our sphere is, and humble as our efforts may be, we shall try, even be it in miniature, to look on the religion of Humanity in all its breadth and its many-sided human relations, neither rejecting *Worship* nor exclusively relying on *Worship*—but treating it as one of the many means of raising the heart to its fullness and its grandeur—but above all things trying to make it clear to ourselves at any rate, that religion implies a long course of mental training, a grasp on science, a true philosophy, a sound logic, quite as much as any kind of prayer or ceremony. Yes! it implies a scheme of education, and a body of educators; a steady devotion to increase knowledge, to make it universal, and to make it fruitful and useful, to knit it up with the life of society, and with our noblest feeling—to consecrate and sanctify and beautify science, as

Comte said,—Religion implies a home training, and a public training, a public commemorating of work, and merit, and public service, and the strengthening and purification of public opinion, quite as much as any congregational act. Finally, our religion implies a rigorous exercise of the duties of citizenship, a devotion to the social wants of our time, a regeneration of the relations of the weak and the strong, the poor and the rich, the managers of the capital of the community and the manual creators of that capital.

Religion as we understand it is the guide to human *duty*—human duty, individual as much as social—a guide at once, theoretical, practical, and emotional. But in any case, for the full conception of religion we need to look on man as a responsible moral being, and as a member of a family, as a citizen, as a child of Humanity. And, again, we must regard him as equally made up of *thoughts*, *feelings*, and *energies*.

In a word, Positivism will do nothing, unless from its very beginning in its humblest germ it can keep its eye fixed on the *synthesis*, the harmony of human *nature as a whole*, and if it will unceasingly tend to make that harmony *complete* instead of partial, universal, not local or sectional. Again, if we take the third great side of human nature, that of work and life, the practical side, that again is not only very complex and many-sided, but also very urgent indeed. Nay, the general state of society may become urgent in a sense that nothing else is, and may engross our immediate efforts, under pain of sacrificing everything if we neglect it. It is quite possible for a time to go on with next to no philosophic doctrine at all, or a very imperfect doctrine. It is possible to suspend anything that can be called moral education, or worship, or satisfaction of the emotions. But there are times, as of revolution, war, anarchy, famine, and the like, when the material existence of a particular society must be guaranteed at once, or it may cease to be ever capable of existence again. Here we must act, and such political and social crises are continually surrounding us.

In this age, in the unstable condition of political equilibrium and in the absence of any accepted political system, we are continually confronted by the risk of being plunged in political disasters and crimes, or else of finding the material comfort of the masses of our fellow-citizens cruelly cut into by the selfish schemes of powerful and rich classes in the mere pursuit of gain or pride. Here again we must act, and that quickly, and it is here that at present Positivism is often able to act most distinctly and most usefully. On the social and practical side of life there is therefore abundant work for Positivism, and work of various kinds. There is the formation of public opinion on international questions, the direct intervention by appeals to opinion in political questions, the many economic problems, the battles of classes, of rich and poor, the claims and duties of capital, the needs and duties of labour, the theory of communism, socialism, co-operation, and political economy, schemes for the relief of distress, or the organisation of charity, of primary education, of the federation of trades, even of amendment of the social and economic Acts of Parliament, all those complicated questions of theory and of practice which occupy not only the Houses of Parliament, but the labours of Social Science Associations, Labour Congresses, of Trades Unions, and Chambers of Commerce. Now on all these matters Positivism has a great deal to say, and even something to do. Not, I need hardly guard myself by saying, that Positivism pretends to have any ready-made projects, or bills, or programmes in its pigeon-holes to answer all these difficult questions of fact, much less that individual Positivists are silly enough or vain enough to think that they have got any revelation on these topics, or have arrived at final truth.

No! simply this, that the coherent body of ideas we call Positivism contains certain social and political principles based on the study of history, human nature, and society which are directly capable of application to the practical problems of the age; and which it is one of the first and most pressing duties of Positivists to endeavour to apply to these problems as they arise. Hence no purpose whatever of Positivism is more important or more urgent than this—the practical formation of public opinion on political and social questions, the formation of a body of persons associated as a school or club, or party, so to act on public opinion and direct and vigorous appeals to statesmen and to the public to modify action on specific questions. Hence we must keep in view that if our action which has its local seat in this room be on one side of it the action of a *school*—a place of education, a lecture-room, and a class-room,—on another side of it it is the *action* of a religious community or Church, meeting to raise our moral and emotional instincts, to solemnise the acts of family and private life, to remind us that we stand as a body of fellow-believers trusting and helping each other, to recall to our minds the great examples of human worth and power in the past, to remind those of us who are parents of the duty we owe to our children, those who are children of the duty they owe to their parents, all of us of the duty we owe to our households, our neighbours, and our country, so, on the *third side*, the action of our body in this form will be the action of a *Club* of citizens—a standing committee we may say of social reformers who watch for every opportunity to develop their political and social principles, and to bring them practically to bear on the public and on the government.

Let us not imagine, therefore, that this place is merely intended as a lecture-room, or on the other hand merely as a Chapel, or again, merely intended to be a Club-room. It is indeed all of these together, all of them equally. We consider a wise and useful political Club to be as much a religious institution as a Chapel, and a really efficient School quite as much a social institute and quite as much a religious place as a club or a chapel. If we can conceive the aims of the *School*, the *Chapel*, and the *Club*, each in their best and highest spirit, combined in one doctrine and to one end, the doctrine being the laws of life and man, the end being the full cultivation of human existence on earth, then we shall get an idea of what our *ideal* (at any rate) has been in founding this place. Alas! it is but too obvious that our ideal will long remain to us but a dim Utopia in the distance!

School, *Chapel*, *Club* in one. For let us not forget how Comte has said Positivism consists of a Philosophy and of Polity, and these two can never be dissevered. Its business is at once to *generalise* our conceptions and to systematise our whole social life, whether practical or emotional.

And this implies a Doctrine, a Life, and a Worship —or, as he elsewhere puts it, Philosophy, Polity, Poetry—which find their place in School, Club, Chapel.

I will briefly indicate the general mode in which these objects will be carried out.

1. *School.*—Courses of lectures of general kind, mainly on leading principles of Philosophy, and of Sociology—especially (1) institutions of society (statics), (2) history and laws of progress (dynamics).

We hope to form in autumn special classes on cosmology, especially mathematics, astronomy, biology.

Positivist Library, formation of, under the care of Dr. Kaines.

2. *Club.—Positivist Society* (President: Professor Beesly), will meet once in each month. There is great importance of this in Paris.

3. *Chapel.*—Direct exposition of Humanity will form part, an essential part, and the formal celebration of Humanity will form part of the work—especially on the Festival of Humanity, January 1—but it will not be continuous, or by any means the exclusive means by which we shall seek to impress on our minds the meaning of Humanity. We leave it to the theologians to *know* God by concentrating their minds on the abstract idea of Creator, and to *serve* God by falling on their knees and repeating formal

invocations. We do not doubt that there is great value to many minds, in some degree to all minds, in such efforts at due seasons and in spontaneous ways, but we think there is no way to know Humanity except by knowing the laws of Nature and of Man, of the Earth and of Society; and this knowledge is always and everywhere a thing of prolonged effort and study and thought. Nor do we know any way of serving Humanity except by doing our duty as men and women, parents, friends, neighbours, citizens; and that is a service that comes only by patient reflection, practical experience, and much converse with the world and with men. For this reason our formal celebration of Humanity will not be continuous or exclusive. Direct commemoration of great types will take their due place. From time to time those solemn consecrations of private life to public duty (that Comte called sacraments) will (as the other day) remind us that our whole life may be made one act of religion in its ordinary uses as much as in its ecstatic moments. But we shall not consider that Religion (as we understand it) is excluded from this place, because we fail, with our present numbers and resources and imperfect training, to hold throughout the year any continuous series of weekly Sunday services or addresses which may be called sermons.

For the present our work will be to a great extent to make more familiar and to commemorate those great types of human beauty, work, and power, the great men whom Comte has grouped in the Calendar. Thereby we shall be dealing with history, the institutions of society, and the concrete and visible form which Humanity has taken on Earth.

Next Sunday will be the anniversary, 200 years after the death, of Calderon, the great dramatic poet of Catholicism, of Spain, of chivalrous society—a poet to whom it specially belongs to Positivism to do justice, so removed is he from the ordinary habits of our industrial, modern Protestant world: but whom Positivist thought will place amongst the most glorious spirits who have combined the types of a whole nation and an entire age.

I conclude with a few words to remind us of the period up to which we are now passing in the Positivist Calendar, and the type of human greatness which we now recall for our instruction. In the Positivist Calendar we yesterday entered on the month of St. Paul, a name to be mentioned by every Positivist with the profoundest veneration and love—one who of all the great names which head the months in that Calendar is that one in which the intellectual power of abstract thought, and the effective force of social sympathy have been the most marvellously balanced and combined—the great Apostle whom Positivists honour as no Christian ever yet honoured him, as no Church, Catholic or Protestant, ever honoured him; one whom, it must be said, Comte revealed and made known, for he places Paul not only above Peter and the Twelve, above evangelists and prophets, saints and apostles, but above Jesus; and not only above Peter and Jesus by virtue of his infinite goodness and richness of heart, but in the line with Aristotle and Descartes by virtue of his profound powers of fathoming the resources of human nature, and between the mighty Julius and the imperial Charles by virtue of his abiding influence over the history of the human race.

I have already endeavoured to show the grounds on which in our picture of religion Paul stands for the founder of the Catholic religion instead of Jesus. I will merely repeat that this ground is mainly the extreme uncertainty of the objective facts of the life of the son of the Carpenter of Nazareth, the extreme vagueness of his teaching, the mixture (at least in the historic records we have) of hallucination or even imposture with violent anarchism, but especially in this, that we have no reason to see that Jesus ever thought of his teaching as anything but a local protest against Pharisaical Judaism. It was the Apostle to the Gentiles who first conceived a religious appeal to the conscience of all men, bond or free, Jew or Gentile, who carried what we call the Gospel out of the narrow local limits of Judaism into the world of Humanity; who first shook himself free from Mosaism and Mosaic prejudices of race and nation, and historic covenants and formal rites, and outward symbols of religious community; who first conceived the idea of the brotherhood of mankind, of the moral bond which unites all mankind, of the possibility of uniting all classes, races, orders, and faiths by a potent moral force that should lie deeper than skin, or family, or tribe, or government, that depended only on the human nature and its kinship to the vast whole which peoples this planet; and finally, who saw as in a vision the regeneration of human life and of human society on the basis of conscience, who conceived of a Church resting on moral authority, not on tables of stone, not on the choice of Caesar, or the suffrage of the people—the man who said: "Now abideth Faith, Hope, Charity; but the greatest of these is Charity." What is this but the Positivist triad of forces. Order, Progress, Love ?—Order, the belief in real truth; Progress, the Hope of an infinite advance; Love, the motive force of an undying social affection ?

So near indeed to the Positive religious ideal does Paul come (when interpreted and illumined by the wonderful insight of Comte), so close to the moral and philosophic basis of Positivism does the transfigured apostle to the Gentiles seem to be, that for a moment one might almost ask ourselves (as in a dream) if the vision of Paul is not after all capable of being expanded and transfigured into a permanent creed for modern man. If our mind ever framed such a question it must be in a dream. We wake, and in cool reflection we see what a gulf there is between the transfigured Paul, seen relatively by the light of analogy, and the real Paul taken literally and in an absolute spirit. The literal Paul, writing to the Romans and the Corinthians, is separated from us by 1800 years whether of time or of moral progress. Between the actual Paul, the actual notions and sayings of the sailmaker of Tarsus, and us to-day, there stands all this :

1. The whole fabric of modern science and philosophy, the idea of natural law, the knowledge of physical and moral law, the logic of philosophy, Descartes, Bacon, Leibnitz, Newton, Hume, Diderot, Condorcet, Gall, Comte. Before this vast and mighty fabric of truth, the crude guesses of the mere pupil of Gamaliel are like the stray guesses of a child.

2. There stand the whole eighteen centuries of human history, and the progress of civilisation, the revolutions, and the laws of progress, and the vast realms of knowledge about man and human nature and society, which were all closed to him.

3. There stands the fact of our modern Society, its needs, and its forces, and the knowledge that

by political wisdom and science we can act on it. Paul, in his vision of a moral and spiritual regeneration, could think of heaven and the life after death ; but the State in which he lived, and the life here on earth, he could calmly hand over to Tiberius, and Claudius, to Caligula and Nero, to Pontius and Agrippa and Festus. We have come now to think of earth, not of heaven—of this life, not of Paradise. We see that the State is just as vital to human life as the Church—and we place Paul, the true founder of the Christian religion, between Julius Caesar and Charlemagne, the great chiefs of men, neither hiding nor adopting the hallucinations of Paul any more than we hide or adopt the vices of Julius and Charles. To us the great moral teacher who conceived the transformation of the human heart under the influence of Charity (or as we are now taught to say, under the influence of Love), or the majestic founder of the Empire in the West, or the immortal founder of social and moral science—all of these, in the relative spirit of Positivism, are of equal greatness and saintliness. It is of the very essence of the Positivist ideal to fuse science and devotion, philosophy and religion as two sides of one force, and hence there is a peculiar fitness, I think, in the fact that in this Hall, where everything on the walls around recalls to us human, not theological associations, we can still recall with enthusiastic love and honour, the great author of the Epistle to the Romans. This building, as you know, once belonged to the Royal Society, and served the purposes of purely human and physical science. The building to which it was once attached, was procured for that learned Society by the mighty physicist, Sir I. Newton. For twelve years he presided over the society in these very precincts. During the last century a considerable number of those whose names are inscribed in the Calendar as the benefactors of mankind in Science and in industry were gathered together hard by, and possibly some of them in this very room. It has been dedicated to Sir I. Newton, the greatest of those who are associated with this site, for we wished to remind those who come amongst us that the religion of Humanity is unalterably based on physical science, that the laws of this cosmos in fact constitute a most essential part of religion, are the first clauses of its creed. The Heavens, says Comte, declare the glory of Kepler, Galileo, and Newton, who first revealed the laws of the celestial movements. And yet in a building purposely dedicated in a special manner to the memory of the mighty physicist Newton, and designed to promote the exclusive service of Humanity, and the true knowledge of humanity, we begin by a formal acknowledgement of the transcendent debt that Humanity owes to St. Paul, the first reader of the heart, the true founder of the Church in spite of all that he did not see or care for, in spite of all that he cared for, and utterly mistook. Humanity forgives all, Humanity reveals all, Humanity unites all.

For we have many members in one body, and all members have not the same office;

So we, being many, are one body in Humanity, and every one members one of another.

Having then gifts differing according to the grace that is given to us, whether prophecy, let us prophesy according to the proportion of faith;

Or ministry, let us wait on our ministering; or he that teacheth, on teaching;

Or he that exhorteth, on exhortation: he that giveth, let him do it with simplicity; he that ruleth, with diligence; he that sheweth mercy, with cheerfulness.

Let love be without dissimulation. Abhor that which is evil; cleave to that which is good.

Be kindly affectioned one to another with brotherly love; in honour preferring one another;

Not slothful in business; fervent in spirit; serving Humanity.

(*June* 1881)

MEDIAEVAL CHIVALRY

Amidst the manifold discussions about Religion which distinguish this age of ours, I wonder that we so often talk of Religion as if it were simply a matter of intellectual problems and subjective hopes—the system of the Universe and the like; the sorrows and the aspirations of the Soul; the creation of man.

About these things men will discuss for ever; and each mind will find its favourite answer. It seems to be forgotten that the ultimate, main, daily business of every religion or philosophy is to improve daily life, to act on the practical work of the toiling masses, to have a social result.

When any scheme of thought or life presents itself to us the question to put before it is this: What has it to say to the industrial world of to-day?

Tried by this test, how strangely empty appear some of the most popular forms of what is called Religion.

Take the vaguer forms of Deism or of Theism —do they answer this question ?

They may satisfy some speculative minds— but what have they to say to the social question ?

Turn to Pantheism—the contemplation of the beauties and glories of the Universe—the poetry of Nature. This may gratify the finer intellects.

But how does it act on life, on industry, on the social system ? On the sins of the great cities, the want, the cruelty, and the arid wilderness of labour ?

What is the relation between this and a sense of pleasure as we watch a sunset, a starry night, a comet ?

To turn to Christianity—to Catholicism— what has it to say to the industrial problems and the state of work, capital, labour ?

Test Protestantism—it has even less to say, it has done much to deepen the bitterness of industrial struggle : it even played into the hands of the most anti-social plutonomy. Look to Ireland, to Protestantism there, or even to official Catholicism. All theological schools, by their nature, are unable to transform practical life. This is like singing hymns or poems to a tornado or an epidemic.

Positivism is an attempt to resort to some motive power which shall directly affect practical life. It takes the crucial step of looking for that motive power in Earth, not in Heaven—in Man, not in God—in the visible working life of men and women, not in poetic visions of an infinite and incomprehensive Universe. The key to practical life is *here*. Hence it is that whilst Religion with all the theological and metaphysical schools means simply a key to certain questions, certain attitudes of worship, devotion, Human religion means all this, but also it means Art, Philosophy, Science, Government, Poetry, Industry, Progress—moral, social, even material concerns. All these are essential parts of Religion; they are all equally cultivated, and all are idealised and commemorated in the Calendar.

During the few weeks passed, the Calendar has given us the Christian and Catholic types: St. Paul, Hildebrand, St. Bernard. Positivism is not, like modern Atheism, afraid of Catholicism. Atheism trembles before Catholicism — like Mephistopheles before the Cross.

Positivism, neither adopting nor denouncing Christianity, recognises the moral and social beauty of Christianity, accepts the fact that it deeply coloured the life of Humanity. On the whole, its glorious mission abides and the future must be worked out by the help of that fact.

But Christianity is only one of the many influences which have acted on the development of Humanity. Even in the Middle Ages it was only one side: the spirit of Feudalism was quite as important and quite as noble.

One of the most original of all the discoveries of Comte was to show the essentially double character of the Middle Ages—the contrast between Chivalry and Church—and the superior moral value and beauty of Chivalry and the greater results achieved by Feudalism. Can one fairly contemplate the world in which we live, and yet believe that the existing religious forces are strong enough to deal with it? Are the Churches or the Chapels, the Spiritualisms, the Pantheisms, or the Atheisms able to transform that vast world of modern Industrialism in which we are to-day?

Taken absolutely by itself, Feudalism is utterly imperfect. Relatively, it was an advance, on what went before it, as great as any in human history.

Great results of *Feudalism* are: (*a*) Change of war to Defence; (*b*) Substitution of free labour for slavery; (*c*) Social development of Woman.

1. Change from war of conquest to defence, protection, settlement, an "armed" peace. Feudalism was the defensive organisation of society, it gave a stimulus to the moral value of warlike duty when it was defensive only.

2. Extension of civic spirit to country instead

of city—a local defensive organisation. Substituted the idea of Nation for City.

3. Substitution of social duty for exclusive Patriotism. (Personal attachment, faith, honour.)

4. Development of home life and consequent raising of the position of woman; moral dignity and intellectual eminence of the women of Feudalism. It idealised courtesy, veneration of woman, and Love. Art, Troubadours, Romance.

5. Education within the family, and for the young under the immediate superintendence of women.

5a. Domestic service—exclusion of slavery, noble servitors, training, idealisation of domestic duty.

6. Intervention of women in politics, in war, government, art, pleasure, and knowledge. The types are Geneviève, Héloise, Beatrice, Jeanne d'Arc, Queen Blanche, Isabella of Castille.

7. Extinction of slavery, modification of serfage, gradual relation of lord, tenant, master, and apprentice, passing into distinction of employer and employed.

8. Organisation of all kinds of industry from point of view of *social function*, arrangement of crafts, guilds, unions, *discipline*, in which society had an interest; *organisation*, to effect results; *reciprocal duty*, of master and man, of lord and tenant, tenant and serf, knight and burgher.

9. Institution of Chivalry, in idea very noble

—spirit of protection, devotion of life to a social idea, that social idea being humanity in its widest general sense.

10. Establishment of the great Social Maxim: Protection of weak by strong. Respect of weaker for the more powerful.

By Feudalism life was organised on the conception of reciprocal duty. But this only in type, in essence. All great systems and institutions are to be judged by their aim—their ideal and spirit. Turn to Spenser's Knight, to the Life of St. Louis, the Knight of Chaucer, the Life of Bayard. Read the last words of St. Louis as recorded by Joinville:

"Let thy heart be gentle and compassionate towards the poor, the unfortunate, and the afflicted, and comfort and help them so far as in thee lies. Maintain the good customs of thy kingdom and put down the bad. Be not covetous against thy people, and do not load thy conscience with imposts and taxes."

Read Chaucer's picture of the true Knight:

> A knight there was, and that a worthy man:
> That from the time that he first began
> To riden out, he lovede chivalry
> Trouth and honour, freedom and courtesy
> And tho' that he was worthy, he was wise,
> And of his port as meek as is a mayde
> He never yet no vilonye he sayde
> In all his life, unto no manner wight,
> He was a very perfect gentil knight.

This could not be said of Scipio or Themistocles. Combination of personal self-devotion to human duty, honour, truth, courtesy, gentleness, and social simplicity.

It could hardly be said of any ancient, even of Pericles or Marcus Aurelius. Even these noble spirits have not the feminine traits of the true knight, the visible purification by the influence of woman's heart and moral delicacy.

Even in the sixteenth century we have this type in Bayard, as told by his faithful henchman.

In all of these, especially in St. Louis, we see the great superiority of Feudalism to Church. They are all better than their creed.

For this the Calendar collects types of great leaders of chivalry—under Charlemagne—Alfred, Godfrey, St. Louis, extending from sixth to seventeenth century, but principally from A.D. 1000 to 1300.

Defensive War. — Crusades, Patriotism — the earliest opponents of Saracens to the latest opponents of Turks in seventeenth; Godfrey, Tancred, The Cid, Richard, and Saladin.

The Mendicant friars, Joan of Arc, Bayard, Walter Raleigh. Patriotism, adventure, honour, courage, self-devotion, courtesy, under a peculiar inspiration of social duty.

Hence Chivalry is peculiarly a spirit which Positivism seizes, appropriates, and seeks to develop.

The central idea of Theocracies was *Order*; of Antiquity, *Patriotism*; of the Church, *Moral purity*; of Feudalism, *Honour*; of Industrialism, *Progress*; of the Revolution, *Freedom*; of the Future, *Social duty*.

Note how close is the relation of Honour to Social Duty.

Of all the sides of Feudalism that one which is perhaps its final outcome (defence was its basis), is a provisional organisation of Industry, *i.e.* idea of making daily work a social duty, a social function, part of a regimented scheme.

There was a reciprocal duty of king to people, of people to king, of lord to tenant, knight to squire and to tenant, of tenant to sub-tenant, and so on to serf. Also of master and apprentice, of master tradesmen to working tradesmen—of guild to guild, of craft to craft. There was pride in work, duty to the soil, and again the religious value of Art.

A sense of superiority of social to personal aim ran through the whole field of industry. It is quite true that the exact forms were hopelessly narrow—failed, and left the memory of frightful abuse. It is no more true that the evil memories of Feudalism should blind us to the beauties and services of Feudalism than that the evil memories of Catholicism should do the same.

Catholicism and Feudalism, amidst much that is very black, have left noble traces on the history of Humanity, and it is the very strength and wisdom of Positivism which alone amongst the revolutionary movements proclaims the incalculable services of both, and seeks to recall all that is good and permanent in both.

It is true that Feudalism utterly failed, broke down in horrible tyranny, and it was followed by Industrialism.

Industrialism gave the world freedom, with a vast expansion of material prosperity and productive energy. But anarchy, self-help, individual selfishness was proclaimed as a gospel. Industrialism gave the world a new group of resources. It stimulated thought. It laid the foundations of science. It has added to the force of Humanity, and has made it possible (at last) for Humanity to constitute itself, and know itself, to feel at home on this planet, and to feel at last master of all the resources of this earth.

It is not too much to say that but for Industrialism, Humanity, in all its vastness, unity, might, and future, would not be to-day a possible conception.

By Industrialism I mean the unrestrained energy of human nature to wring from the earth by labour the greatest possible amount of her material fruits: in other words the free pursuit of Wealth as an end in itself.

And yet—if Humanity owes much to Industrialism in the way of freedom, in the way of resource, what a burden has not Industrialism laid on Humanity.

Industry exerted in a sordid selfish spirit leads to widespread social degradation. It became a search after wealth and material products in utter disregard of the producers and even of the very society that is to consume. The erection of this greed into a sham philosophical gospel of selfishness (called Political Economy) which teaches men that their duty to society is to be selfish, greedy, unsympathetic, to believe mankind uniformly actuated by low material objects, and society to exist for a low material object.

Feudalism and Catholicism (even when they most exaggerated their doctrines of class superiority and the curse of labour) had never contained anything so inhuman, so crazy, so corrupting as this gospel of every man doing the best for himself and accumulating the greatest amount of product.

Slavery and caste themselves, those two scandals of the ancient world, had contained social and sympathetic elements better than this peculiar form of official selfishness, which Protestantism and Protestant constitutionalism especially took under their protection.

And then followed the degradation of beauty, charm, health, repose, and spontaneity in life: the monotony and vulgarity of human existence in those countries and places which Industrialism has seized as its own, crushing man and blasting the face of nature, herding men in vast work-houses that they call cities, stunting the race and afflicting it with a new tribe of physical diseases, unsexing the life of women, and grinding the first years of childhood, and stirring up our politicians to wild raids upon the East and the South, till we become hordes of financial and mercantile buccaneers. Lastly, there lies against modern Industry the peculiar atrocity of reviving in a barbarous form the slavery of the black races: a crime which is far from extinct, and is hardly now kept within bounds under the pressure of the thirst for wealth.

What has been the result? Enormous accumulation of capital going on, whilst the creators of this capital are getting poorer and more hardly tasked. Incredible multiplication of useful things, at cheaper prices, whilst all the while the life of the masses who are to benefit by them gets as a whole more hard, less human. The unwieldy extension of unhealthy cities covering whole provinces, so that large tracts of this country seem one endless, sordid, noisome factory yard. The growth of frightful epidemic and contagious and infectious diseases, wasting and stunting the population, so that 100,000 deaths each year, are due to anti-social neglect, and anti-social selfishness—for the poor live without pure water, and pure air, and in unhealthy homes, and with little of art, amusement, refinement, rest, and social intercourse possible to them (1881).

Here, as we approach the twentieth century, in this England in its glory, there are some millions of actual paupers, hardly differing in life from prisoners, some millions of men and women and children dragging out a life of almost intolerable labour with barely enough to keep them in their untended homes; whilst almost the entire working population are housed like troops under canvas in rooms utterly inadequate for the full growth of human powers, physically, morally, and intellectually. Whilst, when we turn to Ireland, we have a population more squalidly wretched than anything to be seen in Europe, as bad as the lowest types of rudimentary civilisation in primitive savages, worse than anything in the Middle Ages.

Industrialism is ever making gigantic steps towards new triumphs of material progress, and yet under it Humanity does not materially advance.

It is preposterous to ask us to believe that this can be right and lasting, that this is the appointed destiny of mankind. And when any Religion claims our assent in virtue of its beautiful sentiment, or its profound mysteries, or its splendid history let us say to it, short and sharp, "What do you propose to do with the portent of modern poverty, the suffering, the hopelessness, the degradation of the vast labouring mass ?" And if it has nothing to say, let us turn aside.

And if it has only to say, " We offer spiritual hopes to self, and we ask it to turn away from material cares," then we may know that it is little better than hypocrisy, and that it is hoping to cast out the devil of practical selfishness, by means of the devil of spiritual selfishness—to ask men to help their neighbours on earth by helping themselves to Heaven.

All forms of selfishness are utterly bad and worthless. Selfish oppression will never yield to selfish dreams.

And all Theology (refine it as we will), Protestantism, Catholicism, Deism, Theism, Pantheism, even Atheism are at bottom (with all the beauty, sublimity, passion that some of them are capable of), they are all selfish. For they concentrate all the attention on the individual man's own soul, or man's own intellect, and his superterrestrial life and his personal hopes, or on his personal pride and defiance. So, the Atheist's Superman.

They are all necessarily and essentially selfish —that is, anti-social—because they draw off man's mind and hope from Humanity.

There is only one way by which the social sympathies can be disciplined, hallowed, and stirred up to take permanent command of our nature, and that is by systematically holding out to them, as the basis and end of human life, Humanity — the duty of the individual to Humanity.

The heart, the brain, the energy can be stimulated perhaps by forms of Theology. The love of God gave us the *Imitation of Christ.* Take the sermons of Bernard, of Fénelon, the *Christian Year* of Keble. Pantheism gave us Wordsworth and Shelley. Atheism has done grand things in Science.

But in face of the horrors of modern anarchy in labour, the unbridled lust of wealth, the tremendous power of selfish capital, the mountain of human suffering and misery which cries out aloud, " How long, O Man, how long," a mass of appalling want and pity—in face of that nothing can chain up this fierce power, but the sense of social duty to a visible Humanity of which we are each children and servants.

Observe ! the evils of this terrible modern Industrialism are not due to exceptional or conscious vice and wickedness. But to mere anarchy, and vicious principles and ideals.

The very masters for whom these millions toil and groan believe (they are told—they are told from the pulpit, as they sit in their cushioned pews) that they are benefactors of the race.

The very men for whom agents and bailiffs wring pence and sixpences from the half-naked men and women who herd in Irish hovels, are amongst our most respected M.P.'s and Lords; they take the chair at Charity dinners, and fondly believe they are the mainstay of modern society.

No one pretends that the individual men are vicious, only that the system is vicious, rather there is no system. The evils have been growing for centuries, and now have grown with furious rapidity during 100 years. Every fresh triumph of Industrialism has had its battle-fields strewn with crushed and dying humanity as the destroying path of a conquering army.

Just as, in spite of its wealth, and civilisation, and government, and law, and culture, and poetry, and art, and force in peace and in war, the Roman Empire was heaving with some want till Christianity came to stem the torrent of immoral lawlessness in public and private life, and men like Paul, Augustin, Ambrose, and Gregory, found in the vision of the all-seeing eye, the spotless spirit of God to whom all things were pure—the one hope amidst this vast welter of uncleanness and lawlessness—so now thoughtful spirits will begin to doubt if any agency can stem the torrent of industrial selfishness except the image of Humanity as the object of our social duty in practical things as well as in speculative things.

Now here Positivism would revive the great feudal conceptions of the Feudal ages—that:

The daily work of each is—a system of reciprocal duty—in a scheme of distributed parts.

The practical life of each is a social function. Labour is a social function.

In order to labour to good result the parts must be distributed.

Industry must be reconstituted, that is, a proper distribution of leaders and followers.

The ownership of capital is always and everywhere a social function.

Every capitalist, every labourer, has his duty, his part to the community.

The essence of healthy co-operation is good faith, fulfilment of social duty, and reliance of man on man.

This good faith, bond of each to each, takes two forms.

1. The powerful must protect the weaker.
2. The less able must respect the more able.

The leaders, therefore, as possessors of capital, owe to their workers, protection. Nor has this protection any limit beyond the general claims of the community, and the future of man. The true recompense for this self-denial is not the vulgar stimulus of wealth, but the moral stimulus of public respect and honour for the fulfilment of a great social and human duty.

The local and permanent home of the labourer must be secured to him, just as the tenant had a right to have occupation of his holding.

Again, it is the business of the capitalist leader to protect his workmen against the unexpected consequences of external distress, just as much as it was of the Lord to protect his barons or his fief from foreign marauders.

If the capitalist cannot extend the same minute supervision to his workmen as the general does to his soldiers, he is not relieved from the general responsibility of being in spirit called on to see to their welfare.

Such are the general *principles* with which Positivism would deal with modern Industry.

Institutions

1. To make it a central part of Religion itself that the holding of all wealth is a social function —that it has no right, but a duty, involving continual self-denial and anxiety, just as much as office and government does.

2. To have a body of men continually enforcing this by theory and in practice, in general and in detail. To arrange society on this basis.

3. To teach the whole community that capital is only entrusted to the wealthy by the community, for the purpose of fulfilling the duties of wealth.

4. That the first of these duties is the reasonable satisfaction of the wants of the producers of wealth.

5. That this reasonable satisfaction includes all that is necessary for the free, moral, and mental development of the citizen and his family.

5*a*. Limitation of population by mutual consent of parents.

6. That the first basis of such development is the possession in property by the labourer, whether in town or country, of his own home, residence.

7. That it is the duty of the capitalist to take care that people employed have property in their houses.

8. That a portion of the wages should be fixed and not dependent on varying profits.

9. That another portion should be a real participation in profits.

10. That the capitalists must collectively provide against over production, or any change in production or machinery, which might cause wide distress in the employed.

11. That the State should itself provide certain large industrial centres, as types, thus to supply the wants of those who are from time to time out of employment.

12. That rich men (knights) should aid with money, etc., in case of legitimate strikes, etc., which they judge to be just.

12*a*. Abolition of women's labour, restriction on men's.

13. Great reduction of hours of labour to

seven with frequent holidays and Saturday rest.

14. Completed by gratuitous public education, the free access to art, architecture, music, painting, drama, as at Athens, and cities of Middle Ages.

Picture of Labour in the Future

Workmen, relieved from excessive labour, wives and daughters set free, education etc., free, having control of political forces, would have opportunity to devote themselves to culture and to civic life.

Organised Socialism and Communism would be satisfied because all the ends of both would be attained without (1) The revolutionary disturbance of violent socialism (*liquidation sociale*); (2) oppressive and grinding force of official socialism. Positivism is a *moral* socialism, the socialism of free opinion. To this in the end will come:

1. The Retrogrades, finding it impossible to continue the battle of egoism.

2. The anarchists, weary of a contest which leads to no results and has no future.

It may be said, it is a Utopian picture and an impossible vision, how is it to be done?

How? easily enough. If all the efforts that men of commanding energy, and consummate practical sagacity now make to pile up useless heaps of money which their ill-taught children waste in folly, if all the patience, and the self-denial, and the genius of the financiers and the traders, and the manufacturers, now bent on ruining each other, on convulsing markets, and scrambling into a good thing over the disasters of their neighbours, if all the forces of the State now used to coerce poor savages to open markets, if all this force were now directed to provide for the welfare of the workers, for the good of society —if the zeal and skill now given to piling up wealth were used as wisely and systematically in the using wealth, in the due distribution of it—the end would be attained.

Ah, but how? Certainly by no system of selfishness, by no appeal to self-help, by no vision of personal salvation, by no dreams about the loveliness of the Universe, or the beauty of the Universal Mind—by nothing personal, by nothing superterrestrial at all, by no Theology, no Metaphysics, no Pantheisms.

No! this end can be attained by one thing —*a real religion*—a religion of unselfishness, a human religion—by again filling mankind, society, men's and women's hearts from birth to death with the idea of overwhelming and concentrated duty to a Providence to which they owe everything, and by which alone they can do anything, and that a Providence here, visible on earth, the great human family of which each of us is a child, to which we belong by our wives, and our children, our fathers and our mothers, our brothers and our sisters, our friends, and every high and pure sentiment of our souls day by day.

(*January* 1, 1882)

FIRST ANNUAL ADDRESS

For the first time we meet on New Year's Day in a home of our own. Gradually, we trust, this room will be the familiar seat of our union and our work. We do not seek to make it especially a chapel, though it has long been used as a chapel. It is quite as much a school, or even a club room, as it is chapel. Positivism is a system of Action, and a system of Thought, as much as it is a system of Devotion. Its characteristic feature is to combine these three in one mode of real life, under the inspiration of our common Humanity. We do not enter here into rivalry with the worship of any theology; we shall imitate none, as we shall attack none.

And as we have taken this simple but not ignoble building as we found it, so we shall make no pretence to present in it any complete system of worship. We certainly believe that Humanity has not outgrown the need of Worship; nor will be unable in the future to evolve all sufficient expression of the devotional spirit. Worship is no doubt the centre of every religion, and in a normal state the familiar worship precedes intellectual training and external life. But it is not so in the early efforts of a movement, especially of one which rests on a vast system of demonstrated truths. Comte used no regular system of public worship. His successor has devised none. Neither do we presume to bind the future and to anticipate the wants of those who will have the numbers and the power to found an adequate system of cult.

Worship after all is the outward and spontaneous expression of solid convictions. Where these are, worship is. Every time that a dominant belief touches our hearts with reverence and love, and issues in visible deed in life, an act of worship is the result. The worship of an educated, happy, and industrious people in the future will be their life itself and every act of life. It will not be limited to formal words, or outward observance. Much less will it consist of the exclamations and the invocations which sound to us so idle in church and chapel. Let us not narrow down one great side of human life to any vain imitation of a transient phase of the human imagination. The ejaculations of the Christian services are as little suited to the worship of the future as the sacrifices of bulls and kids. In this place we intend neither to chant invocations nor to offer incense. We have far more before us than we can do, whilst we try, however imperfectly, to make clear to ourselves and to others the foundations of our faith and practice.

The place in which for the first time we commemorate Humanity has peculiar associations for us. It belonged to that ancient building (but recently destroyed by fire) which Sir Isaac Newton obtained for the Royal Society; and where, surrounded by the profoundest minds of his age, the mighty founder of systematic physics so often taught, and studied, and discussed. This very room, they say, at some time during the last century contained the Museum of the Royal Society, the nucleus of the actual British Museum. And if these very walls have not contained them all, certain it is that the spot, the building of which for a century it formed a part, has been sanctified for us by the presence of some of the greatest benefactors of the human race, by many of those philosophers and men of science whom the Positivist Calendar recalls. We cherish these associations whilst we would not overrate them. We, to whom everything is yet to be done, are glad to be able by however slight a touch to hold on to traditions of the past. And by the name which we have given to this hall we would impress on those who enter it how completely all that is good in the future must rest for its basis on Science—Science in its noblest and fullest meaning, the Science of Nature first, of Society next, of the Human Soul at last.

It would indeed be an evil day for Positivism if ever it fancied it could dispense with Science, in its most solid, earnest, and most exact form—with daily converse with Science, and a lively eagerness to assimilate all that Science from day to day discovers and teaches. If Positivists ever came to think that the mighty roll of discovery is closed, that the potent synthesis of the sciences, which was the main work of Auguste Comte as a philosopher, had given them some royal road to scientific knowledge, or had put them as *illuminati* above the need of Science—muttering in their hearts, as did the Emperor of old, *Sancti sumus et supra scientiam*—if Positivists ever came to think that religion or worship can give them dispensations or indulgences to exempt them from the duty of hard, patient, humble efforts to acquire a solid scientific training—when the right use of these very things *is* religion, *is* worship—they would end like any of the short-lived emotional sects which start up out of the ruins of theology in England and America, they would straightway pass through quietism into charlatanry. There is no help for it. Once lose touch of the real, and any self-delusion is easy. They who think they know more than their neighbours, without taking the trouble to study what their neighbours know, are on the high road to set themselves up as impostors. And it is in full consciousness of this that the first week-day schemes of work that we propose to attempt are systematic and practical courses in mathematics and physics.

It has been to us all a singular satisfaction that this hall was opened by our beloved chief himself. The first words spoken in it in public came from the lips of that eminent friend and disciple of Auguste Comte, who for twenty-four years in good report and in evil report, in neglect and in popularity, has carried on the work of Comte with a spirit so devoted and a force so impressive. Few of us know with what difficulties and opposition he had once to contend, how unflinching his ardour, how fixed his faith in our great inheritance; with what energy he has grasped one problem of philosophy and science after another, how gentle, chivalrous, humane a nature he has shown. It is easy now to see his worth. He is a public power now. Crowds flock to his teaching. Journals claim his opinions for their party. Some of the influential members of the present Government of France have long been careful students of his words. His school has made itself felt as an influence at last in the intellectual, social, and political atmosphere of Paris. But he is the same now in his success that he was in the heat and burden of the day, when twenty years ago he met in the dwelling of our venerated master, and with a few devoted friends taught week by week the priceless thoughts of the great philosopher.

From him we have heard in set discourses, in brilliant talk, by practical example, how rational religion must rest on a rational education, and how the basis of all rational education is a thorough grounding in Science. The principle, Affection—yes! but the foundation is Order—that is the order of things revealed to us by Science. It is this which marks off the Positive belief from all forms of theological and metaphysical faith. The Shakers, or the Salvation Army, can all say with every Christian congregation and Church, that their principle is Love and their end is Progress, but they cannot say in any intelligible sense that their foundation is Science, and the immutable reign of Law as manifest in Science. That is our ground alone amongst all the religions of the world. Let us never forget or impair it.

On the other hand, though the whole Positivist fabric rests on a comprehensive system of training in Science, we are not slack to claim for it the character of a real religion. Now by religion we do not refer to supernatural creation any more than by worship we mean ejaculations to a power which cannot truly hear us. By religion we mean the sense of an abiding Providence over our lives, the desire to control our natures and to join with our fellowship in serving in our places to that great end. And all this graven on the habit of our daily life by a system of teaching to inculcate it, and a system of expression to clothe it with emotion. This is religion, if anything be religion. And this is what we mean; or at least what we aim at realising. If we think that the forms of expression may wait for a time, we do not think that religion can wait or the observances of religion. We are not slack either here or in Paris to resort to those outward aids to belief which in all ages have had a religious character. We have hardly met in this hall in public on twenty occasions, and yet three of these occasions have been for that outward profession of faith, which with us take the place of the Catholic sacraments. Within a few months we have celebrated in this hall those formal acts of communion—the Presentation of the infant by its parents, the Admission of the young to the rank of citizen, the Destination of the man to his public profession in life,—two of these here given by M. Laffitte in person and one by deputy. We have also in this place commemorated the second centenary of the immortal poet of Spain, the great Calderon, whilst the same thing was being done in Paris, in Madrid, and in South America. And we have just endeavoured, on the Day of the Dead, ere the whirl of another year begins, to recall our thoughts to the memory of those who formed our common Humanity.

In France, M. Laffitte has on many occasions during the past year celebrated these simple yet solemn acts, by which we seek to connect our private life with the life of the community and the race to which we belong. Death has fallen heavily on our friends in France this year, but the cheering consolations of Humanity have been duly heard around the open grave. Can any man doubt if this is a religion? Day by day, and year by year we meet in private and in public to offer our expressions of reverence, to assert our desire towards a worthier life. Week by week we meet to deepen our convictions and warm our energies. Our children are in public brought to be dedicated to a useful life. At the opening and the close of their education this solemn profession is renewed. A man who takes up a profession receives its duties in the face of his fellows, as a priest receives his orders, as a king receives his crown. At death we consign the loved remains to the grave with words of real hopes and solemn resignation. And continually we commemorate in turn the great saints and martyrs of Man, and the paramount Humanity into which their lives are incorporate at last.

If this is not religion—if the inexhaustible

conception of Humanity has not already produced even in a few scattered seekers after light, as we are, the reality of a living religion—the matter becomes a mere dispute of words. We know and feel that we have something by which to live and to die. Nor are we careful to answer those feeble souls who murmur that religion is a matter of God and of Heaven, or those feebler souls, on the other hand, who can see no religion where there are no hymns, no genuflexions, and no priests.

Sometimes I wonder if candid and thoughtful men fully realise to themselves how unparalleled a phenomenon is this growing influence of Auguste Comte. His teaching has been before the world about thirty years (1882). He has been dead twenty-five years. His writings are extraordinarily difficult to master; and they range over every known science, and every side of philosophy, politics, and life. Yet what is it that we see? We see this. The rooms where he lived are kept undisturbed as a pious duty. The legacies given by his will (he left no estate whatever) are by his followers paid to this day. Year by year a crowd of men from Paris, France, and other parts of Europe gather round his tomb, and commemorate his life and death. In many parts of France, in many cities of England, in Scotland, in Ireland, in many parts of Europe, and in America North and South, organised groups of persons are associated to carry out his teaching. Two periodicals exist which both profess to expound his doctrines. In France and in England a scheme of teaching is in full activity whereby his thoughts and precepts are explained in a series of lectures, addresses, sermons, and services. This has been all growing, slowly and steadily making its way for a generation, and at this moment is far more vigorous, far more master of itself, and better understood by the public than at any time before.

This cannot be said of any other modern thinker. What philosopher of England, France, or Germany has organised schools of enthusiastic followers to explain or develop his ideas? Kant, Hegel, Fichte, Humboldt, Cousin, Hamilton have readers, but have they anything like this? Is there an organised propaganda of any of them? Of all modern philosophers, Bentham and Mill unquestionably come nearest to this influence of Comte. But Bentham and Mill in many ways run in the closest lines with Comte; and Mill was at one time his ardent disciple and follower. But is the philosophy of Bentham and Mill growing and broadening and leavening the world by a spontaneous action of associated bodies of students? Is there any hall like this devoted to the exposition of the ideas of Mill? Fine as was his character, and many as were his friends, is there an annual commemoration of his life as a paramount religious duty ? There is but one philosopher in all modern Europe who has left an organised movement in living contact with the life of our age.

In these days thirty years are an unusual period to count the steady and unbroken advance of any sort of religious idea. [Sixty years in 1918.] Most of them in England and America are nearly exhausted after thirty days of spiritual excitement. But the most careless can hardly treat this religious conception of Humanity as a case of spiritual excitement. We may remember that Mr. Mill, hostile as he became at last, spoke of it as majestic. He spoke of Comte as the equal, or rather the superior of Descartes and Leibnitz. The first scientific lectures of Comte were attended by Humboldt, Fournier, Broussais, Blainville, some of the first men of science of their age. The judgement on his philosophic capacity by Brewster, Mill, Littré, Lewes, Grote, and Molesworth may well outweigh the off-hand criticism of specialists in a moment of controversy. It would be childish even for the most irritable opponent to deny the high philosophic rank of Comte. His successor and disciple in Paris at this moment is perhaps one of the most widely and richly instructed of all the minds of France. A large proportion of those who follow him are men of scientific training whose lives have been given to special studies. Are they all men to sacrifice their lives for a merely grotesque fancy? Whence, I ask, is it that Comte alone amongst philosophers has created this profoundly religious enthusiasm, and alone amongst preachers of religion has rallied so many ardent minds that are passionately given to science? Is it not that he is the one modern thinker who has distinctly felt how Philosophy, Science, Duty, Life, Religion are but different phases of one great problem—aspects of one great Power, and that Power Humanity itself?

It would be well (I often think) if those who know Comte only through avowed criticism and the epigrams of current literature would try to know him in a fairer way, as his system is presented in practice. Do they see anything like a system of priestcraft here or in Paris? Do *we* live under the iron rule of a joyless asceticism, intoxicated with morality, as Mr. Mill so oddly puts it? Is there any mummery, any ritualism, any hysterical appeal to a phantom either here or in the Rue M. le Prince? Are *we* the enemies of freedom of mind, of life, of science, and the rest? Are even these sacraments of Auguste Comte's conception such idle imitations of a dead superstition? I read now and then that Positivism is "a relentless enemy of culture." Positivism is "Catholicism *minus* Christianity"; Positivists "reject science"; they would reduce society "to a Jesuit college"; they "banish learning, research, humour, wit, beauty"; they find a new "revelation" in the dreams of a Frenchman. And so forth, and so forth.

Do candid men see this here, do they find it in Paris? Is there anything like Catholicism, is there any Papacy, or tendency to a Papacy here? Are we such gloomy Puritans in daily life; is M. Laffitte impenetrable to humour, to wit, to joy of life—M. Laffitte, one of the brightest, wittiest, heartiest of the countrymen of Molière? Do the despisers of Science organise classes for the teaching of Science? Are we who from time to time address the public here such mental slaves, cast in one mechanical mould, repeating a few formulas?

I say to candid men—Look to what comes of the teaching of Comte in fact. Those who keep up his home, and execute his testament, who year by year assemble round his grave with new ardour and in larger numbers, M. Laffitte, M. Robinet, M. Magnin, who lived in the closest intimacy with him till his death, who for twenty-five years since his death have carried on all the institutions he founded, his course of teaching, and his social rites and observances—these are the men to whom we should turn to see what the system of Comte becomes in practice. In this hall we are in the closest alliance with these men. Do men find here this slavery, this mummery, this "obscurantism"? It would be better, if men desired to judge Positivism, to see what Positivists do in fact twenty-five years after the death of Comte, instead of constructing epigrams out of sentences in his books. It would be very easy for literary men in a critical vein to construct epigrams out of the Bible, or the Koran, or the Prayer Book, or the works of Bacon, Descartes, and Leibnitz. It would be easy to find passages to jest about in any one of these. The logical and rather prosaic acuteness of Mr. Mill would have found even more absurdities in these than he found in the sublime, poetic, and social visions of Comte. Better than literary epigrams would it be to see what in a generation after his death his school are doing here and in Paris, and especially his successor, pupil, and friend, Pierre Laffitte.

We are not "Comtists." We have nothing to do with "Comtism." We are not even "believers in Comte." We are Positivists, who hold by conviction to a body of Positive, demonstrated, and demonstrable truth which Auguste Comte had reduced to organic unity and provided with its head and heart. Comte is not to us in any sense that which Christ is to the Christians, or even Mahomet to Mussulmans, and Confucius to Chinamen. His writings are in no sense a Bible, a Koran, a Book of the Law. Comte is to us one of the greatest and maybe the latest, but only one of the great roll of mighty thinkers by whom man's knowledge has been reduced to principles and grouped in order. Whether his place will be beside Descartes and Aristotle, merely as thinker, the future will decide. But as moral teacher we think he has introduced a new life into the society of mankind, at least as original and potent as that of St. Paul, St. Augustine, or Buddha. His works stand as part of a great body of teaching which opens with Aristotle and comes down to modern Biology. Professor Beesly said last year on this Day that we are not to make a new Leviticus out of the *Polity* of Auguste Comte. I will add, Neither let us make it a new Gospel. Gospels and decalogues disappear with miraculous inspiration and divine revelations, just as infallible Heads of Churches disappear along with absolute Creeds. I yield to no one in veneration for the teaching of Comte; but he who teaches a demonstrable belief must always be ready to submit to the test of demonstration. And profoundly as I hold that the future will owe to Auguste Comte the ultimate religion of Humanity, I will not hesitate to say that whatever in his teachings or writings shall finally fail to convince the enlightened judgement of our descendants will disappear from the world as completely as the blunders of Aristotle in science and the hallucinations of Paul in theology.

This thought is particularly needed in England, and with English hearers. The forms and mental habits of Protestant Christianity are still familiar to the educated minds amongst us. When we first come to the religion of Humanity we are strongly inclined to think from inveterate theological prejudice that the essence of religion is summed up in prayer and in praise. The books wherein we may learn the truths of religion must (we fancy) be Scripture of some kind, and our Teacher himself (we are apt to suppose) must be a sacred, infallible being. Short of this, the careless opinion of the day does not quite see what religion can be. Let us be on our guard against this imitative spirit. Much of the difficulty which meets Comte in England is due to this. We have a natural tendency to Anglicise the abstract phrases of Comte's French instead of translating his ideas. And then we have a tendency to force the uncouth terms so formed into the ideas of Calvinist devotion. Of course the effect is odd. Positivism is no revival of Calvinism or Catholicism, no adaptation of Christianity in any form; it has not even issued out of either. The immediate precursor of Comte, as he has often told us, is Condorcet; Positivism is the issue of the Revolution, as our era in the Calendar (1789) for ever warns us. But we are as little Jacobins as we are Catholics. We accept some great traditions from both. But Positivism in its religious and social affinities goes much further back than the Revolution or the Church. Its field is the history of human religion in its entirety. It has sympathies with the great social and religious uses in the worship of many gods, and even with the primitive worship of nature. Comte is often reminding us that the fine era of theology as a social and humanising force is the era of many gods—not the era of one God. The Monotheism of the Middle Ages, and still more the Christianity of the modern Churches and of modern Protestantism, is a fragment, a survival, perhaps a corruption, of the great age of divine beings and divine interposition. If the personal morality of the future has to base itself largely on Catholic and Puritan traditions, the social and civic morality of the future will be coloured not a little by the noble ideals of antiquity. As to forms, we need borrow none—neither Catholic, Protestant, Pagan, or Jewish. Men will pour no libations in the future. We shall adore neither sun nor stars, seraphim nor cherubim. We shall chant no litanies; neither shall we wrestle with the Lord in spirit. All that is of the past.

This hall, as I said, serves us at once as chapel, as school, and as club; that is to say, for religious communion, for education, and for political action. I will speak of each of these sides of our movement in turn.

Three times during the past year this hall

has served for one of those public acts of profession whereby we seek to give dignity and solidity to private life by connecting its leading epochs with the social life in which we are bound up. Nothing could be fitter for the opening of this hall than the first simple rite which we joined in on the opening day, on the Presentation of an infant daughter of our secretary. As we listened to M. Laffitte's words of confidence and hope, we could feel almost as if our small and feeble body were, as that child is, beginning its life, with an unknown future before us, and our work to be decided for good and for evil by the spirit in which we shall determine our destiny. And so too, when on the Admission of a young man to the full responsibilities of citizenship we listened to M. Laffitte's memorable suggestions to a young man entering on active life, we might all feel, in some sort, how we are commencing a life of activity in which everything useful has still to be done. Lastly, on the Destination of Mr. Hall, who goes out as Consul to Japan, we recalled the ties which bind the man to the community, and the social functions from which no man can absolve or free himself. The Discourse has been printed and lies on the table [now in *Creed of a Layman*, 1907].

In the way of school, what we have attempted is this. Dr. Bridges has given us a course of lectures on Biology, the laws of life, the influence of the brain on the destinies of man. Mr. Lock has treated in full the scheme of Positive Education. We have now arranged to begin a systematic course of teaching in Science. A class is being formed by Mr. Harding to study the elements and early history of Geometry—a class will be opened later by Dr. Senier for the study of the elements of Physics and Chemistry. We hope to extend these classes in time to other sciences, so as to make it the nucleus of a regular system of positive education.

The Positive Library is now being collected and completed. We owe almost the whole of the works at present collected to the generosity and efforts of Dr. Kaines. We have said a good deal at times of the uses of that careful selection of books which was made by Auguste Comte. A short account of it will be published. The books now collected may be referred to, or borrowed on applying to the Librarian.

Everything here is perfectly free. The lectures, the classes, the use of the books are gratuitous. It is an essential part of our principles that all teaching should be free to all. But we accept help, as freely as we give what we offer, without condition and without form. I again remind all those who think that they gain anything in this room of the social duty that they owe to themselves, to us, and to the public to avow that debt and to acknowledge it in act.

Positivism being something more than a philosophy, and in no sense a mere human theology, is occupied directly with practical and political questions. We make politics, in fact, a substantive part of religion. One main use of religion is to breathe a true spirit into politics. The main cause of the selfish spirit which so largely reigns in political fields is the practical severance of political maxims from all religious duty. For that theology in its decrepitude is directly responsible. The claim made by politicians and political writers to treat politics on a basis of expediency or force apart from duty or creeds is at bottom simply a claim that might is independent of right. From time to time we seek to assert the grand political doctrine of Positivism, that politics must be controlled by morality. This was the spirit of the addresses that have been published (1) against the Coercion Acts for Ireland, (2) in favour of the cessation of the Transvaal War, (3) in favour of the reversal of our Opium policy in China, and (4) in condemnation of the Tunisian policy of the French Government. We have no reason to fear the appeal to events on any of these issues. The Coercion Acts have proved to be a blunder, producing little but irritation on the one side, desire for victory on the other, stimulating passion where the need was to calm.

I suppose that some reason will one day

be offered for the arrest of Mr. Parnell and his political supporters, other than the purpose of silencing determined political antagonists. Speaking for my own part, I have yet heard of none; and I see no ground for believing that any other exists. It is melancholy to see a statesman like Mr. Forster drawn on (as it was predicted to him he would be drawn on) into one of the most distinct breaches of word which can be charged against an English Minister. When he told the House of Commons that the object of the Bill was to enable him to arrest the village tyrants and the dissolute ruffians, he, no doubt, did not intend to use it for the arrest of political leaders whom a jury had acquitted in the public tribunals of their country. That is, however, literally what he has done.

But in condemning the Coercion policy of the Government we had no party feeling. We have eagerly welcomed the wise but difficult act of justice that it has carried out in the Transvaal, and the yet wiser and perhaps more difficult task of withdrawing from Afghanistan (1882). Both of these are gains so great and so significant that we are not over-curious in criticising the time and the mode in which they have been achieved, nor are we eager to point out the difficulties which are still left behind them. It is enough that the act is done, and Mr. Gladstone and Lord Hartington, Mr. Bright and Mr. Chamberlain deserve the gratitude of all good citizens. Of the three criminal wars we have lately waged in Africa, of the fourth we have lately waged in Asia, no one now remains. The temple of Janus is closed for us, and by a strange and almost unusual circumstance the Birth of Christ and the New Year have been celebrated in the British Empire without a war or an armed occupation. Neither black, nor yellow, nor brown, nor red skins, so far as I know (but one ought not to be too sure), are now being riddled with bullets in the name of the Queen. An event so unusual reminds us how much we owe to Mr. Gladstone.

In all these political questions of which I have spoken the result has justified the ground we took. Not only has it been borne out by events ; but it is now the ground of the larger and wiser part of public opinion. I do not rate overmuch the occasional utterances of a small group of men of so little account as ourselves. The world is a big place, and the governing classes of this country care little for the opinions of people who are neither in the House of Commons nor even in the Borough 500, who are very seldom seen on a platform, and who do not write in journals. But our opinion, if not a very loud one, has a certain quality of its own. It is (literally) without any boasting almost the only continuous criticism in this country which is perfectly free from party feeling. If we remonstrate with the Whigs it is out of no wish to help the Tories. And if we criticise Radicals, it is as Republicans ourselves that we speak.

Our opinion, such as it is, is the opinion of men who hold by a set of principles, which are more than political cries, which they have held for twenty years, principles which are to them the most sacred and vital of truths. I think I may add that it is known to be the opinion of men who, by the very condition of their union, can hope nothing and fear nothing from any statesman and any party, who will serve no party and accept nothing from any party. We are not irreconcilables. We do not, like the revolutionists of Paris, denounce Opportunism as a doctrine. When we vote as citizens, and when we take any practical part in politics, we are always open to compromise, and are ready to support a politician on general grounds. But in the mere field of opinion, in forming a judgement on affairs, complete freedom is necessary. Party spirit of all things most poisons the clearness of judgement and the unflinching temper of justice.

I read the other day a defence of our official policy on Opium by one of the most able and accomplished officials. I am not about to deal with his charges of weakness and insincerity on the part of the rulers of China. Be it so. But in this elaborate and able defence—the best that can be made, I suppose, of the Opium policy, there is no answer, no notice at all of the direct ground taken up in our Petition to the House of Commons against the Opium policy, viz. the English Government compels the Chinese Government by a standing threat of war to admit a certain odious poison at a fixed duty, on the sole ground that the poison brings in a large revenue. The temperance ground, the poison ground is a minor affair to us. Our main point is the gross international oppression. Imagine England attempting to force on France or Germany by threats of war a particular tariff for her cotton and her coal! How much more enormous would this be if the compulsory tariff related to ten millions worth of adulterated gin. But to make the parallel complete, we have to imagine that the British Government itself manufactured and adulterated the gin and kept it as a royal monopoly. Here is the ground of our protest, to which not the smallest real defence has ever been urged. We have only to suppose the proceeding in Europe, where after all justice is not yet absolutely triumphant, to see how vast is the gulf between Morality and Policy in our public dealings with the Far East, even under the rule of Mr. Gladstone, Lord Hartington, and Mr. Bright. Liberal newspapers, even the best of them, keep silence on all this. They suppress such appeals as ours. Their first business, and sometimes their last also, is to keep up Mr. Gladstone's majority.

On opposing the disastrous policy of the French Government in Tunis we were in thorough accord with public opinion at home, and perhaps we may fairly say with the mature opinion of France itself. Our French friends have exercised, we may hope, a real influence on public opinion. The appeal to the deputies by the Positivist Society of France signed by M. Magnin and M. Finance, two eminent working-class leaders in Paris, was worthy of them and of the cause. The energetic pamphlet of Dr. Robinet, if it was even more vigorous in its terms, was not more decided in its principle. I regret that the condemnation of the Tunis expedition was withheld for a time by the hesitation of some (and of M. Laffitte himself), who were willing to trust the assurances of M. St. Hilaire, and who were inclined to accept the statement that the expedition was an inevitable act of self-defence. But now that the condemnation of the policy is made, it is certainly ample and clear, and as it has been formally put out by the Positivist Society, the hesitation of some is a matter of little moment.

The successful advance of our French friends has been mournfully clouded this year by a series of blows from the hand of Death. I shall not pass over in silence the death of M. Littré, nor shall I make his work in relation to Positivism the occasion either of eulogy or of depreciation. The high position of M. Littré in the world of European letters (for I rank his *Dictionary* as perhaps the greatest literary achievement of this century), this vast reputation as a man of letters neither fascinates us nor imposes on us particularly. To us gigantic literary power is not altogether unlike gigantic wealth, or gigantic muscular power. It may go with moral meanness, or with intellectual shallowness, or both. Of M. Littré it is enough to say that his industry, knowledge, and fertility were very much greater than his philosophical force or his nobility of nature. As I see it, he really devoted his life to what he understood to be the best side of Comte's teaching, and the true meaning of Positivism. Grievously as I think he often misunderstood both, it is enough for me to claim him as one who has done the cause good service. I am quite unable to adopt, I regret in fact from what I can understand, the vehement hostility he inspired in the old friends of Comte. The grave, I think, should cover these discussions now. Let us leave it to the future, with hope, to determine the true services to Humanity of one who lived and died, as he avowed, a Positivist. The Great Revealer, Death, has shown us now, as it does so often with those we value most, how much the best and the truest gain in death, how little they are fully seen in life.

Of all the tasks that the religion of Humanity has to accomplish none is more important than its power to bring out the meaning and the uses of death. Watching as we do with sympathy and respect the celestial dreams of the Christian faith, we say deliberately and distinctly that the Christian treatment of death has failed. Those who find in it consolation and hope we shall not seek to rob of their consolation and their hopes by any public argument to show them that their hopes are a baseless dream. But when challenged and interrogated we answer boldly, that this Christian theory of Paradise demoralises character and deteriorates life. Still more so does the Christian (or un-Christian) theory of Hell. The world does not practically believe it, and hence in effect there is extant no religious view of death at all. In the next place, the current idea of life beyond is an idea of an unworthy life or else of a life horribly cruel. And finally, by transporting the soul after death to a world of visionary inanity, it saps the grandeur and the reality of the soul after death in this world of man, in the world of human memory and progress. Shakespeare and Dante, St. Paul and Gutenberg, are far more alive to-day, are far more potent realities and personalities than they were when they ate and drank, breathed and walked, little known, little heeded, amongst the busy masses around them. Their flesh, their bones are gone; their souls go marching along. Do we care now if these men to-day have robes of amaranth and golden harps? Dante's tomb beside the Adriatic, Shakespeare's house at Stratford are more precious than any celestial crown.

It will be no small part of the mission of religion in the future to recall men to the habit of honouring and perpetuating the dead. It is heart-rending to think with what cruelty and disregard and unconcern we treat the memory of all whom we no longer see and hear. A decorous funeral, conventional mourning clothes, a memorial public or private, sometimes a public subscription—and all is over. The grave is not visited; the memory is not cherished; the name is not uttered: every reminder of the departed life is hustled from us sometimes with impatience and sometimes through reverence. We are not personally callous or ungrateful. We grieve in secret often. We think in our hearts silently of the parent, of the child, the wife, or the husband. But shyness, habits of reserve combine with Christian theology to wrap the dead in silence and to eliminate their influence from life. It seems hardly decorous, hardly congruous, to bring into the daily intercourse of men the memory of those whom we are taught to think of as blessed saints in Heaven. Christianity has torn up from our habits the old human reverence for the dead; and it has failed to make real to men its audacious promise of a superhuman beatification.

The religion of Humanity deals with death in a real way, a friendly, a human way. It robs death of its terror by showing that it is not the destroyer of life, that it deprives us of sensation but not of personality, of consciousness but not of activity, of visible contact but not of spiritual communion with men. We cease to eat and to breathe; we do not cease to live. The loved ones do not hear our words with the ear, but they hear them with the heart; we wound and fatigue others no longer; we inspire them and we soothe them. Year by year we meet again at the grave of the dead. Years after death we solemnly rehearse their merits. To us they are not far off in realms of bliss, but amongst us, beside us, of us, as we knew and loved them, only cleared and purified by the revealing halo of death. Each week Auguste Comte went to the grave of his dear friend to meditate and to gather hope and calm. Each week the friend and successor of Auguste Comte goes to *his* grave with the same end. But the other day a company of his friends and comrades gathered round the grave of a dear friend seven years after his death, whilst his young widow rears their child in her perpetual widowhood. And they tell us, these votaries of the Christian Heaven, they tell us with triumphal scorn that Positivism is utterly powerless to face the problem of death. I say this (and it is but a few weeks since I myself stood by the grave of one very close and very dear to me—a loss that makes life henceforth a different thing to me for ever whilst I live), this I say—if there is one ground more than any other which I would choose as the test and touchstone of the faith in Humanity, it is this ground of death, and our thoughts and feelings about the dead.

As I recall the loss of Madame Robinet I cannot forget all that the future has to offer us of advance in the political influence of women. In few things has the Positivist scheme been more misunderstood than in its relation to women. To the practical as well as to the intellectual energies of women it opens an almost unbounded field. Because Positivism has no sympathy with the noisy and barren clamour about the rights of women—a clamour as barren as that about the rights of man—it has been hastily assumed by some that it is silent on the development of women's minds and women's work. If it were, it were condemned at once, unworthy of further consideration by the seekers after a better future. Let us recall the favourite axiom of M. Laffitte, which he has derived from Comte—that the test of civilisation is the standard which any given society has reached in cultivating the resources of women.

It will not be forgotten that the education of women in the Positivist system is the same as the education of men ; and the education of men is a scheme so comprehensive and arduous (for it goes through the whole range of the sciences, ending with a general philosophy) that few men as yet have mastered it—I know personally of no one in England or in France, Positivist or not, who could stand that test except indeed M. Laffitte himself. After this, it is indeed idle to doubt if Positivism insists on the intellectual development of women. But it is sometimes thought that it insists less on the active powers of women and their practical careers. Here again, as I said before, it would be well, I often think, to look at the practical conduct of Positivists themselves, and rely less on a rather crude and not very well-informed logic to answer this question. Are those women whose lives have been given to Positivism and absorbed by it, whose lives form the happiest school of Positivism, are they women without energy and stamp of character, are they without practical careers, without influence, standing aloof from the social and political movement of our time ? I trow not. They are in their way and within their means what Madame Robinet was, centres and leaders in the political and social movement. Her home, her *salon*, was the seat of intense, continual, political life, one of those indestructible centres of force which make up that electric battery of Paris, and a *salon* as distinct, as personal, as truly the reflex of her nature as was ever that of Madame Roland herself. But her activity was not at all limited to that of a *salon*. During the siege of Paris, during the two sieges —the siege by the Prussians and that by the Government of Versailles—and still more during that opprobrium of modern France, the massacres and proscriptions of May 1871, Madame Robinet made her political energy felt throughout the quarter. Her sympathies with the persecuted, the proscribed, and the exiles were real and deep. Her heroic self-denial, her courage in protecting the victims, her generosity in giving them sometimes the very bread of her children was not forgotten. Her funeral was a political event. The clubs of workmen and of many political schools other than our own sent deputations to the grave, and more than a thousand persons, representing many thousands more, brought their tributes to her premature tomb.

Here was a woman who was a true politician in the great political centre of modern Europe. And yet with what scorn could this woman have rejected the proposal to give her a vote, to drag her on to platforms or to waste her time in committees to obtain the rights of her sex. I can imagine I hear now the hearty and contagious laugh of that clear sensible nature, if one of our lady parliamentary agitators had sought to enlist her name on the committee. She would instinctively have felt that it would be to ask her to give up her influence, to sacrifice the political field where she was strong for one where she could have no sympathy, and where she would very soon have lost herself in barren rivalries and contests. She was a political power in Paris just because she was a woman, by virtue of being a woman, of dealing with politics as only women can. In struggling to enter the political arena as a man she would have forfeited her strength, her nature, her ascendancy. She possessed all this by virtue of that nameless "*verve*," directness, sympathy, and passion which when it is united to a sound judgement and a courageous nature give women that inimitable power in politics—a power which vanishes like a charm when it becomes a matter of votes and rights, majorities and committees.

I think all this is nobler and healthier, and is far more truly political force than that of some so-called political women who drive about from one committee and from one platform to another, repeating the stale gossip of the Commons' tea-room, the party calculations of whips and wire-pullers, of the loungers of the lobbies or of the correspondents of country newspapers, and who think that *that* is politics, unless perchance they think it to be found in giving political dinners to women excluding men, or devising a new costume of a neutral sex. Political activity for women by all means! But it must be really action—not the rattle of female busybodies in search of a new sensation. It must be the activity of women, not of men, carried on in the ways proper to women and in which they excel, not in the ways of men; womanly in its ideals, in its purity, in its sympathy, in its unselfishness; womanly in its lightning instinct of perception and in its directness of purpose; womanly in its courage and its tenacity, and womanly also in its appealing to persons not to masses, in its action in the home and the social gathering, not in the public meeting, the club, or the parliament.

This is far too big a question to be treated to-day. But the key-note of all that Positivism has to say of it I take to be this. The intellectual work, the moral work, the practical work of women is just as noble as that of men, just as much indispensable to the progress of Humanity, requires powers no less difficult and training no less assiduous. But the work is not exactly the same, and it has to be done in ways not exactly identical. This question of women's votes, women's professions, and women's equality of rights is no separate thing, to be settled on its own mere merits, as the apportionment of a poor-rate or a water-rate might be settled. It goes deep down to the whole social, domestic, moral, and physical constitution of Society. It results from that great truth on which Comte insisted so often, that Society is made up of families, of groups of men, women, and children, not of individuals. You cannot recast political functions and professional life without recasting the family and the home. When the relations of men to women are transformed in the forum they must be transformed in the house. Politics, social institutions, home duties and morality are not things as distinct as a mountain and a tree. They are the sympathetic organs of one organic social life.

The social functions of women are not exactly those of men because the domestic, the moral, the physical functions of women are not precisely those of men. Those who deny that still have to admit, with a sigh it may be, with eagerness it may be, that women are not men. So long as mothers are not fathers, so long as wives are not husbands, so long as daughters are not sons, so long as sisters are not brothers, so long as nurses are not grooms, so long as women can sew, and feed a child, and brighten a home (on the average) better than men; so long as men make (on the average) better navvies, better seamen, better coachmen, better colliers than women; so long as men are bigger, stronger, and hardier than women, so long as women are gentler, more beautiful, more tender, quicker, readier, purer than men ; so long as women and not men bear children and suckle infants—so long the social functions of women will not be the same as men's. I will not absolutely assert that all these things may not one day be reversed. When they are, the "rights of women" will be a perfectly rational demand.

Those who talk so easily about throwing open all professions to women appear sometimes to forget that this involves on the same plea of equality the throwing open of all professions to men ; that by the same rule their infants will have to be washed and dressed and put to sleep by male nurses, for the female nurses will be soldiers or policemen ; their girls schooled by male governesses, their sick tended by male attendants, the father must be sent to rock the cradle, whilst the mother is driving a cab or a steam-engine. They forget that this scheme—which is really one to abolish sex so far as social institutions can abolish sex—involves far more than alterations in the suffrage or the rules of admission to two or three learned professions. It involves (unless it is to be a mere social diversion) a recasting of our entire family life, our moral life, our practical life, far greater than any social revolution ever dreamed of by Jacobin, Anabaptist, or Mormon. I well know that those who claim political rights for women have no present intention of going so far. But that is because they have no system of social philosophy to rest on. No reason has ever been offered us why, if the professions of men are to be open to women, the professions of women are not to be open to men. And on the rule of mere supply and demand the one implies the other, the arrangements of society and life will all be an open question. Those who tear up old social habits seldom know how far they are about to proceed. It is vanity and ignorance alone that think it nobler to sit once a week on a committee than to train up a child in the way that it should go.

If we are ever asked why Positivists decline to advocate the opening to women of politics, of professions, of trades—let us reply that we prefer to advocate wives, mothers, sisters; womanly work, and womanly nature in general; in fact, we advocate that primeval institution—the female sex.

The Parliament that meets next month will have other work before it than Bills to enable a few rich spinsters to vote provided they never marry. In the first place the House of Commons which has sought to reform so many institutions will now have the task of reforming itself. One is glad to find Ministers and parties roused up at last to recognise that which the Positivist school has steadily urged now for thirty years—that the executive force of modern States cannot possibly be efficiently exerted on the ancient English traditions of Parliamentary government. It is no business of ours. But in the meantime we repeat our principles that the part of a Parliament is not to govern directly but to hold the public purse, and to form the ultimate Court of National Appeal.

But that to which we all look is Ireland. I am not about to enter on the clauses of the Land Act, or to discuss the schemes that are afloat for the pacification of Ireland whether by the modern imperial system of martial law or by the medieval system of private war carried on by gentlemen and barons at the head of armed retainers. I shall deal with none of these things. We are not now sitting in our political club where the details of practical politics are properly discussed. I confine myself to the assertion of great moral and social axioms, on which everything that claims to be religion is bound to have axioms, and to make their doctrines heard. And the first of all the principles that we have to assert is unflinching sympathy with our Irish countrymen. That sympathy is the feeling we have for a generous, suffering, and heroic race, whom no oppression can crush, and whom no bribes can turn from their undying purpose to win their country back to their own people; a sympathy that is not to be cowed in us by the clamour of any party at home or all the parties united, which is not to be stifled in us by all the indignation we feel at systematic crime and lawlessness.

In this matter of Ireland our position ought to be placed beyond all mistake. In the main, we are with the Irish people, in their two great ends: (1) the practical abolition of landlordism as a system; (2) the practical government of Ireland as a nation distinct from the English. But the first does not mean the abolition of property in land, nor the confiscation of rights of property; and the second does not mean the separation of Ireland from England as a foreign State. On the terrible series of crimes which have been darkening Ireland now for two years, until crime has become hardened into a system, our position is also no less unmistakable. On every ground of reason and feeling these horrible midnight crimes alike revolt us and shame us. We repudiate always the settlement of social questions by force; to us all terrorism is peculiarly odious; we denounce the doctrine that the end justifies the means; we denounce all anarchy and Nihilism, all pure destruction everywhere; we say that there can be no progress without order, and no progress that is not the development of order; and, lastly, we condemn all secret political action of every kind. No crimes can be to us more odious than the crimes which are becoming a national habit in Ireland.

Yet we raise our voice against the temper which is growing up around us to look on the Irish people as abnormally demoralised and savage! One race and one class after another has been goaded by political and social passions into crimes to which these are slight and trivial by comparison. English proprietors and African slaves have committed atrocities ten times as great, yet neither the English nor the African race were permanently demoralised. English soldiers have committed barbarities many times worse, and have developed a spirit of savagery far less excusable in crushing rebellion in Ireland, in Scotland, in the West Indies, and in the East Indies. The atrocities in Paris, but ten years old, were in bulk and bloodiness a thousand times worse. The insurgent peasantry of 1789 in France, the insurgent serfs of the Middle Ages, revelled for years in outrages to which those of Ireland are a feeble contrast. And yet in no one of the cases I mention has history admitted that the nation itself was essentially depraved.

So it is with Ireland! We deplore and loathe these savage crimes; yet we do not lose sympathy with Ireland or with Irishmen. Our thoughts go back to the seven centuries of wrong and cruelty which England has inflicted on Ireland. What Ireland is to-day that English government has made her. Our thoughts go back to the huts of Connemara and Kerry where the lot of the peasant is the hardest in all Europe, where the potatoes and the buttermilk are wrenched from the white lips of half-starved children to swell the revenues of city companies and English lords. Our thoughts go off far away to the millions of Irish homes in all parts of the habitable world where day by day there is renewed the memory of the lost homes and the abandoned graves in the Old Island amidst a burning sense of exile—all owing to "the rules of the estate" and the insatiable advance of rent.

It is clear that there are large tracts in Ireland where rent is *an abuse*; I mean where the natural conditions of agriculture and pasture are such that the whole produce of labour scarcely provides a decent living for the labourers. In such cases, and they number tens of thousands of families, rent can only be wrung out of the health and decencies of life. It is the first duty of Society to see that it does not arm any individuals in the community with legal power to destroy the health and decent life of their neighbours. There are other large tracts of Ireland (perhaps two-thirds of the whole) where, although *some* rent can fairly be payable, the unlimited power of raising rent on pain of summary eviction suffices to render the life of the cultivator one of chronic struggle and terror. Again, there are also large estates (perhaps one-half of the whole) where the relations of landlord and tenant are not mutual, where it is all pure gain on the one side and pure loss on the other, where the owners of the soil are not landlords at all—unless landlord means an irresponsible satrap who spends at a distance the tribute he exacts by his own unscrupulous collectors. The relation of landlord and tenant is often a kind of joint interest such as Roman lawyers call a lion's share partnership—where all gain went to the stronger and the loss to the weaker, one which Roman lawyers held invalid. In the first class of case I say that rent is a social crime. In the second, I say that the arbitrary nature of rent is a social danger. In the third, I say that the existence of landlordism is a social nuisance.

I am very far from saying that there are no fair rents in Ireland, no well-managed estates, or no good landlords. But I say that more than two-thirds of the soil of Ireland is held on conditions which on one or the other of the grounds I state are incompatible with the well-being of Society. What is the answer to this in the current opinion of the day ? The answer is this. The well-being of Society is a thing we will not discuss. Social evil or social danger is a thing too late to be considered. Law and proprietory rights are paramount. The right to the rent is a property duly acquired according to law ; the rights of absentee landlords are rights guaranteed by law and purchased centuries ago. What is all this but the cry : If there be laws in Venice—I'll have my bond—my pound of flesh according to the bond ?

The answer of Portia to Shylock is as true to-day as ever. Society exists for the sake of its members. The well-being of Society is not only a thing that must always be discussed, but it shall always be paramount, and is for ever inalienable. To enforce laws that endanger the lives of citizens is not to enforce laws but to commit crimes; bonds which deal in human flesh must be torn up. Property law and rights exist for the sake of Society. Society does not exist for the sake of them. And when property and rights are in hopeless contradiction with Society, property becomes plunder and rights become wrongs. The welfare of the people of Ireland is the paramount object to be gained. If the laws of the Tudors, of Oliver, of the Georges have failed to secure it, they must be superseded by laws of Victoria.

We may acknowledge that the Land Act of last session has gone far to assert this principle. Let us do full justice to the courage and patriotism with which Mr. Gladstone has proposed, and the English people has accepted, a principle of so highly exceptional a kind, so peculiarly difficult to recognise in a practical way, one which had to be forced on the very people whom it was designed to help. Mr. Gladstone has had to defend his measure of relief against such an insurrection as is usually aroused by a measure of oppression. It is a measure so new and in principle so drastic that it evidently staggers advanced French republicans. It is true that it is far less than was absolutely necessary, but it was perhaps more than any English statesman has ever attempted for a century. Yet, feeling all this, and repudiating the system of terrorism and mere spoliation which is the alternative offered by Irish farmers, I think we must admit that the Land Act, as the Irish leaders insist, has not dealt with the true evil. The real evil of Ireland is landlordism. From a social point of view it would be the true good of Ireland if landlordism ceased to exist.

I am far from saying that private property in land should not be recognised by law, or that properties should be limited by law. Nor do I say that the actual owners should be deprived of their estates without proper compensation. I say it would be a good thing for Ireland if landlordism did not exist. I mean by landlordism that unique system of culture where the owner of the soil enjoys its products but does not contribute in any way to the work of production; where men, women, and children toil under an ungenial climate on a barren moor under the eyes of zealous officials, and the proceeds of their toil is sent off to a person whom they never saw, who never saw them, who takes from them but gives nothing, against whom there is no appeal, and who consumes the produce in London, Paris, or Vienna. Economically, socially, politically, morally, what has he got to show as his equivalent for his portion of their daily bread wrung from their lives and their sweats?—Nothing but parchments.

Now, in the eye of the future, as in the balance of social well-being, parchments are not enough. All wealth, says Comte, is social in its origin and should be social in its destination—*i.e.* all wealth is the result of the joint work of many, and its true use is therefore for the good of Society. Landlordism is the denial of this social nature of wealth and thus it is a negation of social equity.

I may be asked if this principle is not just as true in England as in Ireland. Certainly it is. The principle is as true but the facts are not the same. In England it is exceedingly rare that the owner of the soil takes all and gives nothing, draws rent but contributes no share, whilst this is the rule in Ireland. And thus it may be right in Ireland for Society to interfere to hasten the extinction of landlordism in a way which could not be asked, perhaps could not be justified, in England. But the principle is the same. In England too the special class of idle landowners must pass away. The rich, whose profession it is to amuse themselves, will one day be an anachronism, a class whose sole serious purpose is either to kill animals or to play at games. Whether farmers become proprietors or proprietors become farmers, or peasants become proprietors or farmers become peasants, or all of these in different degrees and different proportions in different places, certain it is that the three classes who divide the soil of England must be reduced to two classes or to one class. The idle class will have to disappear. In a healthy society an idle class are mere parasites ; but in a country where the labouring class can hardly win their daily potatoes, an idle class, living on the labour of ill-fed peasants, is a criminal class.

In Ireland, however, there is another side to the question. For fifteen years we have insisted that the difficulties of Ireland were twofold, not only social but national; and that the national question was quite as important as the social or economic. For fifteen years we have made constant and unflinching appeals to English opinion to recognise the fact, a fact social, historic, political, and economic, that Ireland has a national life of its own ; and that her people will never be satisfied, and ought never to be satisfied, till that national life is respected. I am well aware how odious to a large mass of our countrymen is the mere suggestion of such a plea. But we who through good report and evil report have never at any rate hesitated to say what we thought just, are not to be overborne by public opinion now—be it the opinion of Tory, Whig, or Radical. We assert to-day (1882) more unhesitatingly than we did fifteen years ago, in 1867, when we petitioned against the punishment of the Fenian insurgents, we assert to-day more unhesitatingly that the alienation of the Irish nation from the English nation has had real justification, is a growing and not a diminishing thing.

We insist that the national sentiment of Ireland is a permanent, indestructible, and noble sentiment, entirely in accordance with sound political truths, and entirely in harmony with the course of the European movement. These great Imperial aggregates with their hard compressing systems are in their nature tyrannies and oppress free local life. We do not call for a separation of Ireland from all connection with the Imperial Government; but for fifteen years we have called for a Government of Ireland separate in effect; Irish and not English in spirit; a Government of Ireland in Ireland, by Irishmen, just as Canada, Australia, New Zealand, Hungary, Prussia, have Governments locally distinct though subject to one imperial crown. The satisfaction of this most just and honourable claim is the first condition of healthy political life in Ireland. Land Acts, Church Acts, Coercion Acts, Arms Acts are mere by-play without this.

It underlies them all, and really precedes them all. Every fresh gain to Ireland, every measure of reform which adds to the material prosperity and the moral self-respect of Irishmen increases and stimulates the national demand. If English statesmen could make Ireland prosperous by the Act of one session, it would only be to make her demand for national existence deeper and louder in the next.

We know the answer of Englishmen of all parties. It is this. Irish nationality is a word that shall be stamped out as treason :—Home Rule in any form is a thing we will not discuss. Now we are not to be frightened here by the use of even so big a word as Treason. Treason or not, the reality of the Irish nation is a thing which will be asserted here. There is no political doctrine whatsoever which is above discussion. The men who say Home Rule shall not be discussed are in the same position as those who told our forefathers that Divine Right should not be discussed, or the King's Prerogative, or Established Churches. When rational politicians will not discuss a doctrine they have lost all confidence in its justice and they mean to enforce it by blood and iron as Bismarck does, in defiance of justice. That temper cannot last long in this age in this Empire. We have heard of many things which we were told could not be discussed. Well, in three months they have been undone.

We were told that no discussion could be allowed as to the cession of the Ionian Islands, as to the separate government of Canada, as to the evacuation of Afghanistan, as to the withdrawal from the Transvaal. They have been discussed and they have been carried out. When people have come to the point that they refuse to discuss a principle, we know they are near to yielding, for they have lost all heart in their own right.

Besides, for my own part, I am far from convinced that the whole of the English nation will refuse to discuss this claim of their Irish fellow-citizens. English workmen have neither interests nor passions to alienate them from Irish labourers. And though at present they are often ignorant of the claims of the Irish, they have never shown any disposition to resent them. The claims of the Irish nationality, I will not say to absolute independence as a State, but to distinct recognition as a substantive people, are gaining and growing every day. For my part, I believe that the policy of the Land Act has been wrecked by the fatal act of temper committed when the Ministers of the English people threw into prison, untried and uncondemned, the representatives of the Irish people. Each day makes it clearer that the government of Ireland is becoming impossible whilst this policy is maintained—and not the government of Ireland only, but the government of England. It is the English Parliament which has wrought the historic mischiefs of Ireland. It is the English Parliament which is now itself menaced in turn with paralysis. In the interests of England and of Ireland, Ireland must be released from the English Parliament.

All this is a big field, and we must pause on the verge of a vast programme for the future. Changes so great, so difficult, are hardly within the range of Acts of Parliament, of Alliances, Leagues, and Associations. Politics must be transformed by a moral change, which will change opinions first, then habits, and finally remodel institutions. It must be a solid scientific body of truths centred round the idea of a paramount Providence—a real, universal and human Religion.

ANNUAL ADDRESS, 1884

(*January* 1, 1884)

NEWTON HALL

THE opening of the New Year must find us in a spirit of reasonable confidence and just hope; and, humble as our movement is in these its early days, we cannot fail to see its growth within, whilst the cause we have at heart is making a yet more manifest way in the world around us. Our activity as an organised body in this hall has become far more solid and mature; we are feeling what it is to be a living community with a sense of a common conviction and brotherhood; and the union between the different groups of Positivists in England has become much closer and more real. The formal adhesion of our fellow-believers in Chapel Street, and of the group in North London, to the central organisation in Paris has removed all appearance of division in the ranks of English Positivists; whilst the definite attachment of the latter group with our own has brought us the earnest of a closer ultimate association of all groups, with such local independence as is necessary and wise.

Real as the progress has been in the organised Positivist communities, our grounds of hopefulness are stronger when we watch the way in which Positivist principles are leavening and impressing public opinion. Positivism is in the air: for Positivism is the systematic and vitalised form of these convictions and tendencies which are the dominant forces of our time. These convictions, aspirations, and tendencies are the result of various movements; and we see them in the world in strange divergence and conflict. Positivism is the common ground on which they meet; it supplies the key of their combination; it harmonises all whilst it justifies each. And thus (as I say) Positivism is in the air.

If there is a thing which especially distinguishes our epoch it is the revived interest in genuine and vital Religion. The Churches, the sects, and the theologies of all kinds, whilst they are yielding ground in all sorts of ways, and surrendering one tenet after another, one privilege after another, are certainly not losing in passionate assertion of Religion as the centre and mainspring of life. One of the noblest and most touching facts of our time is the social enthusiasm of the orthodox in the cause of a living Religion, even whilst every foothold of the older orthodoxy seems breaking away from under them. Well, but this passionate assertion of Religion as the centre and mainspring of life is a doctrine of Positivism—nay, it is the centre and mainspring of Positivist doctrine.

On the other hand, it is just as clear a note of our epoch to submit to the teaching of all acknowledged science. Intense as is the religious zeal of a thousand organised Churches, the conquering creed of Science is advancing with great strides. Trace the relative positions of Religion and Science as they stood when, a generation ago, *The Vestiges of Creation* appeared in 1844, and when no decent person ventured to question publicly the miracles in the Bible, and as they stood when, but the other day, Charles Darwin was buried in the Abbey, with the loud and eager approval of almost every dignitary of the Church. It is true that the Churches insist that there is no antagonism whatever between the Bible and Science, between the creeds and demonstration. It is for them, not for us, to establish the harmony; but their claim to accept the conclusions of Science is a striking example of the paramount ascendancy of Science in modern thought. "Come what may, revelation or no revelation, creed or agnosticism, come what may," cry all competent and trained intellects together, "we will not gainsay the evidence of Science." But the paramount ascendancy of Science is a Positivist doctrine; it is the basis of Positivist Religion. Here again is a ground where we join in the current of all modern thought. The dominant tendency of all sound intellects to-day is found to be in fact the peculiar spirit of the Positivist (in other words), of the Scientific system of life.

Here we see how the two great movements of our time are both cardinal principles of Positivism; but we go further and show that Positivism alone attempts to combine and harmonise both. The doctors and preachers of the Churches are continually vowing that they have no hostility to Science, that Christianity is not really incompatible with Science, but they have never yet given to the world a scientific explanation of the Athanasian Creed, of the narratives of Old and New Testament, or of the birth, death, and resurrection of Christ. On the other hand, the great authorities in Science, though they often declare that they will suffer religion in its due place, and a very narrow and shadowy place that is, have never made any serious attempt to present us with a Science of Religion, or a Religion of Science. Religion and Science meet for the most part, as the French Minister and the Chinese Ambassador might meet in the absence of interpreters, neither understanding the language of the other. Now, Positivism has reconciled these two powers who have stood so in mutual repulsion and misunderstanding. Positivism does offer to the world a Science of Religion, and a Religion of Science. And Positivism is the only system yet offered to mankind which even seriously attempts the task. It is as earnest for religion as it is for science. It asserts that both are equally necessary to man, and alike indispensable to progress.

In Positivism Science is the creed of Religion. Not only is there nothing incompatible between them; but they are different modes of the same truth. The intellectual grasp of the laws that govern the world and man is Science; whilst the devout submission of the heart and the will to conform our life to those laws is Religion. But to do this Religion must surrender theology, and all supernatural hypotheses whatever. On the other hand, Science must no longer be confined to a purely intellectual field. It must be fused with a profound human sympathy and reverence; and it must gird itself to a career of human duty. Religion will never be scientific, and therefore will never hold its own, till it rests on demonstration altogether, and not on hypotheses and figments. And Science will never be religious, and therefore will never dominate human life, till it does not stop at an intellectual assent to certain truths, but works in the spirit of love, awe, and duty, and in full loyalty to the moral nature of man. There is but one issue from the dilemma—but one solution of what would seem an irreconcilable paradox. The dependence of man on an overruling and permanent Humanity gives us at once a Science of Religion and a Religion of Science. Science reveals to us the conditions, and laws, and resources of Humanity. And Religion teaches us to serve Humanity with veneration, affection, and a surrender of self.

And see how completely Positivism is in line with the central movements of the time in the minor questions which stir us in thought, politics, or religion. One of the most powerful and hopeful of the ideas of our age is the growing aversion to war, the increasing respect for morality and justice in questions of nation, race, and government. The Chief of the Liberal Party owes his unparalleled ascendancy to the belief (whether justified or not is unimportant) that he represents it more honestly than any modern statesman. Whatever his shortcomings and that of the party he leads, they are for ever asserting as a principle their respect for international morality. Well, international morality is the very basis of all Positivist teaching in politics, a principle for which they have contended in England for twenty years; a principle which Churchmen, Nonconformists, Humanitarians, and Quakers, Radicals, Socialists, and all schools in turn have proclaimed and deserted under strong pressure of party or sectarian interest, but which I make bold to say that Positivists have maintained unflinchingly in Europe, in Asia, in Africa, in Polynesia alike—without any backsliding at the call of party, creed, or person—in the dominant and ever-present sense that all nations and groups of men, civilised or savage, heathen or Christian, black or white, of whatever creed and of whatever race, are brothers of our own, and children of our common mother Humanity.

So too—in respect of all forms of national union, for Home Rule in its widest and not in any special sense, for local self-government, for regard for local and national sentiment—principles which lie at the bottom of half the agitations of our time—these again are eminently principles for which Positivism has contended from the moment that it raised its voice in England. In home affairs, the great domestic feature of our age is the better organisation of popular education. What enormous strides has this made in the thirty years since the first appearance of Positivism. But popular education is the *raison d'être* of Positivism. To found a sound system of education is in our eyes to establish a real Church. Church to us means an educating body, as Religion implies an educated nature, and a religious and happy nation means an educated and humanised nation.

The great political fact of our age is the growing influence of the people in the direction of government, in the spread of republican ideals, in the concentration of government on the welfare of the masses. Well, but the republican spirit of government, the admission of the masses to the fullest advantages of citizenship, the duty of the State to concentrate its care on the great labouring community—all this is the foundation of Positivist politics. It is in this spirit that we have fought the battle of the Trades Unions, of the Workmen's Societies, of their political enfranchisement, that we have offered them, and claimed for them, the privileges and honours of equal citizenship. We were Republicans as they used to say in Paris—of the eve—Republicans before it was the fashion, and social reformers before princes and marquises took Socialism under their patronage.

Socialism we are now told is the coming force of our age, and Conservatives are gravely advised to find their account in countenancing it. If Socialism means (as I think it does) the substitution of the State or the community for personal responsibility in the management of wealth, the removal of all social suffering by the direct interference of the State—then assuredly we are not Socialists. But so far as Socialism means the entire regeneration of our social and industrial life, the diversion of all wealth and all social forces from personal ends to public and social ends, in the interest and enjoyment of all, and not of privileged owners—then we are Socialists and more than Socialists. For we intend to carry out that complete transformation of the products of labour—not by laws that the rich and powerful can evade and turn to account, but by all the resources of public opinion, by education, habit, religion, until it becomes a living and second nature to us all. We shall thus transform not merely every corner of industry, but art, science, philosophy, power of every kind, mental or moral (which Socialists so often and so strangely overlook). We shall give a social direction to every form of power, and not merely to capital in land or in movables. If Socialism is to be the spirit of the future, the field is clear for the social reorganisation of Positivism—one deeper and far more sweeping than is dreamed of by any Socialist school of our age.

On such difficult and special problems as those of Ireland, of the homes of the poor, of religious education, of the separation of Church and State, of municipal government, of the reform of the Parliamentary system, Positivism has for a generation asserted those principles which are now the commonplaces of the subject. We called out loudly for justice to Ireland, for respect of her noble national sentiment, for redress of her obsolete and cruel Church system and land system, for equity towards her devoted patriots long before the Liberal Party had discovered that it is impossible to govern even England until we are just to Ireland. The Liberation Society itself has never raised its voice so clearly and emphatically against State Churches as did Auguste Comte when he proclaimed it to be the foundation of civil government to be free from any trace of privileged religion. Comte has said more true and trenchant things, about the homes of the poor than can be found in all the echoes of the *Bitter Cry* that we have heard so often of late. Comte has pointed out, and we have repeated, the causes of the inevitable weakness of Parliamentary government long before it ever occurred to our statesmen that the very existence of the nation is bound up in the issue of reforming, not the suffrage without, but Parliament within.

And hence it is that Positivism is in living touch with the dominant spirit of our age ; for the great problems are all finding their solution on the very lines which Comte anticipated just thirty years ago, and which we have unflinchingly repeated through good report and evil report, when they were odious and when they are fashionable, neither daunted by opposition nor intoxicated with passing success. We see Positivism advancing on all sides, quite independently of any growth in our own body, by its powerful affinity for the actual situation by virtue of the spontaneous adoption of its central principles. On all sides we see these great maxims of Positivism gaining ascendancy—Man grows more and more deeply religious—Positive Science is the basis of human life—Order is the root of all progress—Live for Humanity—Live in the light—Reorganise Society on a republican type, and with a human and not a theological programme—Feeling impels us to all action, and thought is the instrument of activity—Wealth is the creation of Society, and should be devoted to the service of Society—Politics must be brought under the control of morality—the welfare of the whole people is the true end of government. All these are the ideas of our age and they are the central truths of Comte's system. And therefore I say—Positivism is everywhere in the air.

II

I turn now to a brief review of our special work in this place. I shall divide it again into the three heads of worship, politics, and education. This place, as we have often said, is designed to be at once temple, school, and club. It has no analogy in my mind to the *Church*, which is in some exclusive and limited way confined to meetings for prayer and sermons. I entirely put aside that notion of religion which reduces it to the expression of religious emotion. For my part, I cannot call the repetition of invocations, hymns, and thanksgiving as in any special sense a service of Humanity. The only *service* of Humanity that I can understand is the doing our duty in our homes, as citizens and as men, in a wise, courageous, and unselfish way, and the training of ourselves and of others to do that duty in that high and disciplined spirit. The utterance of invocations, however beautiful, and even if they are deeply and truly felt in the uttering, is only a part of that duty—or rather it is not so much a part of duty as one of the ways of preparing us for our duty—one which, if we do not beware, may easily become mechanical and pharisaical. Hence it is we do not call our meetings here in any special sense, *services*. We have to serve Humanity, wherever we are, and whatever we are doing all day long. We only meet here to warm our hearts and clear our brains the better to do that service. And we think that we are warming our hearts and clearing our brains, not only when we meet to fill our souls with reverence and gratitude in recalling the debt we owe to Humanity in the sum, but also when we meet to study the laws of life and the problems of geometry, or when we meet to form our judgement on a great public question, or when we meet to welcome a child born into our community, or when we meet to enjoy a majestic piece of choral music, or even when we meet in the kindly spirit of social intercourse. Let us serve Humanity at every moment of our lives, by just, wise, kind, and ever brave conduct. Let us meet here to grow, so far as we can, more wise, just, brave, and kind. This is to us at once a temple, school, and club. This place is in no exclusive sense a church: there are here no services in any artificial and narrow sense of that term.

I take first those special occasions on which we have met in the past year to commemorate some great event or day, which in a peculiar way appeals to our imagination and sympathy, and fills us with a sense of reverence and gratitude. On the first day of the past year we met, as now, to recall to our spirits the conception of Humanity as a whole, and to ask ourselves what we had ourselves done, and what we were about to do to make manifest that Humanity to men, to become a part of it ourselves. On the 28th day of January, the last day of Moses, the day in our Calendar set apart to Mahomet, we commemorated the great career of Islam as one of the mighty religious forces of the past, then entering on the fourteenth century of its long history. On the 5th of September, the day of Comte's death, twenty-six years before, we commemorated that anniversary for the first time in our hall. The noble discourse of Dr. Bridges in this place, in which he traced how in Auguste Comte were united the tasks of Aristotle and of St. Paul, has been printed, and can be had here by any one who applies for it to us. Our commemoration of the 5th included a dinner and social meeting at which some eighty of our friends joined, and where we saw three things at least which are rare enough in these days: first a convivial meeting animated not only with a brotherly but even with a religious sense of communion; next, the memory of a foreign philosopher forming the ground of a social gathering; and lastly, the association on a perfectly friendly and equal footing of all classes, ranks, and professions.

Such things are possible and natural in Paris where the *virus* of aristocratic manners is for the body of the people a thing of the past. But in England it can only be effected by habitual resort to an ideal which is at once intensely religious and at the same time profoundly republican. More recently we have celebrated that simple rite—or sacrament, as Comte has called it—the Presentation of young children to the community—when three families of our body brought their children to be presented (or, as the Churches say, christened) and publicly acknowledged the solemn social responsibility which their nurture and education imposes. It was but yesterday, on the last day of the year, that we commemorated the Day of all the Dead, by the performance of the poem of George Eliot, " O may I join the choir invisible," which our friend Mr. Henry Holmes has set as a cantata. The success of that noble piece, as a work of art, is due unquestionably to the zeal and genius of our friend Mr. Holmes, to whose efforts in the cause we are all most deeply grateful—unrewarded as they are by anything beyond the exceeding great reward of being able to rejoice in his glorious art, and the unmeasured thanks of us all whose spirits he has stirred so deeply and raised to such a height. The occasion I think will prove a memorable one in the history of our movement, and in the history, perhaps, of Art. The poem, as we know, was the work of one who was the intimate friend of some of us, profoundly impressed with the thoughts of Auguste Comte, a regular subscriber to our funds, and seeking in every line and word of that poem to express one of the greatest and most subtle of all the conceptions of Comte. Our friend Mr. Holmes, to whom the idea of illustrating this woman's work was suggested, I may say, by a woman, has taken it up in the same spirit. This poem, then, in its musical form, will be always remembered as the first work of high and real art (in England, at least) that Positivism has yet produced. How vast is the field which its boundless resources will offer to the poetic imagination and the Art of Humanity that is to be!

Our Sunday meetings have been regularly

continued throughout the year excepting during the four summer months. It must be distinctly understood that these meetings are in no way an imitation of, or in competition with, the Sunday services of Church and Chapel; they are, in no peculiar sense, designed to be acts of worship, or even to take the place of worship; they are part of our general work here, which is to spread the spirit of Positivism; they are only religious acts in this sense that they are meant to awaken in us a sense of the general power of Humanity, and of our duty towards it. They have dealt with the historical side of Positivism, its general explanation of history, its political aspects, the duties of citizens, and its great social truths, its philosophical aspects and those principles which are in a special sense religious inasmuch as the harmony of life depends on them. Mr. Beesly and Mr. Fleay thus treated in two courses the Theocracies and Early Polytheism; Mr. Morison and Mr. Lushington, the course of modern history. I myself dealt with the general principles of public life. Dr. Bridges then illustrated the seven great truths of the Positive Polity. Mr. Beesly explained in a course of four lectures Comte's *Appeal to Conservatives.* Mr. Higginson gave us the Positivist view of Faith and Valour. Mr. Lock, in three lectures, explained what we mean by Home, Country, and Humanity; and Mr. Ellis has examined the value of Christian Socialism and has expounded the Positivist view of the Commemoration of the Dead. These Sunday Addresses have been designed to illustrate great features in the past of Humanity or the future of Humanity, leading conceptions and types in Philosophy and Poetry as Positivism conceives both. But they are not in any conventional sense Worship in themselves—nor do they take the place of Worship.

We have endeavoured to complete these general presentments of Comte's system of life and thought by special explanations of his works in classes. To this end Dr. Bridges continued his readings in the "General View" of Positivism on Wednesday evenings, and this was followed by a class on the Positivist Library or selection of great books, in which Mr. Lock and myself took part. The special classes in Science which were so admirably opened last year by Mr. Percy Harding and continued by Dr. Senier were this year maintained with quite equal success by Dr. Fitzpatrick, in whose most instructive course on the History and Elements of Biology we all of us found so much interest and profit. It is a new and most significant sign of our age when we find a busy London physician, amidst his professional duties, devoting some part of his evening to systematic lectures in popular Biology, and volunteering to us not only his own time and thought, but the whole of the illustrations and instruments which so signally assisted to explain and give life to his teaching. Dr. Fitzpatrick will give us on two Sunday evenings two lectures of a general kind, in which he will resume the historical and social value of Biology as seen in the light of the general view of Positivism.

It is proposed to open a class for the study of Astronomy, the history and elements, on a similar plan, which Mr. Vernon Lushington will conduct.

Let us express also our hearty thanks to Madame Princep, who has volunteered to form a class for the study of French, and who has continued it steadily with such persevering self-devotion and such entire success. Our school here is intended, not for the study of things in general, nor for literary culture of any kind, but for the systematic training in the history and principles of the seven real sciences. But a knowledge of French is so closely bound up in the due understanding of Positivist teaching, and the closer alliance of the peoples of Europe, that we must always regard it, in such a case as our own, as occupying along with the training in the Arts the place of the most indispensable of all the instruments of education.

The past year has brought us also over and above these continuous classes and meetings a new form of work, the beginning of a regular training in Art. In February we opened the singing class, which has been continued with hardly any break until the end of the year. We have had, by the generous help of our friend Mr. Lushington, the direction of one of the most experienced and skilful teachers of the Art now living, and I know that I but express the gratitude of all who have benefited by that teaching in assuring him that his care has been thoroughly felt and enjoyed. During the vacation the nucleus of this class was continued by Miss Rodd, and thereout of it has grown that choir which we hope will be a constant feature of our gatherings. Not only have they been able to give life and joy to our social meetings, but they have sung for us in our recent Sunday meetings that manly "Psalm of Life," the music of which we owe to Lady Macfarren. It is far too early yet to pretend that we have even begun to enter the serene temple of Art; but we stand as willing catechumens at the portal gazing on the shrine within, and waiting to be duly robed and called. We have been able to brighten our social gatherings with some graceful pieces both of voice and instrument; we have had two new pieces composed for our worship by two accomplished musicians; and we are forming the nucleus of a permanent choir. Let us never forget that Positivism has as much to say on Art, and especially on the Art of Choral Music, as on any other subject whatever. Whatever it may have been in theology, in a human and positive religion, Art is in some sense an essential element of all the highest modes of religious expression of feeling—certainly in the collective form. And it is one of the services to our cause which Mr. Holmes has rendered that he has enabled us to see a glimpse of how the Art of the future will devote itself in the glow of social enthusiasm to idealise the great truths of Humanity, and to make every fibre of our being vibrate with the thrill of ideas, fused in the glow of imagination.

It is the experience of all, I think, that this musical practice, the classes for singing, the formation of the choir, and our social gatherings, have brought us together as a body and have given us new interests and bonds of fellowship which it would be vain to look for in lectures and classes alone. The readiness to help, to take a share in the common life, the willingness to give in time or value, the consciousness of becoming useful one to another, and of giving and receiving at once in the general interchange of human sympathy and brotherhood—and I instance in this the graceful and generous decoration of our hall by the ladies who sing in the choir—all this, I think, has spontaneously risen up in this way, and will grow to larger and more permanent things. But it marks, I am sure, a vitality in our movement. It has brought, as I know, new happiness to the existence of many; it has given new interests to the lives of many.

This marks, I may say, the formation of a living community. It is little enough to boast of, for it is nothing more than what may be seen in scores of communities with a common belief, both old and new. But it may serve to show to others what we have long felt thoroughly ourselves that Positivism is something else beside a set of scientific doctrines, or the programme of a political party. It is the common spirit of a religious communion which can fill the lives and mould the conduct of those who enter it. Here we have busy professional men and women whose days are spent in the absorbing routine of daily work giving up their nights to teach freely all who will choose to come and learn—I instance particularly the two ladies who have taught after their own toilsome day was done the French and singing classes. We have merchants, lawyers, clerks, workmen spending their evenings in the steady work of a class in science, in order to follow up a systematic education. Everything, be it observed, in this place is free.

All lectures, all classes are free — lectures, singing classes, French class, scientific classes, the use of the Library, our musical celebrations, to a great degree our publications are free—not only free without fee to our own members, but free to all who choose to attend. We make little boast of it; for we hold it to be the true basis of all real education, and the true test of a social religion. But such is the fact; and our friends and our opponents would alike do well to remember it. This is a free school—so far as I know, the only truly free school now open. It is perhaps the only place in all these islands where a systematic education in science, in history, in philosophy, in art is freely offered to all who will accept it, not only without fee or payment of any kind, but without condition of membership, and without the least trace of indirect profit. This, then, I take it, is our answer to the Churches who cry out so loudly: "What have you to give the people in place of the Gospel of Christ?" This is our answer to the Communists who ask: "What do you offer the people if you decline to counsel Revolution?" To both our answer is the same: "We offer them education—social, political, scientific, artistic. Not pretending that this is all. We claim for them social acknowledgements and advantages. But as a means we offer them not insurrection, but education. We give them, so far as we can, what we have spent our lives in acquiring—some little systematic knowledge of those things which the world has agreed are of solid and unquestionable value to know—a knowledge as we think which will do more in a permanent and noble way to elevate their lives and raise them in the scale of humanity than either the Gospel or Revolution—more, indeed, than what some now offer them—Gospel and Revolution combined."

Our publications within the year have been these: Mr. Fleay has published his three Lectures on Education, to which has been added a short preface by myself. Mr. Vernon Lushington has published his Discourses on Mozart at our Mozart celebration last December, and that on the Day of all the Dead, which he gave here at the end of the year. Dr. Bridges has published his address on Auguste Comte on the 5th of September. All of these may be had for a few pence together with our other publications. One word may be useful about these publications. They are all without exception published not only without any view to profit, but without any margin for possible profit—usually at the cost of the authors, who not only present their work to the publishing fund, but pay for the cost of paper and printing. They are sold for the most part at cost price, or in most cases below the cost price, and the proceeds of such sales are devoted to the issue of fresh publications. The publishing fund is thus formed by the gifts of the authors themselves and by special contributions to that account. In these days of so much frivolous literature and of extravagantly cheap publications it seems needful to make this explanation. I do not myself look with great hope to the wholesale distribution of tracts, or to the lowest minimum of price. I think myself that a serious Essay of 20 or 30 pages is well worth 3d., if there be anything in it. I rather doubt the value of a reader who cries out that he ought to have it for 1d. It would be easy, of course, to scatter our literature at merely nominal prices by the bushel or the ton. But I look with little favour on that steam-engine method of propaganda; nor do I think that the spirit of Positivism can be conveyed in the form of a penny tract. And that is our answer to those busy gentlemen who come to us or write to us and say: "I don't want to be at the pains to read these books, or to hear your courses of lectures. Give me something which will tell me all about Positivism in half an hour." I am sorry to say we are not able to supply that demand.

One publication of a more important kind is now engaging our thoughts. We propose to issue a volume in which we shall give biographies of the 558 names of great men in the Positivist Calendar—ancient and modern. This will be a compendious but careful Biographical Dictionary for the most eminent men in every age and field. Our friend Dr. Kaines has already prepared the nucleus of such a Dictionary. We propose to accomplish it by a distribution of labour amongst many hands.

III

I turn to the political and social side of our work in this place. The Positivist Society, under the Presidency of Mr. Beesly, has met regularly throughout the year for the discussion of the public questions of the day. It has put out statements and manifestoes in support of the Municipal Government Scheme for London, in support of the Bill for abolishing the Parliamentary Oath of Members, for the remission of the sentences passed under the Blasphemy Laws, and with reference to the position of the Government in Egypt. It has discussed these and many other questions, such as the Burial of the Dead, the House of Lords, the French attack on Tonquin, and the Housing of the Poor in London.

The Positivist Society of London has been in regular existence now for seventeen years, and is the oldest of all the Positivist bodies in this country. It is a matter of peculiar satisfaction to us all to know that under the prudent and energetic direction of Professor Beesly it has largely increased the number of its enrolled members and the field of its general action.

The question of the theological oath as a condition of a place in Parliament, and the scandalous revival of vindictive penalties for attacks on the religion of the majority, raise questions which, however small in themselves, go to the foundation of modern government, and can find no settlement short of the essential position of Positivism. That essential doctrine is—that matters of opinion without any exception whatever concern the conscience and not the magistrate; that the separation of Church and State must be complete and uniform. What we believe or what we disbelieve is subject for argument, for appeal to public opinion, but never for disability, exclusion, or penalty of any kind. There is no half-way house, no compromise possible in this. To exclude one kind of non-belief is logically as wrong as to exclude all beliefs but one. The entire theory of persecution, of State religions, of the political tyranny of a dominant sect—everything that the Liberal Party have solemnly repudiated in Ireland, every one of these principles is violated by the retention of the Oath. The exclusion of Nonconformists, Catholics, Jews has step after step been surrendered as impossible in the conditions of modern thought and government. It was a miserable inconsistency to maintain the exclusion of atheists, more especially when atheists and sceptics are suffered as if in mockery to take the very oath they are known to despise. It is significant that some of the loudest of those who maintained the exclusion were the very Nonconformists, Catholics, and Jews who so long had been themselves shut out.

When we turn from home to foreign affairs, whilst we deplore the criminal ambition of France, which is plunging her into more than one war as wanton as any that Europe has ever waged in the East, it is a satisfaction to us to feel that our brethren in France have issued one of the most powerful and uncompromising appeals on the side of justice and of peace that was ever addressed to a reckless Ministry. And that appeal has all the more force in that it represents the sober opinion of the immense bulk of the nation not involved in the Parliamentary intrigue, and because it comes from earnest Republicans who are in many things sincere supporters of the actual Government. It is wonderful to observe what excellent lessons in sense and justice our politicians and journalists can give to the French, when they are found to be doing precisely what these very journals and parties have applauded our own Government for doing on a score of occasions. When our neighbours enter on a wanton and cruel war to secure some territorial or commercial object, the folly and wickedness of such a policy is obvious to every one of those who at home retail the watchwords of party on platform or in the press. It would be amusing, if it were not so sad, to watch how they cast at the French the very words we have so often addressed to themselves in a similar case.

Egypt still remains, as was always evident

from the first, the dilemma and shame of Mr. Gladstone's Government. Before the close of the session the Positivist Society put forward a statement wherein it recognised the good intentions of a Government, which we have steadily supported in the main. We there welcomed the solemn assurances of Ministers that the occupation of Egypt was shortly to end. Those assurances were doubtless sincere at the time. But the new war in the Desert, the anarchy of Egypt, and the imminence of a renewed occupation and ultimate annexation reopen the question afresh. Deeper and deeper we are sinking into the mire of a false situation, unable to draw back, unwilling to go forward, without a policy, without an aim, without honour, without self-respect. From the day when they first set out to coerce and domineer in the valley of the Nile our rulers were told that their solemn protestations would prove a mockery, that they would be forced into maintaining the very abuses they pretended to remedy, and driven into the conquest they so loudly repudiated. All that they were warned against has come true. They have utterly crushed out of Egypt all life and power of self-government; they are now practically conquerors, hated by the mass and secretly thwarted by the whole ruling caste. The misery of Egypt is increasing, the wretched government of it, the rivalry of the nations, the scandals, the horrors, and the anarchy are at their worst—and Mr. Gladstone and his colleagues are now directly responsible for all. The unhappy fellah is tortured and plundered worse than ever, the administration is more hopeless and crazy than ever, the European usurers are more greedy, the finances are more hopelessly burdened, the whole nation is weaker and more disorganised than it was two years ago, and in the midst of it stands the great Liberal Government of Mr. Gladstone, answerable directly now for everything, yet incapable of mending anything—committed to an incalculable adventure in the deserts of Africa, or in the alternative committed to hand over Egypt to the risk of civil and religious confusion. Such is the result of grandiloquent professions, a readiness to listen to practical men, leaving free hands to commerce and finance, and a desire to promote national covetousness in decorous ways, but without the audacity which covetousness needs [1884; see *Memoirs*, ii., 1911, pp. 167-173].

There are reasons, we are told, for the delay: Egypt will soon be able to maintain herself, and the army of occupation will be withdrawn—this day six months. Does any reasonable Englishman not standing on a platform believe this? We are told to-day that it is the cholera, now it is the Mahdi, now it is the Canal or the interests of British commerce that compel a delay which all deplore and none could foresee. Ah, there are false prophets in England as well as in Africa. The cholera is nothing new; the Canal and British commerce are much what they were ten years ago. These phrases may serve the turn of a debate in Parliament, but they cannot deceive the nation. We went in arms to Egypt to crush the Egyptians into submitting whilst we played our commercial game as best suited our own pocket. We did not intend to annex the country in any formal way so long as the Egyptians were quiet and suffered the commercial game to go on. We are still staying in Egypt because they have never yet submitted to us absolutely. And we shall stay there because they never will submit. Ministers were told that when the native army and Government were annihilated Egypt would be the prey of the savages of the desert. They were told that when we once had occupied Egypt both civilly and militarily it would be practically impossible to come out. They were told that, having plunged Egypt into anarchy, it would be odious and dangerous to annex it and yet impossible to quit it. Yet Mr. Gladstone, with the professions of Midlothian on his lips, went on. Mr. Chamberlain, with all the Nonconformist Anti-Jingoes around him, the very Quakers and the Founders of Peace Societies, and the leaders of the campaign of '81 hounding them on—they went on into this great crime, and in this great crime they all still stand. What is all that the late Government did in comparison with the danger and guiltiness of this? The Zulu War has been undone; the Afghan escapade is undone; the Treaty of Berlin is accepted and Cyprus is a flea-bite. But the annexation of Egypt would be a permanent danger, a formidable burden, a conspicuous breach of faith. And if final annexation does prove the result of this ill-starred war, those who in time to come shall write the history of our epoch will record that the great blot and burden was laid on it—not by Lord Beaconsfield and the Party of War, but by Mr. Gladstone and the so-called Party of Peace. For my part, I see no half-way between complete and immediate withdrawal or complete and immediate annexation. The former would be a humiliation to the Ministry, the latter a humiliation, a burden, and a danger to England. Of the two evils I prefer the former. The Canal could, if needful, be easily guarded in the interest of the commerce of the world. We withdrew from Afghanistan and from Zululand. Let us withdraw from Egypt. It is true that withdrawal is what practical men are wont to call impossible. For my part, I am ready to face the consequences. Great national crimes and disasters arise because there are so many things that practical politicians are pleased to call impossible.

IV

These times, I think, should make serious men reflect if there is anything in our current religion or current philosophy which is capable of resisting the strain of selfishness in its personal or national form—if there is any principle in the theologies and the moralities before us which can keep our national life noble and true. The foremost of English living philosophers succeeded with infinite self-sacrifice and patience in forming an Anti-Aggression League on principles of justice and common sense with a view to resist these incessant acts of wanton aggression and plunder. In that attempt of his many of us most heartily joined. At the first breath of the Egyptian expedition the League fell to pieces, and the very chairman at its first meeting was one of the most eager supporters of the policy of aggression in Egypt. International morality cannot be based on sense and justice barely. Party, ambition, gain overmaster it. It can be based on nothing but religion. And unhappily in this matter the Christian religion is an oracle of double meaning. The other day one of the most powerful leaders in the Church, a man of whom I can never speak without regard and respect—in the distant days of our boyhood he and I sat side by side in the same form at school; as a boy he had the same moral influence he has as a man—he spoke of us as devoting our attention only to the things that are seen, whilst he urged his hearers to set their eyes on the things that are unseen, and by faith and prayer to God to prepare themselves for their work on earth. That eminent teacher in the Church (Canon Liddon), and the powerful party he leads, exercised over the mind of Mr. Gladstone and of the nation no little influence during the war in Turkey. No voices were louder or more earnest in denouncing the iniquities of the Turk, the enormity of Lord Beaconsfield in encouraging our national ambition and greed. Where were their voices, their counsels, and their moral indignation when Mr. Gladstone destroyed the Egyptian national army and embarked on the career which has made him the master of Egypt? Silent, and cold, and most docile were they. The Egyptians were not Christians, there was the cause of the Gospel to consider, and something was said about the suppression of slavery. Having no adequate political theory, the Churches, like the Chapels, and the party as a whole, recognised in war practical merits for which they had no defence in conscience, to which the elastic other worldliness of the Gospel could be easily reconciled and adapted.

The eminent apologist of Christianity most certainly misconceived the spirit of Positivism. We too look on the Unseen. We have a future world on which in the turmoil of life we find it peaceful and inspiring to fix our vision. We too would withdraw for meditation and inspiration into our hearts—we would commune with our souls and be at rest—thinking on the mysterious ways of Providence and the feeble resources of Man. All this is ours as much as any Christian preacher's. But our Providence is here, in the mighty workings of the civilisation we inherit and have yet to transmit. Our Unseen is the glorious vision of a renewed completeness of our race on earth. The Unseen on which our eyes are fixed is not unreal because it is Unseen. It is real. It is not only real to us, but it is real, certain, and an everyday truth to every sane mind, and to every man whatever his creed or his Church. We can appeal to a hope as sure as the future of England or the human race. Our future world is the coming of Man into his kingdom here in a nobler, richer life,

> Laboriously tracing what must be,
> And what may yet be better.

And we hold that this practical and human vision of the Unseen can govern and harmonise men's minds more powerfully and more truly than any celestial vision of the mere imagination—because it is in a line with man's thought and act; it is so real that it can form a solid basis for duty, so perfectly human that it will keep all our sympathies genuine and sound. We at least will not continue on our knees. We will work, learn, and love—in the world, erect upon our feet.

In Positivism, as I understand it, the religion, the religious service, the object of worship, and the end of worship mean things wholly different, different in kind and not only in form from religion, worship, object, and end of worship in the current orthodoxy of Church and Chapel. Nay I go further and say that the business of Positivism is to disabuse modern Christians of the narrow and artificial conceptions of religion and worship into which they have stiffened, and to enlarge their conceptions into the grand and solid idea of Religion which was partly seen in the more distant past, and will only be made fully manifest in the distant future. Religion, in its modern Christian form, is an appeal to certain emotions and nothing more. It addresses the heart; but it has no more to say about the grouping of the sciences, or the function of government, than music or painting has. Now I call that not religion at all, but a special kind of nervous excitement. It may be beautiful, it may be purifying, but it is not religion. We mean by religion the fusing into one force the entire nature, the ordering of our ideas and of our human society. The imitation of the character of Christ will tell us nothing as to the housing of the poor and as to the laws of human history. But these are the very things we need to know to enable us to do our duty. Religion is not exhausted by reverential feeling for the Ruler of the Universe. It means the combination of reverence, knowledge, and enthusiasm of nature which makes a man do his duty in the world with his whole heart and his whole mind. Religious service is the doing it in that wise and enthusiastic way. The object of worship to us is not a superhuman Person, but the collective goodness and wisdom of mankind so far as mankind is worthy of honour. And the end of this worship is not to glorify that Being. It means with us—to give force to our brains, hearts, and energies in the doing our duty.

Now if this be so, we shall actually be opposing the spread of true Positive belief, if we use language or adopt habits such as cause ourselves and others to think that we accept the old evangelical way of presenting religion and worship. It would be better not to use the words religion, service, worship, and prayer or the like, if we use them to express the same things as Christians mean but merely with a change in the object addressed. Not only is the idea of Humanity in no sense whatever comparable with that of God; but the positive notion of serving Humanity is not comparable or analogous with the Christian notion of serving

God. Serving Humanity is a practical thing like serving your country or your city. Serving God is nowadays too often reduced to the idea of singing a hymn or uttering a prayer on one's knees, or going through what is so oddly called some religious exercise. If we were to try to revive Evangelical or Catholic rituals, Christian sacraments, prayers, and associations, simply, as it were, changing the name of the person addressed, we should be committing exactly the same mistake as the Judaising Christians did of old, when James and Peter could see nothing in the teaching of Christ but a new way of treating the Mosaic rites, but one more added to the Hebrew sects of that age. Positivism absorbs not only the Christian habit of mind about religion, evangelical and Catholic, but it absorbs all other forms of Monotheism; it absorbs the religions of Polytheism, of Greece, and Rome, the religion of the Theocracies, of Egypt, India, and China, and the religion of Fetichism (let us never forget it)—that is of Poetry and of Nature.

I go so far as to say that if the end of Positivism were ever taken to be to get groups of people to meet once a week in a place made to look like a Christian vestry or Sunday school, and there simply repeat the formulas of Positivism, invocations and thanksgivings to Humanity, utter responses, canticles, and benedictions, read a passage out of a book of Catholic devotions, and then go home and think that they had been performing a religious service to Humanity, and that this act of theirs was in itself the religion of Humanity,—then I think, if that came to be the end of it, they would have been better employed in some innocent work or enjoyment. I would rather that such a place did not exist at all—it would only be adding one more to the sects—and I should think that these worshippers would have been better occupied, better as regards their own spirits and for their usefulness in the world, if they had gone to some Catholic or Evangelical Church and worshipped frankly in the old way.

I am very far from saying that this is a picture of any body of Positivists of whom I have ever heard. But I give it as a warning of what Positivism might end in if we ever came to think that we could take the religious habits of modern English Christians and simply substitute the new for the old object of worship, reading Humanity where we find God, and Auguste Comte where we find Christ. I do not hesitate to give the reason for this—frankly and rationally. Positivism entails entire openness and perpetual resort to demonstration. The whole idea of religion and religious service in Christianity turns round the centre of a Conscious and All-seeing Person. The idea of communing in spirit with that Perfect and Supreme Being, of entering hereafter into bliss in His presence—these are all conceptions utterly unique, which it is impossible to transplant by simply changing the words. And these hopes and yearnings, where they have got possession of the whole soul, have a certain quality that is truly ecstatic, transcending this world of sense entirely. To attempt to simulate these hopes and yearnings and then to adapt them to the abstract idea of an assemblage of earthly men and women must necessarily be but a pale and artificial imitation. Almighty God, Perfect Son of God, Eternity of Heaven are ideas with an intensity and a passion (as all who have known them can witness) such as no real and human idea can possess.

Trasumanar significar per verba non si porria—it is impossible in sober words to express that which transcends the sphere of man, says the poet. Transcendental ideas like these can and may form *by themselves* a religion of a kind, when devoutly and honestly believed in as truths. *Our* conceptions, I say it boldly and frankly, cannot, *of themselves and nakedly*, form a religion. *Our* religion is a complete system of action, feeling, and thought. The whole force resides in its breadth, reality, completeness, and steadiness —not in its convulsive moments of ecstasy, or in its mere and direct appeal to the emotions. Humanity, human progress and welfare, the continuous life in others are ideas, as we hold, far richer, more real, more fertile, more intelligible, and more useful—but they are not so in special ways: they are not ecstatic at all; they have not the power to throw the whole soul into that delirium of devotion which the old figments certainly once had, and doubtless with certain minds have still.

Hence our Humanity, Progress, Subjective Future have not the quality to form by themselves, taken alone, adequate objects of such worship as Christianity has thrown round the ecstatic prostration of the spirit before its own imaginary beings; and the Christians are quite right when they say: "You cannot pray to Humanity in that rapturous way in which we pray to God, you cannot feel that ecstasy in contemplating the growing perfection of Christ. Your life in others gives you no such delirious indifference to death and torture as we feel in the sense of Paradise opening before our eyes."

They are right. And what is our answer? It is this. We want no ecstasy, delirium, or rapture which loses hold on the solid ground of reality. We ask for nothing absolute, nor incomprehensible; for that comes to mean anything that an hysterical spirit can bring itself to fancy. We desire no indifference to death and torture; we wish only to be able to meet both as men — but not as more. We reply then: "We have outgrown your transcendental dreams, and we shall not imitate your prostrations and your invocations. We have outgrown your ideas of Providence and of Heaven; and so too we have outgrown your ideas of worship and of service." The religion of Humanity loses something perhaps of intensity, but it gains enormously in breadth, in reality, in steadiness. It may be less passionate but it is far more rational, far more constant and certain. It does not carry the emotions into such excesses, but it holds and binds the whole nature in one—brain and energy working with heart, steadily and evenly always. The courage of the modern soldier is not the wild fury of a savage warrior, but it is a far stronger and more certain force: the patriotism of a modern European is not the jealous passion of a Spartan or a Carthaginian for his city, but it is a far nobler and more civilised spirit. The trust of a wise man is not the blind faith of the child or the barbarian, but it is a far more solid and efficient power.

The religious ecstasy of Simon Stylites or an Indian fakir is a far more passionate thing than the sober devotion of the most sincere modern Christian. But his religion is a far lower and far weaker force. The religion of Mahomet has moments of transport more intense than Christianity itself. And the religion of Dahomey or of the Red Indians has moments of transport wilder than those of Islam. It is a law of civilisation that, as it gains in breadth and completeness, it loses something in special intensity.

And the moral of this is that the religion of Humanity can in nothing imitate the purely emotional agencies of the religion of Christ. It means not petitions, nor invocations, nor uttered words of any kind. It means work, education, duty, love. A religious service is any sort of good work done for the benefit of Humanity, with the desire to serve Humanity. A good and useful lecture in science is a religious service; the showing a good example to a child is a religious service; the good influence on our fellow-citizens is a religious service; the careful and honest discharge of our daily task is a religious service. Every man and every woman worships Humanity, not in any exclusive or peculiar way when he comes here, or when he uses that beautiful word, but when he and she are in their homes and are making their homes beautiful by gentleness, love, patience, and self-denial; when they are in their workshop or their counting-house, earnest in doing their work in a true spirit of social usefulness and zeal; when they are in their school or class-room or their study, patiently mastering the great inheritance of science and the vast story of the past. And they are worshipping Humanity in the market-place, or the club, or the household when they are building up a healthy and pure public opinion amongst their fellow-citizens;

striving to make this England of ours a more wholesome place for those who toil, a more unselfish nation in the republic of the West, a less harsh and dangerous neighbour to the weak and uncivilised peoples who are yet our brothers in the human race.

In Te misericordia, in Te pietate,
In Te magnificenza, in Te s' aduna
Quantunque in creatura è di bontate.

THE END

Printed by R. & R. Clark, Limited, *Edinburgh.*